CAMBRIDGE
UNIVERSITY PRESS

UNIVERSITY of CAMBRIDGE
ESOL Examinations

D1810843

Cambridge English

Objective First

Student's Book
without answers

Annette Capel Wendy Sharp

Third Edition

CAMBRIDGE
UNIVERSITY PRESS

University Printing House, Cambridge CB2 8BS, United Kingdom

Cambridge University Press is part of the University of Cambridge.

It furthers the University's mission by disseminating knowledge in the pursuit of education, learning and research at the highest international levels of excellence.

www.cambridge.org
Information on this title: www.cambridge.org/9780521178785

© Cambridge University Press 2012

This publication is in copyright. Subject to statutory exception and to the provisions of relevant collective licensing agreements, no reproduction of any part may take place without the written permission of Cambridge University Press.

First published 2000
Second edition 2008
Third edition published 2012
5th printing 2013

Printed in Dubai by Oriental Press

A catalogue for this publication is available from the British Library

ISBN 978-0-521-17878-5 Student's Book without answers with CD-ROM
ISBN 978-0-521-17879-2 Student's Book with answers with CD-ROM
ISBN 978-0-521-17909-6 Teacher's Book with Teacher's Resources Audio CD/CD-ROM
ISBN 978-0-521-17881-5 Class Audio CDs (2)
ISBN 978-0-521-17880-8 Workbook without answers with Audio CD
ISBN 978-0-521-17882-2 Workbook with answers with Audio CD
ISBN 978-0-521-17883-9 Student's Book Pack (Student's Book with answers with CD-ROM and Class Audio CDs)
ISBN 978-1-107-64891-3 For Schools Practice Test Booklet with answers with Audio CD
ISBN 978-1-107-64892-0 For Schools Practice Test Booklet without answers

Additional resources for this publication at www.cambridge.org/objectivefirst

Cambridge University Press has no responsibility for the persistence or accuracy of URLs for external or third-party internet websites referred to in this publication, and does not guarantee that any content on such websites is, or will remain, accurate or appropriate. Information regarding prices, travel timetables and other factual information given in this work is correct at the time of first printing but Cambridge University Press does not guarantee the accuracy of such information thereafter.

Cover concept by Tim Elcock

Produced by Kamae Design, Oxford

Map of Objective First Student's Book

TOPIC	EXAM PRACTICE	GRAMMAR	VOCABULARY
Unit 1 **Fashion matters** 10–13 Fashion; describing people	Paper 5 Speaking: 2 Paper 4 Listening: 3 Paper 3 Use of English: 4	Comparison: adjectives and adverbs Adverbs of degree	APPEARANCE AND CLOTHING Phrasal verbs
Exam folder 1 14–15	Paper 3 Use of English: 4 Key word transformations		
Unit 2 **The virtual world** 16–19 Computer games; the Internet	Paper 1 Reading: 1	-ly adverbs Review of present tenses	COMPUTERS Collocations Word formation
Writing folder 1 20–21	Paper 2 Writing: 1 and 2 Informal letters and emails		
Unit 3 **Going places** 22–25 Travel	Paper 5 Speaking: 2 Paper 4 Listening: 2 Paper 3 Use of English: 1 and 4	Modals 1: Obligation, necessity and permission Prepositions of location	TRAVEL AND HOLIDAYS Topic set – travel and holidays Phrasal verbs Collocations
Exam folder 2 26–27	Paper 3 Use of English: 3 Word formation		
Unit 4 **Endangered** 28–31 Animals	Paper 1 Reading: 3 Paper 3 Use of English: 4	as and like Compound adjectives	ANIMALS Word formation Topic set – parts of animals Expressions with time
Writing folder 2 32–33	Paper 2 Writing: 1 Transactional letters and emails 1 (formal)		
Unit 5 **Mixed emotions** 34–37 Describing frightening and positive experiences	Paper 4 Listening: 1 Paper 3 Use of English: 2	Review of past tenses: past simple past continuous present perfect past perfect Irregular verbs	EMOTIONS Collocations – adverbs of degree
Exam folder 3 38–39	Paper 3 Use of English: 2 Open cloze		
Unit 6 **What if?** 40–43 Winning prizes and celebrity culture	Paper 1 Reading: 2 Paper 3 Use of English: 1 and 3 Paper 5 Speaking: 4	Conditionals with if Conditionals with unless Parts of speech	WINNING AND CELEBRITY Phrasal verbs with keep Word formation
Writing folder 3 44–45	Paper 2 Writing: 2 Stories 1		
Units 1–6 Revision 46–47			
Unit 7 **Life's too short** 48–51 Sport	Paper 3 Use of English: 3 and 4 Paper 4 Listening: 3 Paper 5 Speaking: 3	Gerunds and infinitives 1	SPORT Collocations – sports Expressions with do Word formation
Exam folder 4 52–53	Paper 3 Use of English: 1 Multiple choice cloze		
Unit 8 **Growing up** 54–57 Childhood	Paper 5 Speaking: 2 and 4 Paper 1 Reading: 1 Paper 3 Use of English: 3	used to and would	JOBS AND WORK Collocations Phrasal verbs with get Word formation
Writing folder 4 58–59	Paper 2 Writing: 2 Essays		

Content of Cambridge English: First

The *Cambridge English: First* examination consists of five papers, each of which is worth 40 marks. It is not necessary to pass all five papers in order to pass the examination. If you achieve a grade A in the examination, you will be awarded the *First Certificate in English* and your certificate will state that you demonstrated ability at C1 level. If you achieve grade B or C, you will be awarded the *First Certificate in English* at Level B2. If your performance is below B2, but falls within Level B1, you will get a Cambridge English certificate stating that you demonstrated ability at B1 level.

You will also be given some indication of your performance on the individual papers, i.e. whether you have done especially well or badly.

Paper 1 Reading 1 hour

There are three parts to this paper and they are always in the same order. Each part contains a text and a comprehension task. The texts used are from newspaper and magazine articles, fiction, guides and reviews.

Part	Task type	Number of questions	Task format	Objective Exam folder
1	Multiple choice	8	You must read a text and answer multiple choice questions with four options: A, B, C or D.	Fiction **10** (128–129) Non-fiction **12** (152–153)
2	Gapped text	7	You must read a text with sentences removed. You need to use the missing sentences to complete the text.	**9** (114–115)
3	Multiple matching	15	You must answer the questions by finding the relevant information in the text or texts.	**11** (140–141)

Paper 2 Writing 1 hour 20 minutes

There are two parts to this paper. Part 1 is compulsory, you have to answer it. In Part 2 there are four questions and you must choose one. Each part carries equal marks and you are expected to write between 120–150 words for Task 1 and 120–180 for Task 2.

Part	Task type	Number of tasks	Task format	Objective Writing folder
1	Question 1 a transactional letter or email • formal/informal	1 compulsory	You are given a situation which you need to respond to by letter or email. You may be given some extra information in the form of notes which you need to use in your answer.	**2** (32–33); **8** (108–109); **12** (158–159);
2	Questions 2–4 • an article • an informal non-transactional letter • a letter or email • a report • an essay • a review • a story Question 5 Writing one of the above types of task: • There is a choice of two set books, with a question on each.	4 choose one	You are given a choice of topics and you have to respond to one of them in the way specified.	Essays **4** (58–59); Informal letters and emails **1** (20–21); Articles **5** (70–71); **12** (158–159); Reviews **6** (82–83); Reports **11** (146–147); Applications **7** (96–97); The set book **9** (120–121); Stories **3** (44–45); **10** (134–135)

Paper 3 Use of English 45 minutes

There are four parts to this paper, which tests your grammar and vocabulary.

Part	Task type	Number of tasks	Task format	Objective Writing folder
1	Multiple choice gap-fill, mainly testing vocabulary	12	You must choose which word from four answers completes each of the 12 gaps in a text.	4 (52–53)
2	Open gap-fill, testing mainly grammar	12	You must complete a text with 12 gaps.	3 (38–39)
3	Word formation	10	You need to use the right form of a given word to fill the gaps in a text containing 10 gaps.	2 (26–27)
4	Key word transformations testing grammar and vocabulary	8	You must complete a sentence with a given word, so that it means the same as the first sentence.	1 (14–15)

Paper 4 Listening about 40 minutes

There are four parts to this paper. Each part is heard twice. The texts are a variety of types with either one speaker or more than one.

Part	Task type	Number of questions	Task format	Objective Exam folder
1	Multiple choice	8	You hear short, unrelated extracts, each about 30 seconds, with either one or two speakers. You must choose an answer from A, B or C.	6 (76–77)
2	Sentence completion	10	You hear either one or two speakers and this part lasts about 3 minutes. You must write a word or short phrase to complete the sentences.	5 (64–65)
3	Multiple matching	5	You hear five unrelated extracts with a common theme. Each lasts about 30 seconds. You must choose the correct answer from a list of six.	7 (90–91)
4	Multiple choice	7	You hear either one or two speakers talking for about 3 minutes. You must choose an answer from A, B or C.	8 (102–103)

Paper 5 Speaking about 14 minutes

There are four parts to this paper. There are usually two of you taking the examination and two examiners. This paper tests your accuracy, vocabulary, pronunciation and your ability to communicate and complete the tasks.

Part	Task type	Time	Format	Objective Speaking folder
1	The interviewer asks each candidate some questions.	3–4 minutes	You are asked to give information about yourself.	Speaking folder (162–163)
2	Each candidate talks to the interviewer for about 1 minute.	3–4 minutes	You have to talk about two pictures and then comment on the other candidate's pictures.	Speaking folder (162–163)
3	Candidates have to discuss a task together.	3–4 minutes	You are given some material – diagrams, pictures, etc. – to discuss with the other candidate.	Speaking folder (162–163)
4	Candidates offer opinions relating to the task they've just completed.	3–4 minutes	The interviewer will join in with your discussion.	Speaking folder (162–163)

Acknowledgements

The authors and publishers would like to thank the teachers and consultants who commented on the material:

Brazil: Eliane Sanchez Querino (KNOW-HOW); Czech Rep.: Aleš Novak; Hungary: Ildiko Berke; Italy: Robert Islam (British School of English), Fiona Line (Modern English); Mexico: Lizeth Jerezano Rodriguez, Graciella Toral Garcia; Poland: Dr Andrzej Diniejko (University of Warsaw); Russia: Tatyana Elistratova; Spain: Caroline Cooke, Nick Shaw (Cambridge English Studio), Leanne White; Switzerland: Allan Dalcher; UK: Kathryn Alevizos, David Jay, Julie Moore.

The authors would like to thank Alyson Maskell for her constructive suggestions and meticulous editorial support on this third edition. Thanks also go to Joanne Hunter and Sara Bennett at Cambridge University Press, and to Kamae Design for their creative design solutions.

The authors and publishers acknowledge the following sources of copyright material and are grateful for the permissions granted. While every effort has been made, it has not always been possible to identify the sources of all the material used, or to trace all copyright holders. If any omissions are brought to our notice, we will be happy to include the appropriate acknowledgements on reprinting.

This product is informed by the English Vocabulary Profile, developed as part of English Profile, a collaborative programme designed to enhance the learning, teaching and assessment of English worldwide. Its main funding partners are Cambridge University Press and Cambridge ESOL and its aim is to create 'reference level descriptions' for English linked to the Common European Framework (CEF). English Profile outcomes, such as the English Vocabulary Profile, will provide detailed information about the language that learners can be expected to demonstrate at each CEF level, offering a clear benchmark for learners' proficiency. For more information, please visit www.englishprofile.org

Development of this publication has made use of the *Cambridge English Corpus* (CEC). The CEC is a computerised database of contemporary spoken and written English which currently stands at over one billion words. It includes British English, American English and other varieties of English. It also includes the *Cambridge Learner Corpus*, developed in collaboration with the University of Cambridge ESOL Examinations. Cambridge University Press has built up the CEC to provide evidence about language use that helps to produce better language teaching materials.

The Cambridge Advanced Learner's Dictionary is the world's most widely used dictionary for learners of English. Including all the words and phrases that learners are likely to come across, it also has easy-to-understand definitions and example sentences to show how the word is used in context. The Cambridge Advanced Learner's Dictionary is available online at dictionary.cambridge.org. © Cambridge University Press, Third Edition, 2008, reproduced with permission.

Helen Storey for the text on p. 12, published by Faber and Faber;

Cambridge University Press for the definition on p. 16 from Cambridge Advanced Learner's Dictionary (2005). Copyright © Cambridge University Press;

Future Publishing Limited for the reviews on pp. 16–17 from PC Gamer, 1997. Copyright © Future Publishing Limited;

Gary Stock for the text on p. 19 from www.googlewhack.com/stock.htm. Reproduced with permission;

Penguin Books Ltd and Random House Inc for the text on p. 37 from The Big Sleep by Raymond Chandler (Hamish Hamilton 1939, Penguin Books 1970, 2005). Copyright © Raymond Chandler 1939 and renewed by Helga Green of the Estate of Raymond Chandler. Used by permission of Alfred A Knopf, a division of Random House Inc and Penguin Books Ltd;

Solo Syndication for the text on p. 40 adapted from 'British student, 19, becomes Far East superstar after winning Chinese X Factor' by Liz Thomas, Daily Mail 18.1.10. Copyright © Daily Mail;

NI Syndication for the text on p. 46 adapted from 'Cover direct' by Debbie Hall, The Sun 12.3.00, for the text on p. 47 adapted from 'Flying' by Liz Gill, The Sun 19.7.03, for the text on p. 51 adapted from 'Fitness' by Cheryl Holmes, The Sun 21.5.05, for the text on p. 61 adapted from 'King of Madison Avenue' by Brian Schofield, The Sunday Times 8.2.09, for the text on p. 143 adapted from 'Glastonbudget' by Chris Catchpole, The Sun 1.6.10, for the text on p. 153 adapted from 'Zimbabwe Holiday' by Sean Newson, The Sun 2.6.02. Copyright © NI Syndication;

Telegraph Media Group Limited for the text on p. 80 adapted from 'Shops with the sweet smell of success' by Jacqui Thornton, The Telegraph, 1999, for the text on p. 104 adapted from 'Sounds and colour influence the taste of food' by Richard Gray, The Telegraph 30.5.08. Copyright © Telegraph Media Group Limited 2008, 2011;

BBC Magazines for the text on p. 85 adapted from 'How to be an office god' by Jonathan Green, Focus Magazine May 1997. Copyright © BBC Magazines;

Random House Group Ltd and Simon & Schuster, Inc for the text on p. 116 from The Old Man and the Sea by Ernest Hemingway. Copyright © 1952 by Ernest Hemingway. Copyright renewed © 1980 by Mary Hemingway. Reprinted with permission Random House Group Ltd and Scribner, a Division of Simon & Schuster, Inc;

David Higham Associates Ltd for the text on p. 129 from The Day of the Triffids by John Wyndham, published by Penguin Books Ltd. Reproduced with permission;

Text on p. 133 © Crown Copyright;

The Guardian for the text on p. 141, text (a) adapted from 'Me and my car, Charlie Dark' by Donna McConnell, The Observer 5.6.05, text (b) adapted from 'Doh! James Wood Literary Critic' by Philip Olterman, The Guardian 3.2.07, text (c) adapted from 'Me and my car, Rachel Mari Kimber', The Observer 26.5.05, text (d) adapted from 'Me and my car, Sharon Nnatu' by Donna McConnell, The Observer 12.6.05. Copyright Guardian News & Media Ltd, 2005 and for the text on p. 161 adapted from 'Wrong number lands navy expert in Spielberg's war' by Nick Hopkins, The Guardian 6.8.98. Copyright Guardian News & Media Ltd 1998;

IPC Syndication for the text on p. 161 adapted from 'How to make a small fortune' Woman's Weekly 16.9.97. Copyright © IPC Syndication/Woman's Weekly;

Photo acknowledgements:

p. 10 (1a): iStockphoto/Justin Horrocks; p. 10 (1b): Annika Johnemark / photographersdirect.com; p. 10 (2a): DreamPictures/Getty Images; p. 10 (2b): itanistock/ Alamy; p. 10 (3a): DreamPictures/Shannon Faulk/Purestock/Superstock; p. 10 (3b): iStockphoto/ranplett; p. 10 (4a): Darren Baker/Alamy; p. 10 (4b): Sujata Majumdar / photographersdirect.com; p. 19: F1 Online/Rex Features; p. 22 (1): Tetra Images/ Superstock; p. 22 (2): Gavin Hellier/Alamy; p. 22 (3): John Dakars/Eye Ubiquitous/ Hutchinson; p. 22 (4): Hemis.fr/Superstock; p. 28 (bear, koala): Thinkstock/iStockphoto; p. 28 (parrot): Nature Picture Library/Rex Features; p. 28 (shark): David B Fleetham/OSF/ Photolibrary; p. 28 (orang-utan): K. Tornblom/IBL/ Rex Features; p. 28 (leopard): Jurgen & Christine Sohns/FLPA – Images of Nature; p. 29: John Foxx Images; p. 37: Warner Bros/ Kobal Collection; p. 40: AdrianSheratt/ Rex Features; p. 43: Trinity Mirror/Mirrorpix/ Alamy; p. 50 (L): Leo Mason/Getty Images; p. 50 (C): Photri Images/ Superstock; p. 50 (R): Mike Tittel/OSF/ Photolibrary; p. 52: Popperfoto/ Getty Images; p. 54 (1): Imagebroker. net/ Superstock; p. 54 (2): Hill Creek Picture/Purestock/ Superstock; p. 54 (3): Thinkstock/ Jupiterimages; p. 54 (4): Hervé De Gueltzl/ Photolibrary; p. 57: Thinkstock/iStockphoto; p. 59: Prisma/Superstock; p. 60: Image courtesy of the Advertising Archives; p. 61: UPP/ Topfoto; p. 63 (1): Helene Rogers/Art Directors & TRIP; p. 63 (2): Kathy deWitt/Alamy; p. 63 (3): Stuart Kelly/ Alamy; p. 63 (4): Peter Cavanagh/ Alamy; p. 66 (T): Spyglass Entertainment/Ronald Grant Archive; p. 66 (B): Victor Habbick Visions/Science Photo Library; p. 68: NASA/ Science Photo Library; p. 69: Photosindia/ Alamy; p. 70: Thinkstock/ Jupiterimages; p. 72 (L): Evan Agostini/AP/Press Association Images; p. 72 (C): Henry Lamb/ Photowire/BEI/ Rex Features; p. 72 (R): Jeffery Mayer/WireImage/Getty Images; p. 73: age fotostock/Superstock; p. 78 (1): Jerry Amster/Superstock; p. 78 (2): Getty Images; p. 78 (3): Motoring Picture Library/Alamy; p. 78 (4): Neil McAllister/Alamy; p. 81: Ian McKinnell/ Getty Images; p. 84: Warner Bros/ Ronald Grant Archive; p. 85: Image courtesy of the Advertising Archives; p. 86 (L): educationphotos.co.uk/Walmsley; p. 86 (R): Alexander Caminada/ Rex Features; p. 87 (Christie): Angus McBean/Camera Press; p. 87 (Madonna): Matt Baron/BEI/ Rex Features; p. 87 (Lennox): Ken McKay/Rex Features; p. 87 (Gauguin): Bettmann/ Corbis; p. 87 (Cruise): Broadimage/Rex Features; p. 87: Socrates, marble head, copy from a bronze from the Pompeion in Athens, made by Lysippus, Classical Greek, c.330 BC, /Louvre, Paris, France /The Bridgeman Art Library; p. 90: Travel Library Ltd/ Superstock; p. 92 (L): Gianni Cigolini/Getty Images; p. 92 (R): Ukraft/Alamy; p. 93 (A): Flirt/Superstock; p. 93 (B): Catchlight Visual Services/Alamy; p. 93 (C): Thinkstock; p. 93 (D): Christopher Robbins/Getty Images; p. 93 (E): Shutterstock/ StockLife; p. 95: Popperfoto/Getty Images; p. 97 Bruno Vicent/Getty Images;

p. 98 (1): Eye Ubiquitous/Rex Features; p. 98 (2): Adrian Sheratt/Rex Features; p. 98 (3): Inter Vision Ltd/Travel Pictures Ltd; p. 98 (4): AFP/Getty Images; p. 101: Melanie Friend/Eye Ubiquitous/Hutchison; p. 102: Oliver Gerhard/Imagebroker/ FLPA-Images of Nature; p. 104 (T): Lowell Georgia/Corbis; p. 104(BL): Lori Adamski Peek/ Getty Images; p. 104 (BR): Dale Durfee/Getty Images;

p. 106: Chris Rennie/Art Directors & TRIP; p. 110 (1): Thinkstock; p. 110 (2): Dave Thompson/PA Wire/Press Association Images; p. 110 (3): Martin Black/Imagestate; p. 110 (4): iStockphoto/Hans-Martens; p. 111: M.Powell/The Times/Rex Features;

p. 113: Helene Rogers/Art Directors & TRIP; p. 114: © warrensmith.biz; p. 118 (Lear): King Lear by Shakespeare/Cambridge University Press; p. 118 (Gabriel): Gabriel García Márquez A Life by Gerald Martin/Bloomsbury; p. 118 (Detective): The Last Detective by Robert Crais/Orion Group; p. 118 (Richard): Broken Angels by Richard Morgan/Orion Group; p. 118 (Davis): from A Body in the Bath House by Lindsay Davis, published by Century and Arrow. Reprinted by permission of The Random House Group Ltd.; p. 118 (Bees): Designed by Brian Roberts/Guardian Books; p. 122: MIRA/Alamy; p. 124 (T): Robert Stainforth/Alamy; p. 124 (B) Thinkstock/IT stock; p. 125: Andrew Cowie/ Coloursport; p. 126 (T): TEK Image /Science Photo Library; p. 126 (B): Image Source/Rex Features; p. 127: Thinkstock /Polka Dot Images; p. 130 (1): Thinkstock/iStockphoto; p. 130 (2): Flirt/Superstock; p. 130 (3): Frederic Sierakowski/Rex Features; p. 130 (4): Helene Rogers/ Art Directors & TRIP; p. 130 (5): Charles Thatcher/Getty Images; p. 136 (2): Leslie Woodhead/Eye Ubiquitous/Hutchison; p. 136 (1): Julian Calder/Getty Images; p. 138: Jon Blau/Camera Press London; p. 139: Pixtal/Superstock; p. 140: Dennis Kitchen/Getty Images; p. 142 (T): AFP/Getty Images; p. 143: Courtesy of Glastonbudget Music Festival, Mockstar Ltd, www.glastonbudget.org; p. 145: Everett Collection/Rex Features; p. 148 (1): Gerald Cubitt; p. 148 (2): iStockphoto/mashurov; p. 148 (3): Amy & Chuck Wiley/Wales / Photolibrary.com; p. 148/149 (4): iStockphoto/hepatus; p. 149: iStockphoto/Beboy_ltd; p. 151: A.T. Willet/Alamy; p. 154 (1): ©Universal/Everett Collection/Rex Features; p. 154 (2): Dreamworks/Aardman Animation/Kobal Collection; p. 155 (4): KeystoneUSA-Zuma/Rex Features; p. 155 (3): Chuck Franklin/Alamy; p. 157: Morgan Creek/J. Farmer/ Kobal Collection; p. 161 (L): Bournemouth News; p. 161 (BR): Lefteris Pitarakis/AP/ Press Association Images; p. 162 (L): AlamyCelebrity/Alamy; p. 162 (R): Nicholas Khayat/ Rex Features; p. 163 (L): Leslie Woodhead/Eye Ubiquitous/Hutchinson; p. 163 (R): Robin Smith/Getty Images.

Illustrator acknowledgements:

Laetitia Aynie pp. 13, 79, 80; Dominic Bugatto p. 132; Karen Donnelly p. 45; Nick Duffy pp. 31, 42, 95, 100, 119, 133; Federico pp. 16, 24, 51; Katie Mac pp. 48, 105, 151; Louise Morgan p. 137; Julian Mosedale pp. 65, 74, 75, 107, 112, 122, 142, 150, 156; Roger Penwill p. 86; Jorge Santillan pp. 34, 163; Jamie Sneddon p. 61; David Tazzyman p. 89

We are unable to trace the copyright holder for the photograph that appears on page 142 (T) and the illustrations that appear on pages 11, 37, 39, 47, 77, 116 and117, we would appreciate any help which would enable us to do so.

Recordings produced by Ian Harker, Ian Harker Audio, with Paul Deeley at The Soundhouse Ltd.

Picture research by Kevin Brown.

Corpus research by Julie Moore

New for the third edition of Objective First

In this third edition, there are plenty of new texts, pictures and exercises, as well as new audio recordings. The course has been informed by the *English Vocabulary Profile* (see below), which guarantees suitable treatment of words, phrases and phrasal verbs at B2 level. A CD-ROM and free website material provide additional support.

B2 English Profile English Vocabulary Profile

The *English Vocabulary Profile* is an online resource with detailed and up-to-date information about the words, phrases, phrasal verbs and idioms that learners of English know at each of the six levels of the Common European Framework – A1 to C2. The authors have used this rich and reliable resource to select vocabulary that is relevant to the B2 level. The course deals systematically with areas of vocabulary development that are important for the *Cambridge English: First* examination: topic vocabulary, common words with several meanings, phrases and collocations, phrasal verbs and word families.

CD-ROM

On the CD-ROM there are 96 exercises, eight for each pair of units, giving extra practice in vocabulary, grammar, reading, listening and writing. There are also additional resources for students including downloadable wordlists with and without definitions.

Website

www.cambridge.org/elt/objectivefirst
On this website you will find a number of useful resources for both students and teachers: a free photocopiable *Cambridge English: First* Practice Test with audio, and photocopiable unit by unit wordlists.

Fashion matters

Speaking

1 How important is fashion to you? What sort of clothes do you prefer to wear? Do you ever have to wear things you don't really like? If so, when, and why? Talk with a partner.

2 Describe what people in the class are wearing today. Then list topic vocabulary in sets like these.

Clothes: *suit, sweatshirt,* ....
Footwear: *boots, sandals,* ....
Jewellery: *bracelet, earrings,* ....
Headgear: *hood, helmet,* ....
Materials: *woollen, leather,* ....
Appearance: *casual, smart,* ....

3 Work in pairs. Choose a pair of photos, for example 1a and 1b. Describe what each person is wearing and say something about their appearance.

4 In the same pairs, compare the two people in your photos. These examples may help you.

The one on the left is younger than the one on the right.
This girl's clothes are not as stylish as the other one's.
This man seems to be less serious than the man in the suit.

5 As a class, summarise what you said about the people.

Listening

6 ▶ **02** You will hear some short recordings, where five of the people in the photos talk about what they like to wear. Say who is speaking in each case.

Here is an example. Speaker 1 is the man in photo 3b. Look at his photo as you listen.

In this transcript of what Speaker 1 says, some words and phrases are highlighted. This is to show that parts of an exam recording may make you think that other answers are possible. This is why you must listen carefully and check when you listen a second time.

__I'm not a suit man__. Even for work, I can get away with casual stuff, though I still __like my clothes to look smart__. I love shopping – my favourite place is Paul Smith in Covent Garden. I bought a really nice woollen shirt there recently. Clothes are important to me, but they need to be comfortable as well as __stylish__.

▶ **03** Now listen to the other four speakers and match the correct photo to each speaker. Compare answers with someone else when you have finished.

Speaker 2 ☐
Speaker 3 ☐
Speaker 4 ☐
Speaker 5 ☐

Vocabulary
Phrasal verbs

Phrasal verbs are used in spoken and written English, especially in informal situations. You already know some basic phrasal verbs: for example, you *wake up* in the morning and *put on* your clothes. These phrasal verbs are at A1 and A2 level. However, the ones you will need to learn at B2 will be harder than these because their meaning will be less obvious. *Objective First* will give you regular help in learning phrasal verbs. In your vocabulary notebook you can organise them

- by topic, e.g. phrasal verbs for *Fashion and clothes*
- by main verb, e.g. phrasal verbs with *go*
- by particle (adverb or preposition), e.g. phrasal verbs with *out*

In the recordings there are several examples of phrasal verbs. For example, Speaker 1 says:
*Even for work, I can **get away with** casual stuff.*
Be careful with word order: three-part phrasal verbs like the example are never separated. Two-part phrasal verbs containing an adverb have a flexible word order when used with a noun object, but if the object is a pronoun, it always comes between the verb and the adverb.
EXAMPLE: *I tried on the red jacket. / I tried the red jacket on. I tried it on.*

7 Listen to Speakers 2–5 again and tick the phrasal verbs you hear. Then match them to definitions a–i.

add to	go out	save up
cut down	keep up with	slip on
dress up	pull on	stand out
fit in with	put together	take back

- **a** be easy to see or notice
- **b** create something by joining or combining different things
- **c** return something
- **d** wear smarter clothes than usual
- **e** keep money for something in the future
- **f** reduce
- **g** put something on quickly
- **h** go somewhere for entertainment
- **i** understand something that is changing fast

Corpus spot

Many phrasal verbs contain irregular verbs. Be careful with past tense forms – the *Cambridge Learner Corpus* shows that exam candidates often make mistakes with these.

I **took off** my coat and sat down.

NOT I ~~taked~~ off my coat and sat down.

Phrasal verbs with *go*

8 Complete the sentences with a phrasal verb with *go*. Use the correct form of *go* and an adverb or preposition from the box.

go + | ahead   back   for   in   on   over   up

EXAMPLE: *That new shop has some great swimwear. I __went in__ there yesterday for the first time.*

- **a** The prices of leather bags have .... a lot recently.
- **b** Why are you looking at me like that? What's .... ?
- **c** The design company .... the applicant with the best portfolio.
- **d** I .... to the same shoe shop but there were no more pairs in my size.
- **e** You'll need to .... all the figures in the report to check they're correct.
- **f** Can I wear your necklace tonight? – Sure, ... !

9 Now complete this letter with some of the phrasal verbs from 7. More than one answer may be possible.

Dear Jayne

Last night, Maria, Sally and I **(1)** .... clubbing. I was late back from work, so I just **(2)** .... some black jeans and a sparkly T-shirt, but the other two really **(3)** .... ! Maria chose a stunning purple dress and sprayed her hair gold. Sally **(4)** .... the most outrageous outfit – red leather shorts, a bright green top and knee-length boots with stars on. When we got there, they both **(5)** .... on the dance floor and I looked very ordinary in comparison.

Honestly, I can't **(6)** .... them – they're so fashion-conscious. What would you do in my position?

10 What advice would you give the writer? Discuss in pairs.

1.2

Comparison

1 Read this short text about the fashion industry. Do you agree with its viewpoint?

> Why is it that fashion houses design their clothes for the youngest and skinniest men and women? We may not actually want to look like supermodels, but it is a fact that the most underweight models have dominated the world's catwalks for a very long time. It seems it is not in the interests of the fashion industry to represent an 'average' person. Although 'slimmer' may not always mean 'more desirable' in the real world, fashion succeeds because it carries with it that image of the least achievable figure.

2 These comparison structures are used with adjectives.

-er than	more … than	the most …
the -est	less … than	the least …

a Why do we say *younger* than but **less** serious than; and *the youngest* but *the **most** underweight*?

b Which common adjectives can we either add *-er/-est* to or use *more/most* with?

c What are the spelling rules for forming the comparative and superlative of words like *slim* and *skinny*?

Check the Grammar folder when you see this:

G → page 166

Corpus spot

Correct the mistakes that exam candidates have made with comparatives in these sentences.

a What are the better clothes to wear at the camp?
b He is famouser than all the others in the film.
c You look more tired and thiner.
d I would like to buy a much more better one.
e It's now more easy to get there.
f This is even worser than before.

3 Give the comparative and superlative forms of these adjectives.

bright	brighter	the brightest
big		
thin		
dirty		
casual	more/less casual	
outrageous	more/less outrageous	
good		the best
bad	worse	

4 Now complete the following sentences by using one of the adjectives in 3, choosing either the comparative or the superlative form.

a Have you painted this room recently? Everything's looking a lot .... than before.

b Out of all my friends, Jake wears .... clothes – take his handmade plastic coat, for example!

c Don't dress up for the club tonight – everyone's looking .... there nowadays.

d You can't put those disgusting jeans on again – they're .... pair I've ever seen!

e I'm a bit worried about Sally. She doesn't eat a thing and so she's getting .... than ever.

f My brother has .... taste in ties ever – awful designs in really odd colours!

g There's no way you can fit into my shoes – your feet are a lot .... than mine!

h Market stalls often offer slightly .... value for money than shops.

Grammar extra

Note the use of *a lot* and *slightly* in sentences g and h. These are adverbs of degree, which are commonly used with comparative adjectives. Some adverbs of degree are also used with superlative adjectives, as in this example:

*Kate Moss was **by far** the most famous model of the 1990s.*

Put these adverbs of degree into the following sentences. Which one can be used with both comparative and superlative adjectives?

a bit   a great deal   much

a This ring is only .... more expensive and it's .... nicer than the others.

b Tracksuits may be .... warmer, but shorts are .... the best for running in, whatever the weather.

G → page 166

5 *not as ... as / not so ... as*

You used this structure to compare the people in the photos in the last lesson. Now compare these different types of footwear in the same way, choosing suitable adjectives from the ones below to describe them.

comfortable   elegant   practical   outrageous

EXAMPLE: *The high-heeled shoes don't look as comfortable as the flip flops.*

G → page 166

6 Identify the comparative adverbs in this short newspaper article and then explain how they are formed.

FASHION KNOCK-OFFS

Counterfeit consumer goods – more commonly known as 'knock-offs' – are imitation goods that are offered for sale at much lower prices than the genuine products, and they are a big problem for the fashion industry. Knock-offs are now far more readily available than they were a few years ago, both on the web and on market stalls worldwide. These fake designer goods damage the actual brands in more ways than one, reducing their sales and causing them to be regarded less exclusively, no longer the luxury items they once were. Some people view the matter less seriously, arguing that knock-offs offer a type of free advertising and promotion to the real designer labels. However, there is no getting away from the fact that this is an illegal activity, and the fashion industry is starting to fight back with high-tech solutions that will distinguish the real goods from cheap copies.

7 What do you feel about counterfeit goods? Would you buy them? Why? / Why not?

8 Practise comparison structures by completing the second sentences so that they have a similar meaning to the first. Use the word given.

0 Mary is shorter than her brother.
NOT
Mary is ..... NOT AS TALL AS ..... her brother.

1 These sunglasses cost a bit less than my last pair.
WERE
These sunglasses ....
than my last pair.

2 Coco Chanel was an extremely talented designer.
MOST
Coco Chanel was one of ....
.... in the world.

3 I preferred you with curlier hair.
STRAIGHT
I preferred your hair when it wasn't ....
.... is now.

4 This shoe shop is the cheapest one I've found.
EXPENSIVE
This shoe shop is ....
.... all the ones I've found.

5 Suzanne's host at the dinner party wasn't as elegantly dressed as she was.
MORE
At the dinner party, Suzanne was far ....
.... her host.

6 It takes much less time to travel by train than by car.
LOT
Travelling by train ....
.... travelling by car.

7 Harry wears smarter clothes now he has a girlfriend.
LESS
Harry dressed ....
he didn't have a girlfriend.

8 That model is only 17 – I thought she was older.
AS
That model is not ....
I thought.

Exam folder 1

Paper 3 Part 4 Key word transformations

In this part of the Use of English paper you are tested on both grammar and vocabulary. There are eight questions and an example at the beginning.
You can get up to two marks for each question.

1 Read the Part 4 exam instructions below and then look at the example (0).

Complete the second sentence so that it has a similar meaning to the first sentence, using the word given. Do not change the word given. You must use between two and five words, including the word given.

Here is an example (0).

0 Have you got a belt that is cheaper than this one? ← *first sentence*
LESS ← *key word – this never changes*
Have you got .... than this one?
The second sentence must mean the same as the first when it is complete.

The gap can be filled by the words 'a less expensive belt', so you write:

Example: | **0** | *A LESS EXPENSIVE BELT*

1 mark + 1 mark

Write only the missing words IN CAPITAL LETTERS **on the separate answer sheet**.

2 Think about what is important in this exam task. What advice would you give another student about answering Part 4 in the exam?

3 Now read the advice given in the bullet points.

EXAM ADVICE

- Read the first sentence carefully.
- Think about how the key word given is commonly used.
- Complete the gap with a possible answer. You can use the question paper for rough answers.
- Count the number of words you have used in the gap. You must use not fewer than two and not more than five, including the word in bold. Note that a contracted form such as 'don't' counts as two words.
- Read the completed second sentence to check it means the same as the first.
- Ask yourself whether the words in the gap fit the sentence grammatically.
- Transfer your answer (just the words in the gap) to the answer sheet.

4   Complete these key word transformations, using the instructions in 1.

   1 'A club has just opened in Leeds,' said Maria to Sally.
   TOLD
   Maria .... club in Leeds.

   2 I returned the dress to the shop because it was badly made.
   TOOK
   Because the dress was badly made, I .... to the shop.

   3 Some shops try really hard to help you.
   EFFORT
   Some shops really .... to help you.

   4 Fifty years ago, cars were slower than they are nowadays.
   AS
   Fifty years ago, cars .... they are nowadays.

   5 People wear casual clothes where I work.
   UP
   People .... where I work.

   6 It's a lot easier to learn a language by visiting the country where it's spoken.
   MUCH
   You can learn a language .... you visit the country where it's spoken.

   7 For me, Stella McCartney is doing a lot more interesting work than other designers today.
   FAR
   For me, Stella McCartney is by .... designer working today.

   8 The stall didn't sell much jewellery because of its high prices.
   HIGHLY
   The jewellery on the stall was so .... much was sold.

The virtual world

Speaking

1 How far do you agree with the following statement? Discuss your ideas.

Computer games are anti-social and violent, and their users are mindless nerds.

> **nerd** /nɜːd/ *noun* [C] *informal* someone, especially a man, who is not fashionable and who is interested in boring things • **nerdy** *adjective informal* boring and not fashionable

2 What are the good things about playing games online? Are there any disadvantages?

3 In pairs, decide on the five most important features of any computer game, choosing from a–h below. What else do you look for in a virtual game?

a fast pace
b easy to get into
c lots of action
d puzzles to solve
e single- and multi-player modes
f suitable for all ages
g great background music
h sophisticated graphics

Exam spot

In Paper 1, there is a lot to read in only one hour. By **skimming** the text (reading it very quickly, not trying to understand every word but just trying to get a general idea of what it is about) and **scanning** it (running your eyes over it very quickly, just looking for particular words or information) you can find the answers more quickly and efficiently. These are essential skills to learn.

Reading

4 Scan the four online reviews of computer games to answer a–d quickly.

Which game

a is the cheapest?
b gets the best review?
c seems the least suitable for adults?
d has the most impressive soundtrack?

Where did you find this information? How much text did you need to read?

1

The idea is brilliant: set in the Wild West, this is a clone of the classic game *Doom*. Probably the best thing about this game is its introduction, with unusual camera angles, excellent sound effects and just about every Western cliché there ever was. It goes downhill when you get into the game itself. You spend your time creeping around empty buildings, endlessly shooting at hundreds of bad guys. You collect ammunition, health points and other things that you can use to solve puzzles. But once you finish one level of the game, you go on to another one which is remarkably similar – all rather dull. It's a case of 'Been there, done that' – eight times! However, while you're playing, you can always listen to the background music, which is by far the best of its kind. Turn up the volume and enjoy it.

THE VERDICT

○ *Makes you yawn at times, but good fun for fans of Westerns.* ***** £19.99**

2

This game's all about finding power for your ray gun, which you get by capturing tiny cartoon figures. The ray's pretty weak when you start – it needs electricity after all – so you only move small objects. This gives you enough power to turn on household appliances like fridges or vacuum cleaners, and locate the electrically charged critters hiding in them. You feel pretty hopeless to begin with, but ten minutes and several hundred hits later, you reach the point of feeling more like a superhero as the adventure develops. You overturn sofas, beds and other huge items, leaving rooms in a very messy state. And that's nothing! In higher levels, you walk the streets, so powerful that you can lift cars, trucks and eventually entire buildings. It's a shame that the gun resets to weak with each new level, but there are some impressive gameplay touches that stop you mindlessly breaking stuff – your grandma would approve!

THE VERDICT

○ *A great sense of progression as you go from weak to strong – never thought electricity could be so much fun!* ****** £8.75**

5 In groups of four, choose one review each and skim the text to find out what sort of game it is. Then scan your review to find one good and one bad point, looking out for phrases similar to the ones below. Compare your findings with other groups.

Good points
The best thing about

Bad points
It's a shame that

3

Did you know that car games have a poor relation? Yes, it's their motorbike cousins! Somehow motorbike games never provide the same thrill as car games, but this version comes very close and is easily the best available. There are eight different bikes, nine long tracks and a choice of race styles: Grand Prix or the muddy scrambling type, which gets quite tricky. The intelligence and speed of your 23 computer opponents are high, and guarantee a game demanding enough for the most advanced racer. So get on your bikes and take control!

THE VERDICT

● *A super-slick bike racer that truly does not disappoint.* ***** **£12.50**

4

This game is not demanding, perhaps because it's primarily aimed at kids under ten, though with only six levels and no multi-player mode, it's likely to be a bit disappointing even for the youngest of players. The little guy jogs along at a slow rate, which gets extremely boring at times. Jumping works OK, with a nice double-jump facility for things that are out of reach. Graphically, the game looks good with its bright and colourful cartoony feel, and occasionally there's some really nice background animation too. It's just too bad there isn't more content – games of this type are becoming more and more complex, but not this one! Even kids will get through most of it in an afternoon, as the puzzles and tasks are far too simple.

THE VERDICT

● *Simplistic gameplay suitable for a very young audience* ** **£9.99**

Vocabulary

Collocations

Vocabulary development beyond topic sets is essential for B2 level. Word formation, phrases, phrasal verbs and collocations are all important areas.

Learn which words commonly go together – nouns after a certain verb, adverbs with adjectives, etc. Some words have a close association, for example *bitterly disappointed*. Strong collocations like these are tested in the exam.

6 Read reviews 1–3 and find the nouns that go with verbs a–d. Then choose two more collocates for each verb from the box.

a solve .... (review 1)
b spend .... (review 1)
c reach .... (review 2)
d take .... (review 3)

| advantage conclusion crime fortune |
| goal interest money problem |

Grammar extra

-ly adverbs

All the adverbs below were used in the reviews of computer games. Write down their related adjectives and then say what the spelling rules are for forming these adverbs.

easily   endlessly   graphically   remarkably   truly

Some adverbs do not end in -ly. The most common of these are *fast, hard, late* and *well*. Note also the adverbs *hardly* and *lately*, which have different meanings.

Explain the meaning of the adverbs used below.
a She hardly thought about work while she was on holiday.
b He thought hard before answering.
c There have been a lot of good films lately.
d We arrived late for the film, which had already started.

G→ page 166

Corpus spot

Correct any spelling mistakes that exam candidates have made with adverbs in these sentences.
a Unfortunatelly, I'm quite busy at the moment.
b If I were you, I would definitly spend my evenings reading by the fireside.
c You just have to say your name and the computer opens the door automaticly.
d Entering the restaurant, you immediatly feel comfortable.
e We realy started to work hard the morning before the show.
f You must adjust the laser extremily carefully to get it in the correct position.
g I would like more information, especialy about accommodation.
h The computer completly takes hold of our lives.

Review of present tenses

1 Identify the underlined tenses in examples a–d. Then complete the grammar explanation below.

a The little guy <u>jogs along</u> at a slow rate.

b While <u>you're playing</u>, you can always listen to the music.

c It's a shame that the gun <u>resets</u> to weak with each new level.

d Games of this type <u>are becoming</u> more and more complex.

> The present .... tense is used for permanent situations (example ....) or to talk about actions which are habitual or repeated (example ....). On the other hand, the present .... tense is used for temporary situations (example ....), or for situations that are changing or developing (example ....).

2 Explain the other uses of each tense that are illustrated in these examples.

a <u>We're buying</u> a new computer next weekend.

b If <u>you finish</u> all the levels within an hour, <u>you get</u> extra points.

c Don't talk to me while <u>I'm playing</u>!

d Once <u>you decide</u> where to go, let me know.

e All the planets in our solar system <u>orbit</u> the sun.

G → page 167

3 Correct any mistakes with tenses in these sentences. Some sentences are correct.

a Electronic books are becoming more and more popular.

b This week only, the shop sells all software at 20% off.

c Don't shut down the computer as I'm downloading a film.

d As soon as you are playing this game, you realise the graphics are tremendous – everything is so realistic.

e My neighbour gives me access to his wifi this week but I'm planning to install my own on Monday.

f When you visit the website, you are getting a choice of free downloadable applications.

g Once I find a useful site, I'm bookmarking it for future reference.

4 Choose the correct present tense for each of these sentences, using the verbs in brackets.

a My new game is sensational – as soon as you .... a level, you .... something completely different to do. (finish, get)

b Generally, computer manuals .... , but some are still not accessible enough for users. (improve)

c An upgrade for this application .... soon. (come out)

d In the latest version, a dragon .... overhead and .... when you .... it. (fly, explode, hit)

e The company .... an interface to allow users to personalise their documents. (develop)

f Back-up copies .... time to prepare, but they are essential. (take)

g Whenever you .... , the system .... you to enter your password and then it .... a random security question. (log on, require, generate)

h If a computer .... , you .... the file you .... on unless you .... it regularly. (crash, lose, work, save)

5 Skim the extract from an article about 'googlewhacking' on the opposite page. Then fill each gap with a suitable present tense of one of the verbs in the box. Use each verb once only. There is one extra verb you do not need.

> add become believe change create
> encourage find out google mean
> ~~refer~~ sound spend submit update

Compare your answers with another student.

In which gaps can both the present simple and the present continuous be used? Is there any change in meaning?

Which of the verbs that you used do not have a present continuous form? Verbs not normally used in the continuous tenses are called 'stative' verbs. Do you know any more verbs like this?

G → page 167

Google™

An experienced web user, Gary Stock, came up with the term 'googlewhack', which **(0)** __REFERS__ to a single entry on a Google search page. It **(1)** .... increasingly difficult for googlewhackers like Gary to achieve their aim: the appearance of the message "Results 1-1 of 1" on their computer screen.
For one thing, people **(2)** .... new web pages and **(3)** .... existing ones all the time, which in turn **(4)** .... more and more entries on Google. Also, anyone who **(5)** .... their googlewhack to a website **(6)** .... another entry just by doing that.

Perhaps all of this **(7)** .... like a waste of time, but Gary Stock **(8)** .... that googlewhacking is a meaningful activity that **(9)** .... people to surf the web again, just like during the early days of the Internet. According to many, Google **(10)** .... our lives by broadening our knowledge of the world. People certainly **(11)** .... about new or unusual things by googlewhacking – from 'bartok nosepieces' to 'jillionaire incinerate'! But if you **(12)** .... these phrases on your computer today, will they still be googlewhacks?

Vocabulary

Word formation

Recognise words that are formed from a common base word and record them together to help you remember them. For example, at B2 you should know the noun *truth*, the adjective *true* and the adverb *truly*. Word formation using prefixes and suffixes is tested in the exam. You will also need to know some words with negative prefixes, as in this word family: *happiness*, *unhappiness*; *happy*, *unhappy*; *happily*, *unhappily*.

Many nouns have a related adjective formed with the suffix *-y*, as shown at the end of the dictionary example for *nerd* on page 16.

6 Make adjectives in this way from the nouns below. The first three are used in the reviews. What are the spelling rules in c and d?

    a trick   **b** mess   **c** mud   **d** ice

7 Many of these adjectives came up on pages 16–17. Divide them into two meaning groups, positive and negative. Which adjectives contain a prefix or a suffix? Which one contains both?

accessible	colourful	dull
excellent	favourable	hopeless
impressive	mindless	sophisticated
tricky	unhelpful	

Three of these adjectives are tested in 8, and some may also be useful in the writing task on pages 20–21.

8 Use the word given in capitals to form a word that fits in the numbered gap. Look at the words on either side of the gap to decide whether an adjective, adverb or noun is needed.

Tablet computers are growing in **(0)** __POPULARITY__ . They generally weigh far less than laptops and are much more **(1)** .... for people on the move. Many **(2)** .... that are developed for tablets incorporate a pen-friendly user interface and/or the **(3)** .... to handwrite directly into a document. They are very **(4)** .... when it comes to viewing photo slideshows or movies, though reading books **(5)** .... on a tablet can be **(6)** .... , depending on the screen display.

0 POPULAR
1 ACCESS
2 APPLY
3 ABLE
4 IMPRESS
5 ELECTRONIC
6 TRICK

Writing folder 1

Informal letters and emails

1 Look at the extracts below. Which two would you describe as informal? How did you decide?

A This is to inform you of the decisions taken at last week's meeting. Please note that all members of this department are strictly required to be present at such meetings and action may be taken in future to ensure this.

B I want to let you all know about our staff get-together last week. It's a pity more of you weren't there as it was a terrific occasion. Why not come along next time? There's free coffee and biscuits!

C Anyway, let me tell you about the party Jack is having on Saturday. Well, just about everyone is coming – even that weird guy Sam from college! Jack says he wants us all to be there, so you'd better not miss it. Why not come down for a few days? You can stay at my place if you want.

Decide for each extract who could have written it, who it was probably written to and why.

Exam spot

In Paper 2, you may have to write an informal letter or email. Think carefully about who you are writing to and why, before you decide whether to use informal language. In Part 2, you may be given an extract from a friend's letter or email to reply to, which can also give you clues about a suitable style.

2 Read this writing task and find the style clues.

Here is part of a letter from an English friend:

Guess what? My parents have given me some money for passing my exam, so I can splash out on something really special. I can't choose between buying a new computer game or saving up a bit more and getting some clothes. Which do you think would be better?
And can you suggest what exactly I should get?

Write a suitable **letter** to your friend.
(120–180 words)

3 The sample answer below would get a low mark, for several reasons. What are they?

Dear Frankie

What brilliant news in your letter! I wish to offer you congratulations about the exam. Moreover, how nice to have some spare cash.

You say you can't decide if to buy a computer game or some clothes. Don't you think that if you choose some new clothes you must save up a bit more money first? Clothes are not as cheap than computer games and I know you like expensive designer outfits. If you choose computer game, which one? There are so many available and to my mind they are all the same. In my opinion you should spend the money in something else. Why don't you get yourself a new dictionary, for example? Then it would be easier for you to study, wouldn't it?

I hope you will consider my suggestion seriously and I look forward to receiving a reply from you in due course.

Yours sincerely

Correct the errors in paragraph 2 and rewrite paragraphs 1 and 3 in an appropriate style.

4 Work in pairs. Plan how will you answer the task using the advice below and on the next page. Then write your answer.

Content ideas

Decide whether you think your friend should buy a game or clothes and note down some reasons to support your view. Then think about one specific game or item of clothing. What is special about it? Compare your ideas.

Game: topic, best points, price
Clothes: material, colour, style

Language input

You need to include these functions:

Congratulations   Opinion   Advice/Suggestion

Organisation

A letter needs adequate paragraphing, to make it easy to follow. In the sample answer, paragraph 2 is too long and the ideas in it are muddled. It is important to plan what you are going to say in note form before you start writing.

- Use this plan for your letter.
  - Opening formula
  - Paragraph 1 Initial greetings and congratulations
  - Paragraph 2 Opinion about which item the friend should buy
  - Paragraph 3 Description of one specific item
  - Paragraph 4 Final remarks
  - Closing formula
- Try to use linkers within each paragraph, to improve the flow of the letter. Choose appropriate ones from the list of linkers in 5 opposite to present your ideas in a clear order.
- Do not include any postal addresses, as they are not needed in the exam.

Style

Here are some typical features of informal writing. There is at least one example of each in the sample.

Contracted forms, for example *I'm, don't*
Phrasal verbs
Phrases with *get, take, have*, etc., for example *take a look*
Short sentences
Simple linking words, for example *Then*
Direct questions, for example *What about …?*
Some exclamation marks (not too many!)

Editing your work

It is important to read through what you have written and put right any mistakes. Check your work for the following:

a Is the grammar accurate?
b Is the spelling correct?
c Is there enough punctuation?
d Is the style consistent?

The first letters of the five headings above spell out the word C-L-O-S-E. It is important to think about these five elements (Content, Language, Organisation, Style, Editing) for all Paper 2 tasks. And the word 'Close' will also remind you to finish a piece of writing, for example by signing off a letter. Some candidates in the exam forget to do this and lose marks.

Formal or informal?

5 **Write *Inf* next to the expressions that are informal.**

Initial greetings
It was great to hear from you. ...*Inf*...
I am writing with reference to your letter. ....
Thanks for writing to me. ....

Congratulations
Well done! ....
I would like to offer congratulations on ....
Let me congratulate you on ....

Opinion
In my opinion ....
To my mind ....
I hold the view that ....
Personally, I have no doubt that ....
My own thoughts are ....

Advice/Suggestion
Why not try ....
What about trying ....
It is recommended that you ....
You could ....
I urge you to ....
I suggest that ....
If I were you ....

Linkers
Moreover ....
Also ....
Then again ....
Furthermore ....
Better still ....
As well as that ....
What's more ....
Additionally ....

Endings
Do drop me a line if you have time. ....
I look forward to hearing from you without delay.
....
Hope to hear from you soon. ....
Keep in touch. ....
I hope to hear from you at your earliest convenience.
....

Opening and closing a letter
Match these opening and closing formulae and say when you should use each of them.
Dear Jayne   Yours faithfully
Dear Sir   Yours sincerely
Dear Ms Jones   Love

3.1 Going places

Speaking

Exam spot

In Paper 5 Part 2, each candidate is given a pair of photos to talk about on their own. The task will involve comparing and contrasting the two photos, rather than just describing each one.

1 Work in pairs. Student A look at photos 1 and 2, and Student B at photos 3 and 4.

Student A Who would enjoy these types of holiday?

Student B What are the advantages and disadvantages of these types of holiday?

Now talk about the following questions in pairs.

a Which of the holidays in the photos would you choose? Why?

b If you had a lot of time and money, where in the world would you most like to go on holiday? Why?

Exam spot

In Paper 4 Part 2, you will be asked to complete some sentences. You will need to write a word or short phrase and you will hear the recording twice. The words you write down are in the order you hear them. There is no need to make any changes to these words.

Listening

2 🎧 04 Read questions 1–10 and, in pairs, try to predict what word or words you might need to fill each gap. Then listen to the interview and answer the questions.

Steve says that the temperature was usually around _____ **1** degrees during the trip.

Steve found _____ **2** to be the most useful thing he took with him.

In his cabin, Steve had a _____ **3** under his bed.

Steve says the nationality of the expedition leader was _____ **4**

While Steve was on the cruise, the seas were _____ **5**

Steve enjoyed seeing the wide range of _____ **6** most of all.

According to Steve, the only people, besides tourists, in the region were working at a _____ **7**

Steve says that empty _____ **8** are the only evidence of fishing in earlier times.

Cruise ships are forbidden to get rid of _____ **9** in the Antarctic.

Steve says it's important that _____ **10** isn't disturbed by tourists.

3 Do you approve of tourists being allowed to go to unspoilt areas of the world? Would you go to Antarctica if you had the opportunity?

Vocabulary

Topic set – travel and holidays

4 If you write down new words in categories, it will help you remember them. With a partner, put the words in the box into the following categories:

Transport   Seaside   Accommodation
Movement   People

> airline   backpacker   bed and breakfast
> campsite   caravan   cliff   coach   coast
> crew   ferry   flight   harbour   holiday-makers
> hostel   journey   landing   shore   travel agent
> voyage   yacht

What other words could go in each category?

Phrasal verbs

5 The phrasal verbs *in italics* are to do with travel. Match each phrasal verb in sentences a–h with one of the meanings 1–8 below.

a When we got to the hotel we went to the reception to *check in*.

b Paolo decided he really needed to *get away* to somewhere hot where he could rest and relax.

c The plane is supposed to *get in* at about 10.00.

d Dr Lee *set off* from his house around 6.00 this morning in order to catch his flight.

e When we fly to Japan we usually *stop over* in Delhi.

f When the family went to the travel agency, the travel agent *booked* them *into* a hotel on the coast for two weeks.

g All hotel guests must *check out* by midday.

h Please go to Gate 14 as the plane to Lisbon is due to *take off* in about 30 minutes.

1 to arrive at a destination
2 to leave the ground
3 to pay and leave accommodation
4 to stay somewhere for a short time when you are going somewhere else
5 to arrange for someone to stay in (a hotel)
6 to go on holiday
7 to register at your accommodation
8 to begin a journey

Now, in pairs, talk about your last holiday using vocabulary from the exercises above.

EXAMPLE:

A: Where did you travel to?

B: I went to Australia. I caught a plane and had to set off very early in the morning.

Collocations

6 Link the verbs in box A with suitable nouns in box B. There is sometimes more than one answer. Do the same words go together in your language?

A

> take   book   catch   board   get   go

B

> skiing   trip   sightseeing   ship
> plane   tan   hotel   flight

7 The task below is similar to, but simpler than, the one you will have in the Use of English paper. Decide which answer, A or B, best fits each gap.

The history of airports

The earliest aircraft takeoff and landing (**1**) .... were in fields or on dirt tracks. When it came to landing, a plane could (**2**) .... at any angle, depending on wind direction. However, fields and tracks only functioned well in dry conditions. In order to (**3**) .... year-round landings, concrete surfaces would be necessary.

The word 'airport' (**4**) .... in a *New York Times* article in 1902, where it was (**5**) .... that New York was expected to be the main world 'airport' within twenty years. However, there was competition for this title as a number of other airports began to open in the 1920s – Albany International Airport in the United States, Bremen Airport in Germany, Schiphol in The Netherlands, Sydney Airport in Australia and Rome Ciampino in Italy.

Today, the world's busiest airport is Hartsfield-Jackson Atlanta International, which is (**6**) .... in the United States. It is the world's busiest airport by passenger traffic, serving 90 million passengers per year, as well as by number of landings and take-offs. The airport has 151 (**7**) .... and 28 international gates, and two terminals where passengers (**8**) .... for their flights.

1	**A** sites	**B** spots
2	**A** reach	**B** approach
3	**A** let	**B** allow
4	**A** arrived	**B** appeared
5	**A** stated	**B** told
6	**A** set	**B** located
7	**A** home	**B** domestic
8	**A** check in	**B** take off

Modals 1: Obligation, necessity and permission

1 Look at the extracts (a–g) from the recording in 3.1 and then match them with phrases 1–6.

a you should take warm clothes

b you really need a windproof coat

c you don't have to socialise if you don't want to

d cruise ships are not allowed to go where they like

e they have to take scientists to lead the excursions

f only small parties are permitted to land

g you've got to keep quiet

1 There's no choice.

2 It's necessary.

3 It's forbidden.

4 It's allowed.

5 It's not necessary.

6 It's a good idea.

2 In small groups, talk about the following sentences. Decide why some sentences use *must* and others use *have to*.

a I must remember to buy a newspaper on my way home.

b The doctor says I have to try to take more exercise.

c All cars must be left in the car park, not on the road.

G → page 167

3 Imagine you are extremely rich. In pairs, discuss your holidays in the places shown, using *must, have to* and *don't have to*. Talk about transportation, accommodation, food, activities, entertainment and people.

> When I go to Los Angeles, I tell my secretary that I must stay at the Beverley Wiltshire hotel. My suite must have a private swimming pool and jacuzzi. Luckily I don't have to queue at the airport as I have a private jet, and a limousine to meet me. Even though I'm very rich, I still have to take a passport like everyone else.

Corpus spot

Be careful with modal verbs – the *Cambridge Learner Corpus* shows exam candidates often make mistakes with these.

I **must fill in** an application form for a visa.

NOT I ~~must to fill in~~ an application form for a visa.

I **don't have to show** my passport at the border any more.

NOT I ~~haven't to show~~ my passport at the border any more.

Correct the mistakes that candidates have made with obligation and necessity.

a You needn't much space to park your car.

b Another thing, should I to take my camera with me?

c You needn't smoke in this part of the restaurant; it's a no smoking area.

d It is better when you go by car because you must not get up early.

e We have get to the exhibition early or we won't get a ticket.

f You don't have to swim off the rocks because it's dangerous.

g My doctor says I need give up smoking.

h Lisa must to buy a ticket before getting on the bus.

i I don't have to be late or I'll miss my plane.

4 With a partner, talk about the following situations.

EXAMPLE: *I'm going to travel abroad.*
– *I need a new passport.*
– *I have to have an injection.*
– *I must pack my bag.*
– *I should buy a new pair of sunglasses but I don't think I have time.*

a It's the weekend tomorrow.
b My brother is 18 next week.
c My friend is getting married soon.
d I started a new job last week.
e I've got toothache.
f I'm having a party on Saturday.

5 You can use *permit*, *allow*, *let* and *can* to express permission. Notice that both *permit* and *allow* are followed by *to*, and *let* and *can* aren't.

What did your parents let you do when you were younger? What are you allowed to do when you are 18 in your country?

Using *permit*, *allow*, *let* or *can* once only, complete these sentences. You may need to add other words.

a I wasn't .... to go on holiday with my friends until I was sixteen.
b You .... stay at this campsite without booking in advance.
c Peter .... me borrow his large suitcase when I went shopping in New York.
d They .... us to board the plane early because we only had hand luggage.

G ➔ page 167

Grammar extra

Prepositions of location

Complete the following sentences with these prepositions of location.

| across | at | in | into | off | on |

a The hotel had a swimming pool .... its roof.
b I arrived .... the airport very early in the morning.
c When I walked .... the hotel I was amazed by the decoration.
d I arrived .... Spain last Tuesday.
e We showed our passports as we went .... the frontier.
f I found a bank .... the town centre.
g We sat .... the terrace drinking coffee.
h There was a notice .... the wall telling us about trips.
i I jumped .... the pool to cool off.
j Singapore is an island .... the coast of Malaysia.

Exam spot

In Paper 3 Part 4 remember that a contraction – *don't*, *isn't* – counts as two words.

6 Complete the second sentence so that it has a similar meaning to the first sentence, using the word given. Do not change the word given. You must use between two and five words, including the word given.

1 The travel agent said, 'All passengers for Marseilles must change trains in Paris.'
TO
The travel agent said that all passengers for Marseilles .... trains in Paris.

2 Smoking in the hotel restaurant is not allowed.
FORBIDDEN
It .... in the hotel restaurant.

3 I wasn't allowed to go on holiday with my friends last year.
LET
My parents .... on holiday with my friends last year.

4 This is a 'no swimming' area.
PERMITTED
You .... in this area.

5 It's a good idea to have health insurance when you go on holiday.
GET
You .... before you go on holiday.

6 British passport holders no longer need a visa to visit the USA.
HAVE
British passport holders .... a visa to visit the USA any more.

7 It's not necessary to wear heavy clothing in the summer months.
NEED
You .... on heavy clothing in the summer months.

8 You must telephone the hotel and book in advance if you want to be sure of a room.
GOT
You .... up the hotel and book in advance if you want to be sure of a room.

Exam folder 2

Paper 3 Part 3 Word formation

In this part of the Use of English paper you are given a short text with ten gaps and an example. At the end of some of the lines there is a word in CAPITALS which you will need to change so that it will make sense when it is put in the gap in the same line. In the example below, you are given the verb 'arrive' and it needs to be changed into the noun 'arrival' in order for the sentence to make sense.

EXAMPLE: Their plane's late ..... was due to a thunderstorm during the flight. **ARRIVE**
ANSWER: Their plane's late _ARRIVAL_ was due to a thunderstorm during the flight.

You need to read the sentence carefully to decide what kind of word is missing – is it a noun, a verb, an adjective or an adverb? In English we often use prefixes (letter(s) that go in front of a word) and suffixes (letter(s) that go at the end of a word) to change the type of word it is.

Prefixes

1   The following prefixes all give the meaning of NOT when they come before a word.

il-   ir-   in-   un-
dis-   im-   mis-

We often, but not always, put *il-* before words beginning with *l*, *ir-* before words beginning with *r*, and *im-* before words beginning with *m* and *p*.

Which prefix do we use to make these words negative?

a satisfied   h happy
b patient   i responsible
c expensive   j understand
d legal   k appear
e possible   l regular
f comfortable   m moral
g honest

2   What meaning do you think these prefixes give to the word that follows? Can you think of some more examples?

a *non-*stop   d *un*tie
b *re*train   e *under*line
c *sub*way

Suffixes

3   NOUNS – Typical noun suffixes are:

-ation -ion -ness -ship -ity
-ism -ence -ment -al

Make these words into nouns.

a happy   d recommend   g friend
b intelligent   e act   h pay
c approve   f popular   i tour

4   Not all nouns follow the above pattern. Make nouns from these words.

a true   c die
b succeed   d high

5   ADJECTIVES – Typical adjectival suffixes are:

-ible -able -y -al
-ive -ful -less -ous

Make these words into adjectives.

a wind   d danger   g value
b attract   e end   h access
c hope   f accident

6   ADVERBS – Adverbs are usually formed by adding the suffix *-ly* to the adjective. Be careful with spelling.

complete – completely   reasonable – reasonably
temporary – temporarily   basic – basically
real – really

And there are some exceptions:

true – truly (NOT ~~truely~~)
shy – shyly (NOT ~~shily~~)
public – publicly (NOT ~~publically~~)

Make these words into adverbs.

a steady   **d** annual

b active   **e** extraordinary

c necessary   **f** automatic

7   VERBS – It is less common in Part 3 of Paper 3 to have to form a verb. However, you may be asked to make changes to a verb by using a prefix such as *un-*, *dis-* or *re-* , or to make a noun or an adjective into a verb by using the prefixes *dis-* or *re-*.

Change these words using *un-*, *dis-* or *re-*.

a new   **e** pay

b courage   **f** approve

c do   **g** lock

d build

It is more likely that you will need to change a verb into a noun or adjective. Change these verbs to nouns.

h communicate   **l** identify

i measure   **m** introduce

j satisfy   **n** criticise

k maintain

EXAM ADVICE

- Read through the text carefully to get an idea of what it is about.
- Decide what kind of word is missing – is it an adjective, verb, noun or adverb?
- Make sure that your choice makes sense in the sentence. Some words may need to have a negative prefix.

  EXAMPLE: The waitress took ages to bring us the menu and I found her very rude and .... HELP

  ANSWER: UNHELPFUL

- Check that you have spelt the words correctly.
- You MUST write your answers IN CAPITAL LETTERS.

8   Read through the text on the right and think about what kind of words you need to make. For example, **0** is a noun (PUBLICATION). List the parts of speech for gaps 1–10 and then complete the task.

     1 = VERB

     2 =

     3 =

     4 =

     5 =

     6 =

     7 =

     8 =

     9 =

     10 =

A DISTINGUISHED MAP-MAKER

Example: **0**   P U B L I C A T I O N

In 1538, the **(0)** .... of a world map showed North and South America as separate continents for the first time. The man who **(1)** .... this important map was called Gerardus Mercator. Mercator spent his **(2)** .... in Flanders, where he became known as an **(3)** .... talented map-maker. Besides teaching mathematics to the students at the University of Louvain, he also earned extra money making **(4)** .... instruments.

PUBLISH

PRODUCT
YOUNG
EXTREME

SCIENCE

In 1544, he was briefly imprisoned for his **(5)** .... beliefs and, fearing for his family's **(6)** .... , he went to live in the Rhineland, where he remained for the rest of his life. Mercator's youngest son Rumold became his father's **(7)** .... after his death in 1594, supervising the **(8)** .... of the first complete edition of the Mercator world atlas the following year.

RELIGION
SAFE

REPRESENT
APPEAR

Although Mercator constantly updated his maps with new information, some were **(9)** .... because the earth is round. As maps are flat, it is virtually **(10)** .... to show the right scale, area and direction on one map.

CORRECT
POSSIBLE

4.1 Endangered

Exam spot

Paper 1 Part 3 consists of four to six short texts on the same subject. Read the 15 questions first, so that you know what you are looking for. Then scan the text for the information you need.

Reading

1   Match the animal or bird with the correct photo.

tiger shark   snow leopard
orang-utan   thick-billed parrot
polar bear   koala

Which of the above are endangered? Do you know why?

If you could save *one* of the above, which would you choose? Why?

2   These sentences include words which are used in connection with animals today. Use an English–English dictionary to look up the meaning of the words in bold and then match a–e with 1–5.

a   Arctic animals are now **in danger** because of

b   **Cutting down** the trees where animals live is

c   Many animals **suffer** when rivers and streams

d   There are very few Bengal tigers left because of

e   Some animals such as the white rhino are

1   called **habitat destruction**.

2   **rising sea levels** affecting coastal areas of Bangladesh.

3   ice melting due to **global warming**.

4   **are polluted** by factories.

5   **facing extinction** because people hunt them for their horns.

3   Skim texts A–E opposite. They all come from one source. Which do you think it is?

a   an encyclopaedia   c   an article
b   a novel   d   a brochure

4   You will find that some of the texts are quite similar. It is important that you find the information that actually answers the question. Read the texts opposite and answer the following for practice.

a   Which person went to the zoo with a relative?

You will see that all the relatives mentioned are highlighted in the texts, but only text E has the answer to the question.

b   Which person thought the zoo was value for money?

All mentions of money are underlined – which answers the question?

Now read questions 1–15 and find the answers in texts A–E. When you think you have found the words that gives you the answer, underline them.

Which person

mentions an exhibit which some visitors find amusing?	1
says visitors can decide on the animal they want to support?	2
was surprised at first by the absence of some animals?	3
says that the zoo was as good as people said it was?	4
gives advice on a means of transport at the zoo?	5
says that one particular aim of the zoo has succeeded?	6
mentions a particular problem which is endangering animals?	7
complains about how long it takes to see everything within the zoo?	8
mentions visitors being able to bring refreshments with them?	9
praises the location of the zoo?	10
enjoyed seeing one particular type of animal?	11
was initially unsure about going to a zoo?	12
complains about some people's attitude to less familiar species?	13
says that after visiting a particular zoo they changed their mind about zoos?	14
was unconcerned by the number of visitors at the zoo?	15

A visit to a zoo
Five people describe their visit to a conservation zoo

A Julia

I went to Marwell Zoo with two friends from college last year. It has over 200 species of rare animals, from Siberian tigers to white rhino and snow leopards. Personally, the red pandas were my favourites – they're like cuddly teddy bears. The zoo was only started in 1972, with breeding as its objective, and some species, such as the scimitar-horned oryx, which was once extinct in the wild, have been bred so well that they have been re-introduced into the wild. I was initially amazed by the fact that there are no traditional zoo animals like elephants and penguins there. This zoo specialises in keeping rare and endangered species and there is not room or money enough to keep anything just because it happens to be popular. There are, however, some traditional features like a café and souvenir shop.

B Peter

I took the decision to visit San Diego Zoo. It has a huge reputation and I was interested in whether it would live up to it. I wasn't disappointed. The zoo was founded in 1916 and the founders couldn't have picked a better place – benefitting from breezes from the Pacific Ocean, being close to the city but also having wooded canyons, which make the zoo fun to explore either on foot or by bus or cable car. The zoo is home to a huge number of endangered species. However, one problem for the zoo was that the visitors seemed to be mainly interested in the well-known species such as the polar bear and just walked straight past other more endangered but less well-known species like the thick-billed parrot.

C Karin

I was working as a nanny for two sisters in New York last year and on one of my free days I decided to visit the Bronx Zoo. Animals are kept in large, natural enclosures and the zoo is very keen on visitor education about conservation. You get to go into the largest African rainforest exhibit in the world – and it actually felt like a real rainforest – with lots of different animals like, for example, gorillas. When you come out you are allowed to select which rainforest animal you want your entrance fee to fund. There were crowds of tourists at the zoo when I visited, but the place is so big that it didn't really matter that much. There are a number of inexpensive cafés you can go to, or do as I did and take a picnic – there are loads of places to sit and enjoy the scenery.

D Tom

Many species are now endangered because of what is happening to our planet – things like global warming – but some zoos are actually doing something to try to conserve these species. Whipsnade Zoo in England is one of them. I visited it about a month ago when I was backpacking with a friend of my brother's. He's studying zoology at university in Australia so he was keen to see what conservation ideas the zoo had. We had a really good time and it was worth every penny. There's a free bus that can take you round all the main sights and I would really recommend you take it. The penguin pool is particularly beautiful as it is on top of a hill and has great views. It's a great place if, like me, you're into photography.

E Lara

Last summer, I was staying with my aunt in Toronto and she suggested I take my nine-year-old cousin to the zoo as it was her favourite place. I wasn't sure at first that I wanted to spend a day at a zoo. I guess I had always regarded them as over-priced places with cages and unhappy animals, but Toronto Zoo soon made me think differently! It's quite big – a bit too big if you try to go everywhere, and it's a 20-minute journey getting from one area to another, which is a pain. You absolutely must take a map as well, as it's easy to get lost. There are four main areas to visit and many of the animals are endangered species. I particularly liked the Malayan Woods Pavilion – there is artificial rainfall there, which makes children laugh.

---

5 Do you think zoos are a good way of saving endangered species? Why? / Why not?

What do you think of the zoos mentioned in the article?

Have you ever been to a zoo? What was it like?

Vocabulary

Word formation

> When you look up a word in a dictionary, look also to see what other related words you can find and make a note of them.

6 Which words related to a–j occur in texts A–E?

EXAMPLE: *expensive (C) – inexpensive*

a tradition (A)	**e** conserve (C)	**i** happy (E)
b danger (A)	**f** enter (C)	**j** rain (E)
c decide (B)	**g** zoo (D)	
d visit (B)	**h** see (D)	

as and like

1 Read the explanations below. Some of the examples are taken from the article you have read in 4.1.

- *As* is used to refer to a person's profession:
  I was working as a nanny for two sisters
- *Like* is only used for comparison or similarity:
  they're like cuddly teddy bears
- *Like* and *such as* can be used to mean *for example*:
  different animals, like gorillas
  things like global warming
  such as the scimitar-horned oryx
- Some verbs can be followed by *as*:
  I had always regarded them as over-priced
  Other verbs of this type are *refer to, use, be known, describe, class, accept* and *treat*.
- *As* is normally followed by a subject and verb, while *like* is followed by a noun or pronoun:
  or do as I did and take a picnic
  it actually felt like a real rainforest

G → page 167

Corpus spot

The *Cambridge Learner Corpus* shows that exam candidates often confuse the use of *like* and *as*.

I would like to work **as** a babysitter.
NOT I would like to work ~~like~~ a babysitter.

Sometimes students use *like* or *as* when it isn't necessary to do so.

It was a small flat that looked empty.
NOT It was a small flat that looked ~~like~~ empty.

I expected the water to be crystal clear.
NOT I expected the water to be ~~as~~ crystal clear.

---

2 Complete the following sentences using *as*, *like* or nothing, as appropriate.

  a The large cat looked .... a cheetah.
  b I know it sounds .... foolish, but I want to buy a tiger.
  c You can work .... full-time in the zoo souvenir shop.
  d The new penguin area is very big – it's .... an Olympic swimming pool.
  e She could photograph the animals just .... a professional.
  f He went to the fancy dress party dressed .... a gorilla.
  g Pete regarded his cat .... a member of the family.

3 Complete the second sentence so that it has a similar meaning to the first sentence, using the word given. Do not change the word given. You must use between two and five words, including the word given.

1 According to the brochure, the zoo was 'a perfect place to spend the day'.
  AS
  The zoo was ....
  'a perfect place to spend the day'.

2 In my house, we store our bikes in the garage.
  STORAGE
  In my house, we ....
  for our bikes.

3 Sue taught small children in a school in Sydney before returning to the UK.
  WORKING
  Sue ....
  of small children in a school in Sydney before returning to the UK.

4 My friend, whose name is Edmund, is usually called Fuz at school.
  KNOWN
  My friend Edmund ....
  Fuz at school.

5 They heard what they thought was a dog barking.
  SOUNDED
  They heard ....
  a dog barking.

Compound adjectives

4 A compound adjective is an adjective which has two parts and is usually written with a hyphen. Many have a present or past participle in the second part of the compound, as in this example from 4.1:

a thick-billed parrot – a parrot with a thick bill

Work through the questions in a–d with a partner.

a 1 Who do you think our 'four-legged friends' are?
   2 What is a man-eating tiger?
   3 How would you describe a cat which has blue eyes, long hair and a bad temper?

b Do you know anyone who is:
   1 left-handed?
   2 cross-eyed?
   3 bad-tempered?
   4 sharp-tongued?
   5 narrow-minded?

Compound adjectives are very useful for describing people, both for character and physical characteristics.

EXAMPLE: *My mother's a brown-eyed, curly-haired woman. She's left-handed. She's a broad-minded and self-confident person.*

c Some compound adjectives have a preposition in the second part of the compound.
   1 Where would you sit at a drive-in movie?
   2 How would you feel if you were hard-up?
   3 How much money do you need to have to be well-off?
   Can you think of some more examples?

d The article in 4.1 talked about a '20-minute journey'. Notice that *minute* is singular not plural.

   How would you describe:
   1 a road which was fifty kilometres long?
   2 a girl who is twelve years old?
   3 a film which lasts 75 minutes?
   4 a car which costs £35,000?
   5 a pause which lasts ten seconds?

Vocabulary

Topic set – parts of animals

5 Decide which of the words below are used with each of these creatures. Some can be used more than once. Use an English–English dictionary to help you.

parrot bear tiger rhino

beak feathers fur horn paw tail wing

Expressions with *time*

When you learn expressions such as the ones below, try to write them in a sentence to help you remember them.

6 There are many common expressions with *time* in English, as in this example from the article about zoos.

   … we had a really good time

kill time	ten times three
have a good time	one at a time
tell the time	from time to time
spend time	a time when
pass the time	time for breakfast/lunch
take time off	in time
waste time	at times
	(four) times as much

Complete sentences a–h with one of the expressions above.

a We all went into the aquarium .... through the automatic gate.

b I usually don't have enough .... , so I grab a sandwich on the way to work.

c He says he never puts on weight, but he eats three .... as I do.

d .... people will realise that not spending enough on education is very unwise.

e Although Peter decided not to come with us, he said he hoped we would ....

f I always take a book to the doctor's surgery to .... while I'm waiting.

g She was given a watch as soon as she learnt to ....

h I really hate .... doing stupid exercises.

7 Ask your partner these questions.

   a Can you think of three ways of wasting time?
   b What's the best way of having a good time?
   c What do you do when you have to kill time?

Writing folder 2

Transactional letters and emails 1

Question 1 in Paper 2 is compulsory – all exam candidates have to answer it. 'Transactional' means that the letter or email has a particular purpose, and will require further action by its reader, usually in the form of a written response. The letter or email must be based on the information given in the question. Examples of transactional letters and emails include: writing to a school to request details about a language course; complaining to a company about a holiday; replying to a friend about arrangements for a party. The letter or email could be formal or informal. For the examination there is no difference in the way you write a letter or an email.

1 Look at the following extracts and decide what the writer is doing in each. (Some may be used twice, while others are not used at all.)

a complaining
b suggesting
c correcting information
d giving information
e asking for information

1 I must point out that the article in your newspaper about our International Club gave some misleading information. We actually meet once a week, not once a fortnight, and we begin at 8 o'clock, not 9 o'clock. You also gave the impression that the club was just for young people. In fact, we are very happy to welcome people of all ages.

2 I have always enjoyed working with animals and have spent every summer working as a riding instructor at a local stable. I am available for interview from May 19th this year and I include the names and addresses of two people who would be willing to give me a reference.

3 As I've already said, I think the general standard of accommodation in your hotel is good. However, I think that you should spend more time on staff training as I found some of your staff, especially those in the restaurant, to be unhelpful and on one occasion, quite rude.

2 Read this example of a Part 1 task.

You have just returned from a trip to Florida. You flew there and back with Ocean Air. You decide to write to the airline to complain about your flight.

Read the advertisement and the notes you have made. Then write a letter to the airline, using all your notes.

Write your **letter** in 120–150 words. Do not include any postal addresses.

3 In pairs, discuss what you are being asked to do.

- Do you need to write a formal or an informal letter? How do you know?
- Do you know the name of anyone at the company? How will you begin and end the letter? What kind of tone will your letter take (rude, polite, etc.)?
- How are you going to organise the letter? For example: how many paragraphs will you need, and what kind of linking words will you use?
- Which points do you think are the most important?
- Are there any points you think you can leave out?
- Is there anything you think it would be a good idea to add?

4 With a partner decide what is wrong with the following letter. For example, there are punctuation mistakes, so **a** is ticked (✓). Do the same with **b–j**.

a punctuation ✓
b paragraphing ☐
c length ☐
d grammar ☐
e vocabulary ☐
f opening and closing phrases ☐
g content points ☐
h spelling ☐
i tone (level of politeness, formality) ☐
j linking words ☐

Dear Sir,

I am writing to complain about the flight to Florida that I made with your airline on 12th June this year We were three hours late boarding the plane. No one was able to tell us why. Another problem was the flight attendant she was very unhelpful. I had problems with my hand luggage. She told me she was too busy to help me. I demand some compensation for the problems I had flying with your airline. If you don't send me the money immediately, I will call my lawyer.

Yours faithfully

---

5 With a partner decide which of these sentences you would use in a formal letter and why. You must remember that your letter must have a 'positive effect' on the person reading it.

a I want you to give me back my money.
b I look forward to hearing from you in the near future.
c The food was OK.
d I have decided not to fly with your company again.
e I would be grateful if you could send me a refund.
f The service was satisfactory.
g If you don't do what I tell you, there's going to be trouble.
h I would appreciate an apology from your company.
i Hi Steve!
j See you soon.
k Dear Sir or Madam
l And, another thing, I won't fly with you again because it wasn't very comfortable.

Abbreviations

6 You will sometimes find abbreviations given in the Part 1 task. Decide what the following common abbreviations mean. Use your English–English dictionary to help you.

a	RSVP	**g**	PTO	**l**	c/o
b	e.g.	**h**	kg, km	**m**	approx.
c	etc.	**i**	nos.	**n**	cont'd
d	N.B.	**j**	max., min.	**o**	mins
e	tel.	**k**	Dr		
f	Sq., Ave, St, Rd				

7 Another type of transactional letter or email task is correcting information, usually from a newspaper article. Look at this task. Write your answer in 120–150 words in an appropriate style.

In the summer you had a job at a work camp in Kirby in England.
A friend in Kirby has just sent you this article from the local newspaper. You decide to write an email to the newspaper to correct some of the information in the article.

Read the article and the notes you have made. Then, write an email to the newspaper, using all your notes.

Student slaves at work camp

All summer some 30 foreign students were working long hours for little more than pocket money on a local farm. Sleeping in old tents and with only one shower between 30 people, the students spent their days picking fruit and vegetables. It's a disgrace that visitors to this country who come to these so-called 'international work camps' should have to put up with such dreadful conditions. I think that

Notes
- max. 15 students
- mornings only, weekends free
- modern, wooden buildings with showers
- fun, great atmosphere

In your email you must use grammatically correct sentences with accurate spelling and punctuation in a style appropriate for the situation.

Mixed emotions

1 Put these adjectives in two groups according to positive and negative meaning. Which two are used with *stiff* to describe a very strong emotion?

anxious	content	delighted	frightened
happy	petrified	pleased	satisfied
scared	tense	terrified	thrilled
uneasy	worried		

2 How do the things in the picture make you feel? Use adjectives from 1 to describe your emotions.

Vocabulary

Collocations – adverbs of degree

> Be careful when using adverbs such as *absolutely* and *very* with adjectives. Think about the meaning of the adjective – is it 'gradable' or not? For example, *enormous* is ungradable, because it already contains the meaning of 'very, very big'.

3 Which sentence in a and b is correct? Why?

a I'm very happy to see you. / I'm absolutely happy to see you.

b Sam's very delighted with her present. / Sam's absolutely delighted with her present.

> When combining adverbs like these with adjectives, think whether the adjective already means 'a lot'.

4 Complete the sentences with a suitable adverb from the box. More than one answer is possible.

> absolutely   completely   extremely
> really   totally   very

a Sally was .... astonished to hear that she had won the competition.

b As he entered the dark, empty flat, Alex felt .... uneasy.

c Simon's father sounded .... proud of his son's achievements.

d I arrived late for the film and James was .... furious with me!

e Martin gets .... irritated by people asking him the same questions time after time.

f I was .... relieved to find out I didn't have to pay the bill after all.

> ### Corpus spot
>
> Exam candidates often make mistakes in the spelling of these adverbs:
>
> absolutely NOT ~~absolutly~~
> completely NOT ~~complitely~~
> extremely NOT ~~extreamly~~
> totally NOT ~~totaly~~

Listening

5 **1**|05 Listen to this recording, where a man is talking about something frightening that happened to him. Say where the man was and how long he spent there.

Now listen again and describe in detail what happened to the man. Use these questions to help you.

1 Why was he in the building?
2 What time of day was it?
3 Which two things did he try to do?
4 Why was he there for so long?

Exam spot

Paper 4 Part 1 consists of eight short extracts. For each extract, there is one multiple-choice question. The eight questions will test different things, for example who is speaking, how he or she feels, where the recording is taking place, or what it is about.

6 Here is the question for the extract you have just heard.

1 You hear a man talking about something frightening that happened to him. What was his first reaction?
   A He sat down and cried.
   B He decided to call for help.
   C He tried to keep calm.

All three options are mentioned in the extract. Listening out for sequence words – that is, words which tell you what happened when – will help you to decide what his first reaction was.

Listen again and note down any sequence words and phrases. Which one signals the answer?

7 **1**|06 Before you listen to extracts 2–8, read these questions. Think about the words in bold and what to listen out for. Then listen and answer the questions.

2 You hear a man talking about how to deal with fear. **Who** is he?
   A an ex-teacher
   B an ex-pilot
   C an ex-actor

3 You hear a woman talking to her son on the phone. **How** does she **feel**?
   A furious
   B anxious
   C relieved

4 You hear a woman talking about something that happened in her home. When was she **most** scared?
   A when she heard a burglar upstairs
   B while she was watching a horror film
   C when she suddenly saw a frog

5 You hear a man leaving a phone message. **Why** is he **proud of his daughter**?
   A because she is going to have a book published
   B because she has won a writing competition
   C because she is doing so well at university

6 You hear a woman describing what happened to her on a journey. **Where** did she **end up** that night?
   A on a country road
   B in hospital
   C at her house

7 You hear a man being interviewed about a sailing accident. What was the **worst** part of his experience?
   A being cold
   B feeling hungry
   C avoiding sharks

8 You hear a woman talking on the radio about an incident abroad. **Why** was she able to **escape**?
   A She was by the door.
   B She wasn't noticed.
   C She had a radio.

8 How much can you remember about the last account? Discuss with a partner what happened and note down everything in the order it happened. Then listen to extract 8 to check your notes.

Grammar extra

This unit revises past tenses. Before the next lesson, copy and complete the table of irregular forms. All the verbs below have occurred in the listening extracts. An example is given.

Infinitive	Past tense	Past participle
become	*became*	*(has/had) become*

burst buy creep drive find get hear hold keep
know run see shake sink spend take think weep

Which verb has the same form throughout? Do you know any other verbs which are like that?

G→page 168

5.2

Review of past tenses

1 Look at examples a–j, which come from the listening in 5.1. Decide which tenses they contain. Where there are two different tenses in the same sentence, list both.

past simple	(PS)
past continuous	(PC)
present perfect tense	(P)
past perfect tense	(PP)

a I'd had this interview for a job.
b I got in the lift and pressed the button.
c I've never been in one since.
d I was watching a horror movie.
e It was the next door neighbour's cat I had heard.
f While I was putting away the books, I found something else.
g The others were looking at a map on the table, but I was standing by the back window.
h I knew they hadn't seen me.
i When I realised that they had gone, I ran inside.
j You have recently sailed around the world.

Look again at the examples containing two different tenses. Can you explain why each tense is used? Think about when each action happened.

Past simple / Past continuous

The most important difference between these two tenses is the duration of an action. For example, in example **f** above, the past continuous describes an action that happened over a longer time period than the second action, which happened at a specific moment and may have interrupted the longer continuous activity:

———————**X**—————

While I was putting away the books … I found something else.
Like the present continuous tense, the past continuous is used to describe temporary situations, as in example **d**.

———————————**X**

I was watching a movie. … I turned off the TV.
Note that this use can be an effective way of setting the scene at the beginning of a story, as in example **g**.

———————————**X**

The others were looking at a map … About six of them burst in.

2 Complete this text using the verbs in brackets in either the past simple or past continuous tense.

Quite late one evening I **(1)** .... (walk) home alone from college. The wind **(2)** .... (blow) hard and it **(3)** .... (pour) with rain, so there **(4)** .... (be) no one around. Anyway, this big black van **(5)** .... (drive) past me and **(6)** .... (stop), just where the road **(7)** .... (curve) round. I **(8)** .... (decide) to go on, though I **(9)** .... (feel) increasingly uneasy. However, as soon as I **(10)** .... (get) close to the van, it **(11)** .... (drive) off. This **(12)** .... (happen) twice more further down the same road. Each time, the van **(13)** .... (pull up) about fifty metres ahead of me and then **(14)** .... (wait) until I almost **(15)** .... (draw) level with it, then **(16)** .... (pull away) again. By this stage I **(17)** .... (be) absolutely petrified. So I **(18)** .... (stand) for a moment under a tree. The rain **(19)** .... (come down) in torrents now. I **(20)** .... (shake) and **(21)** .... (wonder) what to do next, when a policeman **(22)** .... (come) past. He **(23)** .... (push) his bike because of the heavy rain. I **(24)** .... (grab) him by the arm and **(25)** .... (make) him stop. Then I completely **(26)** .... (go) to pieces. While he **(27)** .... (try) to calm me down, I **(28)** .... (hear) the van drive off, thankfully for the last time. I've never walked home on my own since.

Past simple / Past perfect

The <u>past perfect</u> is used for actions in the past that occur earlier than the time period that is being described, as in example **i**:

When I realised they <u>had gone</u>, I ran inside.

3 Complete these sentences with the verbs in brackets in either the past simple or past perfect tense.

  a We .... (spend) the last three nights shivering in a tent in the middle of nowhere, so we were really pleased when we .... (get) to the hotel.

  b Jenny .... (tell) us in great detail what .... (happen) to her and .... (explain) why she .... (find) it so scary at the house.

  c I .... (keep) still for over half an hour and I .... (think) it .... (be) safe at last to come out of my hiding place.

G → page 168

4 Look at this set of four pictures from an action story. Describe what happened in each scene, starting with the last one (4), and making reference back to what had happened earlier. Remember to use a range of past tenses.

5 Read this extract from the thriller *The Big Sleep*, ignoring the gaps for the moment. Why do you think the man telling the story wasn't frightened of the gun? Turn to page 47 to find out if you are right!

The gun pointed at my chest. Her hand seemed to **(0)** _BE_ quite steady. I laughed **(1)** .... her. I started to walk towards her. I saw her small finger tighten on **(2)** .... trigger and grow white at the tip.

I was about six feet away from her **(3)** .... she started to shoot. The sound **(4)** .... the gun made a sharp slap, a brittle crack in the sunlight. I didn't see any smoke. I stopped again **(5)** .... grinned at her.

She fired twice more, very quickly. I don't think **(6)** .... of the shots would have missed. There were five in the little gun. She **(7)** .... fired four. I rushed her.

I didn't want the last one in my face, **(8)** .... I swerved to one side. She gave it to me quite carefully, **(9)** .... worried at all.

I straightened up. 'My, but you're cute,' I said.

Her hand **(10)** .... holding the empty gun and began to shake violently. The gun fell out of **(11)** .... Her mouth began to shake. Then her whole face **(12)** .... to pieces.

6 Now fill each gap, choosing a suitable word from the box below. There are three words you do not need.

and	any	at	~~be~~	because	it	had	has
not	of	so	some	the	was	went	when

Can you put these words into grammatical categories? For example, *and* is a conjunction. These words are typical of the kinds of words that are tested in Paper 3 Part 2.

Exam folder 3

Paper 3 Part 2 Open cloze

In this part of the Use of English paper you are asked to complete a text containing 12 gaps. You must write only one word in each gap. The missing word is usually a grammar word, but occasionally, vocabulary is tested. There is an example at the beginning. You must write your answers in CAPITAL letters.

1 Here are some examples of what is tested in Paper 3 Part 2. Complete each sentence with one word.

   a **Quantifiers** – *many, every, each*, etc.
   There were only a .... people at the zoo yesterday.

   b **Collocations** – *set an example, change the subject, be in favour of*, etc.
   I expect you to .... your promise to tidy your room.

   c **Determiners** – *a, some, the*, etc.
   I've lived in .... USA for some years now.

   d **Modals** – *would, should, need*, etc.
   You absolutely .... not use this path through the valley – it's dangerous.

   e **Verb forms** – *done, taking, see*, etc.
   He's .... working on his homework for two hours now.

   f **Phrasal verbs** – *give up, carry on, make out*, etc.
   Susie has taken .... photography.

   g **Pronouns** – *me, it, that*, etc.
   Tom hurt .... while playing football – he had to go to hospital.

   h **Relative pronouns** – *where, what, which*, etc.
   My wife, ... is Brazilian, works in the university.

   i **Comparison** – *more than, one of the worst*, etc.
   Suzanne has twice as .... clothes as I do.

   j **Linkers** – *if, although, before*, etc.
   You won't lose weight .... you go on a diet.

   k **Prepositions** – *on, by, in*, etc.
   According .... the website, all flights to Berlin are delayed this morning.

EXAM ADVICE

- Look at the title so you have some idea what the text is about. The title is there to help you.
- Read the whole text through carefully before you decide on an answer.
- Always write something down, even if you are not sure of the right answer.
- The word you write MUST be spelt correctly.
- Check whether the word you need should be singular or plural, past or present, etc.
- Make sure that the word you write makes sense in the sentence and text.
- You will need to transfer your answers to an answer sheet. Make sure you transfer each answer correctly.

2 Read this text through and then choose the best title from the three below.

  1 DON'T TAKE THE RISK!
  2 NOTHING TO WORRY ABOUT
  3 BALANCING THE RISKS

3 For questions 1–12, read the text below and think of the word which best fits each gap. Use only one word in each gap. There is an example at the beginning (0).

Write your answers IN CAPITAL LETTERS.

Example: | **0** | | *O* | *N* | | | | | | | | | |

What are the chances of slipping **(0)** .... a banana skin, being hit by lightning or being struck by a meteorite? These are not the sort of unlucky events that most people **(1)** .... their time thinking about, **(2)** .... one has already happened to them. **(3)** .... surprising number of people have, **(4)** .... some time in their lives, imagined aliens kidnapping them. Some even have recurring nightmares about it, whereas relatively **(5)** .... are afraid of dying from flu, even **(6)** .... it is something that is more likely to happen. No doubt many people who go rock climbing will be among the people drinking bottled water on the grounds that it is safer **(7)** .... drinking tap water. Amazingly, our fear of flying outweighs our fear of driving, but the statistics show that going by plane is so **(8)** .... safer. The best explanation is that people worry more about the possibility of dropping **(9)** .... of the air than of crashing on land. **(10)** .... an attempt to educate people about the real and imagined risks of life, scientists have constructed a scale of risk **(11)** .... they can use to compare any new and unfamiliar risks, **(12)** .... as those involved in taking new medicines, in terms of real events.

Part 2														Do not write below here
13														13 1 0 u
14														14 1 0 u
15														15 1 0 u
16														16 1 0 u
17														17 1 0 u
18														18 1 0 u
19														19 1 0 u
20														20 1 0 u
21														21 1 0 u

Reading

1 If you suddenly became famous, how would you feel? What would be the advantages of achieving instant success? Would there be any drawbacks?

2 Read the headline and the first paragraph of the article. Why has this girl become famous?

3 Now read the whole text, paying attention to the highlighted parts around gaps 1–7. These give you content clues for the missing sentences.

Exam spot

In Paper 1 Part 2, you will have to complete a *gapped text*, where seven sentences have been removed. This type of text has a clear development of ideas. You should look out for words that refer back and forwards in the text, such as *it* and *this*, as well as references to specific content. This will help you to fit the text together.

British student, 19, becomes instant superstar in China

UNTIL RECENTLY, her greatest showbusiness moment had been winning £45 in the Undiscovered Youth Talent Contest in the small town of Stroud in Gloucestershire, close to her family home. But now, Mary-Jess Leaverland has found fame in China overnight, following her appearance in a regional TV talent show there.

1 [ ] Indeed, thanks to YouTube, she is being talked about not just by her friends at home but the whole world over, and has appeared in TV interviews to discuss her story. The 19-year-old exchange student won Jiangsu province's equivalent of *The X Factor* show by singing in Mandarin. And although there are no million-pound record deals on offer as yet, she is discovering what life is like as a superstar. **2** [ ] She claims to be enjoying this new-found celebrity status. 'It is really strange, but nice,' she said. 'It was the most exciting thing I have ever done in my life. My friends think it is cool because they just know me as me.'

Mary-Jess, who is fluent in Mandarin and Italian, is studying for a degree in Chinese and Music. **3** [ ] Shortly after she arrived in the country,

she took part in a small singing competition for foreigners, which she won. It was through this event that she was talent-spotted for the show *Min Xing Chang Fan Tian* (the name translates as *I Want to Sing to the Stars*). The show's producers were so impressed by her performance that they invited her to audition. *Min Xing Chang Fan Tian* is a live competition on Chinese television, though it is broadcast only in Jiangsu province. **4** [ ] The show follows a similar format to *The X Factor*, and has a judging panel of three experts. These are drawn from local record executives and songwriters.

Mary-Jess won first place on *Min Xing Chang Fan Tian*. To reach the finals, she had sung the Puccini aria *O Mio Babbino Caro* before performing Sarah Brightman's *Time To Say Goodbye*. **5** [ ] Her winning performance in Mandarin was *Yue Guang Ai Ren* (*Moonlight Lovers*), the theme tune to the hit film *Crouching Tiger, Hidden Dragon*. 'I was the only foreign person in the finals and I still can't believe I won.'

She was rewarded with a cash prize of around £3,000, as well as gaining a trophy and a CD recording of

herself. **6** [ ] 'If I hadn't won, I wouldn't have been able to come home for Christmas because I wouldn't have been able to afford the flight,' said Mary-Jess, who has a 17-year-old sister, Chez.

According to Mary-Jess, her singing talent is part of a family tradition. **7** [ ] 'She was a real inspiration but my mum is my main inspiration. We even sing together in a duo when I am home.' For obvious reasons, her mother Liz was unable to watch her daughter triumph. 'I would have loved to be there but I saw some of the videos and seeing Mary-Jess in the limousine and on the red carpet was amazing,' she said. 'I'm just so proud of her and hope she can continue in the industry.'

4 Now use the highlighted words in A–H to help you decide where each sentence fits. Remember that one sentence is not needed.

A As part of her course, she has been spending a year in Jiangsu province.

B This was the song that had won her that original 'best in show' title in Britain.

C Although it pales into insignificance beside the amounts involved in *The X Factor*, this sum was still very welcome.

D She has really missed her family and friends though.

E However, it is no small-scale event, as the region has a population of 70 million.

F Her grandmother was a semi-professional opera singer.

G People keep on stopping the singing sensation in the street to ask for her autograph.

H She has also made the headlines back in Britain.

5 Would you have taken part in the competition? Why? / Why not?

Vocabulary

Phrasal verbs with *keep*

6 The verb *keep* occurs in many phrasal verbs, as in this example from the article.

People keep on stopping her in the street.

Match definitions a–f to the correct phrasal verb. One is used twice with different meanings.

| keep away   keep down   keep in |
| keep to   keep up with |

a stop the number, level or size of something from increasing

b make someone stay in hospital

c understand something that is changing very fast

d stay with something such as a plan, subject, path

e move at the same speed as someone or something

f not go somewhere or near something

7 Use a phrasal verb with *keep* in the correct tense to complete a–h, adding a pronoun if necessary.

a Professor Grant's lectures would be much shorter if he .... the point!

b I rarely .... British news when I was living in Chile.

c We generally .... from the city centre during the day as it's so crowded.

d Sally swims so fast! I never manage to ....

e Mark had the operation on Saturday but they're .... for more tests.

f It's easy to get lost on the mountain, so make sure you .... the path.

g If Ben .... time at the meeting, we'll be finished by three.

h My weight .... increasing – I have to exercise to ....

Word formation

8 Use the word given in capitals to form a word that fits in the numbered gap.

Celebrity culture

Why do we find celebrities so (0) _FASCINATING_ ?

These days, it seems to be almost (1) .... to open a newspaper or magazine without seeing an image of a celebrity in it. The (2) .... often made by the press is that they are only responding to public demand – it seems that people are far more interested in celebrity gossip and scandal than in the (3) .... of our modern world.

Rightly or wrongly, the paparazzi make a very good (4) .... by keeping up with the rich and famous. However, some high-profile celebs are (5) .... hounded by the media. In these cases, does the press go too far? Don't these individuals have a right to some (6) .... privacy?

Then again, celebrities often do seem to lead such interesting lives that it is perhaps (7) .... that we want to find out more about them. In fact, some evolutionary (8) .... have said it is natural for humans to look up to the most (9) .... individuals in a society. In prehistoric times, this would have meant respecting good (10) .... Today's equivalents are our celebrities, whose fame and fortune we are so envious of.

0 FASCINATE	**6** PERSON
1 POSSIBLE	**7** UNDERSTAND
2 ARGUE	**8** SCIENCE
3 REAL	**9** SUCCESS
4 LIFE	**10** HUNT
5 END	

6.2

Conditionals with *if*

1 **1 07** You are going to listen to four short extracts, where people talk about winning the lottery. How would their lives change if they won?

2 Explain what the contracted verb forms are in these examples of conditional sentences. How do the sentences differ in their use of tenses?

  a If I won the lottery, I'd buy a beautiful house in Spain.

  b If I hadn't won, I wouldn't have been able to afford the flight.

  Which types of conditional sentences are a and b? Choose from 0–3.

  0 a situation that happens often

  1 a situation that may happen in the future

  2 a situation that is unlikely to happen

  3 a situation that could have happened in the past, but didn't

  G → page 168

3 Match the two halves of each sentence.

  a If you did more revision, …

  b If it snows, …

  c If I have time, …

  d If Helen comes round, …

  e If there had been a vote, …

  f If they finish early, …

  g If you swam regularly, …

  h If I'd known about the risk, …

  1 we'll get our skis out.

  2 she'll be able to tell you.

  3 Sam and Bernie usually have a coffee.

  4 you'd pass the exam.

  5 I'd never have eaten seafood.

  6 they would have lost.

  7 I like to walk to work.

  8 your body would be in better shape.

Conditionals with *unless*

4 Read these examples and explain the meaning of *unless*.

  a We'll miss the start of the match unless Juan arrives soon.

  b Unless you've already got tickets, you won't be able to get in.

Corpus spot

Correct any mistakes with *unless* that exam candidates have made in these sentences. Tick the correct sentences.

a There will be no improvement in my tennis unless I don't get some training.

b I will not remain silent about the letter unless you give me my money back.

c People hardly ever use candlelight today unless there isn't anything wrong with the power supply.

d There isn't much to do in the city unless you haven't got friends.

e You must stop working so hard unless you don't want to end up in hospital sooner or later.

f If there were no televisions, we wouldn't know much about other countries unless we visited them.

---

5 There are eight mistakes with tenses in this story. Correct the mistakes and fill the gaps with *if* or *unless*. Examples have been done for you.

Yesterday was a very bad day. **(0)** *If* it ~~wasn't~~ *hadn't been* raining, perhaps it wouldn't have been so difficult. The thing is, I never drive to work **(1)** .... it's raining. But it was pouring and I needed to get to an important meeting, so I took the car. It broke down on the way. **(2)** .... I had it serviced regularly, I know it won't be so unreliable, but garages charge so much these days that I don't bother. I decided to call the breakdown company on my mobile phone. Well, I would have done that **(3)** .... my mobile hasn't run out of battery! Never mind, I thought, **(4)** .... I'll find a public phone, I'll be able to call from there **(5)** .... it's out of order! It was, so I can't! By this time, I was in a panic. What will my boss say **(6)** .... I didn't get to the meeting? **(7)** .... people don't arrive on time, he will get really angry with them. Luckily, a taxi pulled up. 'Mason Square,' I shouted, 'and **(8)** .... you will do the journey in under ten minutes, I'll pay you double!' 'Forget it,' said the driver. 'The centre of town's gridlocked. You'd never get there in ten minutes **(9)** .... you went by helicopter.' So I ended up late for the meeting and the boss was furious with me.

6 Talk to a partner. Take it in turns to finish these sentences. Then tell the class what your friend said.

   a Unless I get up early tomorrow, …

   b If I had enough money, …

   c My life would be a lot easier if …

   d If I hadn't come to class today, …

 → page 168

Vocabulary

Word formation

> **Exam spot**
>
> In Paper 3, Part 1 tests vocabulary. You have to fill twelve gaps in a text, choosing from sets of four words. All four words will be the same part of speech and the twelve questions will test a range of different parts of speech, such as nouns, verbs, adverbs, etc.

7 Look at the words in the box. They form four sets and all four words in a set have a similar meaning. Can you group them into the four categories in the table? Be careful: some words can be more than one part of speech. Think carefully about their meanings when you decide which category to put them into.

accepted	attempt	by	delicate	experiment
gathered	gentle	in	light	on	received
tiny	to	trial	try	welcomed

Nouns	Verbs	Prepositions	Adjectives

8 Now read the short newspaper article below. There are four gaps in it. Decide which part of speech is required in each gap. Then choose the correct option to fill each one from your four sets of words.

Speaking

9 Discuss these questions.

   a Should lottery winners receive so much publicity?

   b What are the pros and cons of winning the lottery?

   c If you won the jackpot, would you go public?

Useful language

As I see it …
To my mind …
For one thing … .
For another (thing) …
On the one hand … .
On the other (hand) …
The main advantage is …
One drawback is …

Could it possibly be YOU?

Camelot is to make a final **(1)** .... today to track down the winner of an unclaimed £2.1 million jackpot prize. A **(2)** .... aircraft will fly over Hull trailing the banner: '£2 million winner – is it you?' for two hours at lunchtime.

The city became the focus of attention after a local newspaper **(3)** .... an unsigned letter from an elderly local widow saying she did not want the prize. Her reason was that 'the fuss would finish me off'. If the money is not claimed **(4)** .... 11 pm it will go into the lottery's 'good causes' fund.

Writing folder 3

Stories 1

In Paper 2 Part 2, you may be asked to write a short story. The first or last sentence of the story is given in the question and you must remember to include this. Make sure that the story you write fits with the sentence.

1 Look at these two questions. Discuss with a partner what tenses you would need to use in each story.

   a You have been asked to write a short story for your college magazine. The story must begin with the following sentence:
   If he hadn't answered the phone, it would have been just another ordinary day.

   b You have decided to enter a short story competition. The rules say that the story must end with the following sentence:
   Suddenly, he woke up and realised it had been a nightmare.

2 Now read this sample answer, which works for both questions. Say which past tenses have been used. You can ignore the underlined words and gaps for the moment.

If he hadn't answered the phone, it would have been just another ordinary day. But he had lifted the receiver and had heard the news that turned his life upside down. His girlfriend had been taken hostage and her kidnappers were demanding $1,000,000.

He was in shock but he still moved fast. He found his father's gun and **(1)** _went_ out of the flat. A bus was pulling away and he managed to jump on. He travelled downtown to the city's biggest bank. As he **(2)** _went_ in through the glass doors, people looked at him **(3)** .... Then someone noticed the gun and screamed. 'If you don't move, you won't get hurt,' he shouted **(4)** .... 'I want a million dollars, now. Hand it over.' He waved the gun around **(5)** ....

They stuffed the cash from the safe in a bag. He grabbed it, left the building and headed for the river, where the kidnappers were waiting. He ran and ran, endlessly, but the river got further and further away. He was crying now.

Suddenly, he woke up and realised it had been a nightmare.

3 Look at numbers 1 and 2 in the sample answer. To get a good mark in the exam, you need to use a range of vocabulary. Choose suitable words to replace *went* from the sets below.

   1 A rushed
   B shuddered
   C hammered
   D crashed

   2 A carried
   B threw
   C burst
   D turned

Now, with a partner, choose the most suitable adverbs for gaps 3–5, from the ones below. Use each adverb once only.

anxiously	desperately
nervously	suspiciously
tragically	wildly

EXAM ADVICE

- Read the given sentence carefully and think about the setting for the story.
- Decide whether the story needs to be written in the first person (*I/we … my/our*) or the third person (*he/she/it/they … his/her/its/their*).
- Be careful to spell any names in the given sentence correctly.
- Make some quick notes, to plan the order of events in your story.
- Use the past perfect tense instead of the past simple if you need to make the sequence clear.
- Check your spelling of adverbs and past tense forms of irregular verbs.
- Include a definite ending to your story.

4 Look at the picture sequence below and re-arrange sentences a–i in the order of the pictures. Then include suitable sentence openers from 1–6 where needed. There is one extra opener you do not need.

a ... a crowd of people had gathered and were watching her anxiously as she struggled to reach the bank.

b ... she heard someone whimpering below her and when she looked down from the bridge, she saw a small boy in the deepest part of the river, waving his arms helplessly.

c ... she thought he was dead but when he coughed and his legs started to move, she knew she had saved his life.

d It was a fast-flowing river and she had to swim harder than she had ever swum before, to get to him before it was too late.

e As Jean walked towards the bridge, she was thinking of all the things she could do now that the school holidays had arrived.

f Although he was panicking, she was able to grab him and she started to pull him back to the bank.

g It was a beautiful summer's day, the sun was shining and the birds were singing.

h ... she jumped off the bridge and dived into the rushing water.

i ... she managed it and threw both herself and the boy onto the warm grass.

1 Eventually
2 Suddenly
3 Without a second thought
4 By now
5 At first
6 Last but not least

5 Now do this writing task.

You have decided to enter a short story competition. The rules say that the story must begin with the following sentence:

As soon as he got out of the car, Martin felt uneasy.

Write your story in 120–180 words.

Spend a few minutes noting down ideas for your story and then discuss your notes with a partner. Suggest how your partner's story could be improved. Then list relevant vocabulary you could both use, including a range of verbs, adjectives and adverbs.

Write your story, being careful to include the given sentence accurately and where you are told to.

After you have written your story, remember to check the spelling, punctuation and grammar.

Units 1–6 Revision

Topic review

1 Together with a partner, read these sentences and discuss which are true for you, giving more details. Try to use as much of the vocabulary and language as you can from the units you have just studied.

a I always get out of bed early in the morning.
b If I had some money, the first thing I would buy is a fast car.
c I'm worse at English than I am at Maths.
d I'm always getting into trouble for forgetting things.
e I'm not afraid of anything!
f I think I'm broad-minded.
g I must try to work harder.
h I like to follow fashion.
i Books interest me more than computer games.
j Beach holidays are not for me.

Grammar

2 Read the text below and think of the word which best fits each gap. Use only one word in each gap. There is an example at the beginning (0).

Most (0) ..OF.. us go a little crazy when we jet off (1) .... holiday, but some, it would seem, go completely mad. They see giant rats eating through their luggage and even lose their mother-in-law in (2) .... back of a stolen caravan. So says WorldCover Direct, the holiday insurer. These are just (3) .... of the claims the company (4) .... received in the past 12 months.

A director said, 'One of our policyholders skied into a tree (5) .... he was on holiday and made a claim for injuries. What he didn't mention was that he (6) .... blind and in the process of testing a new radar system for blind skiers.'

But what (7) .... you were in the Mediterranean in August and had had (8) .... much sun? Take a dip in the pool, sit in the shade for a while – or phone your holiday insurance company requesting repatriation (9) .... you were 'feeling a bit hot'? One holiday maker, (10) .... was in Spain, did just that. Another policyholder made a claim because he and (11) .... wife had missed their flight. He failed to mention that she was prevented (12) .... boarding because she had a baby pig in her hand luggage!

Phrasal verbs

3 Complete the following sentences using the appropriate verb.

UP

a If Elizabeth had been able to .... up just a little more money, she would have bought a faster computer.
b Every time I go shopping for clothes, I find that prices have .... up yet again.
c Come just as you are, there's really no need to .... up.
d Sara was walking so fast that I couldn't .... up with her.
e When you manage to find his address, ... me up and let me know what it is.

OUT

f Tourist guides often carry umbrellas so that they .... out in a crowd.
g Sheila decided to .... out of the hotel a bit early so she wouldn't miss her plane.
h 'I don't know how you can .... out looking like that,' Sue's mother said.
i I'm not sure I can .... out how to play this computer game.

Now look at these mixed examples and replace the verb or phrase in italics with a phrasal verb or compound noun.

j If you want to look good in that outfit, you'll have to *reduce* the amount of chocolate you eat.
k We *spent some time* in Singapore on our way to Sydney.
l I really hate shops that make you feel guilty when you *return* clothes that shrink in the wash or fall to pieces.
m We decided to *start the journey* to the castle at midnight, in the hope of seeing the ghost.
n The policeman told them *not to go near* the edge of the cliff.
o My friend had to spend about two hours waiting in the plane for it to *leave*.

Revision of present and past tenses

4 Read through this text and put the verbs in the correct tense.

The statistics on the safety of flying **(1)** .... (BE) immensely comforting. It **(2)** .... (SEEM) that the chances of being involved in an accident **(3)** .... (BE) a million to one – the equivalent of flying safely every day for 95 years. Try telling that to the white-faced, petrified aerophobic, who **(4)** .... (SEE) every frown on a stewardess's face as a portent of disaster. For some years now, psychologist Henry Jones **(5)** .... (TRY) to tell them, and he **(6)** .... (DO) a lot more besides. He **(7)** .... (DEVELOP) both a theory and practice for treating air travel anxiety. Apparently, it **(8)** .... (BE) a widespread phobia. One American survey **(9)** .... (PUT) it as the fourth most common fear, preceded only by snakes, heights and storms. Jones **(10)** .... (HAVE) nearly 500 clients during the last decade. Before they **(11)** .... (COME) to him, some of his clients **(12)** .... (never FLY), others **(13)** .... (HAVE) just one bad experience after years of flying. One man **(14)** .... (TAKE) over 200 flights a year for five years and **(15)** .... (never WORRY) up till then. Then, one day, on a flight to Chicago the pilot **(16)** .... (ANNOUNCE) that they were going to turn back because of an engine fault. The man then **(17)** .... (HAVE) a panic attack and **(18)** .... (TRY) to get off the plane in mid-air. After Jones's course, the man **(19)** .... (OVERCOME) his fears and **(20)** .... (MANAGE) to fly again.

5 Complete the second sentence so that it has a similar meaning to the first sentence, using the word given. Do not change the word given. You must use between two and five words, including the word given.

1 Andrea said she would only go dancing if her mother bought her a new outfit.
UNLESS
Andrea said she .... her mother bought her a new outfit.

2 I have never seen such a terrible film before.
WORST
This is the .... seen.

3 I'm sorry I didn't meet you at the airport – my car wasn't working.
MET
I .... at the airport if my car had been working.

4 This party is 'evening dress' only.
ALLOWED
You .... dress casually for this party.

5 I'm not as frightened of flying as I am of ghosts!
THAN
I'm .... I am of flying.

6 It was a mistake for me to buy you that computer game.
BOUGHT
I .... that computer game.

7 The play started before we could get there.
HAD
The play .... when we got there.

8 I need to wear glasses to drive.
SEE
I can't .... my glasses.

5.2 exercise 5
The man talks about the incident later in the story. He says:
'All five chambers are empty. She fired them all. She fired them all at me. From a distance of five or six feet. Cute little thing, isn't she? Too bad I had loaded the gun with blanks.'

Gerunds and infinitives 1

1 Identify the equipment in pictures a–o, and name each sport.

2 With a partner ask and answer these questions.

a What sports do you really enjoy watching?

b Is there a sportsperson or team who you particularly like watching?

c Which sport can't you stand watching?

d Which sports have you either taken up or given up recently?

e Which do you prefer – watching a sport live or watching it on TV?

f Are there any sports you like doing on holiday?

3 A gerund, which is a verb used as a noun, always ends in *-ing*, but not all *-ing* forms are gerunds. An *-ing* form might be a present participle or an adjective. What is the *-ing* form in these sentences?

a I pulled on the climbing rope to show I was safe.

b Anna was running along the track when she tripped and fell.

c Snowboarding is a very popular sport.

4 Look at these sentences:

1 I enjoy going swimming.

2 After learning to ice skate, I'm going to learn to play ice hockey.

3 I want to take up rowing.

4 Climbing is a fairly safe sport nowadays.

5 It's not worth going to watch our local football team because they always lose!

Find an example of a gerund above which:

a follows a preposition.

b is the subject of the sentence.

c follows an expression.

d follows a verb.

e follows a phrasal verb.

5 When we put a verb after a preposition, we usually use a gerund. Complete the following sentences with a preposition and one of the verbs in the box.

do   drop   get   learn   play   swim   teach

a She was doubtful .... to the training session on time.

b Steve is very proud .... to scuba dive so quickly.

c I've been very successful .... the children to ride their bikes.

d The boy was in trouble .... his muddy sports clothes on the changing room floor.

e I believe .... some exercise every day in order to keep healthy.

f You don't have to be good .... to enjoy it.

g I'm looking forward .... against him again in tomorrow's match.

G → page 169

6 Infinitives are forms like (*to*) *do*, (*to*) *say*. They are usually used with 'to', but not always.

Look at the following sentences, which show the most common uses of the infinitive.

1 I'm going to the pool *to have* my swimming lesson.
2 I want *to enrol* for netball practice next term.
3 They are unlikely *to hold* the Olympics in Cambridge.
4 They let me *do* the judo classes even though I had never done judo before.
5 You must not *run* with the ball in some sports.
6 We encouraged them *to run* faster by cheering loudly.

Now say which of the infinitives above:

a follows an adjective.
b follows a modal auxiliary.
c follows a main verb.
d is used to express purpose.
e has an infinitive without 'to'.
f follows the object of a verb.

G → page 169

Corpus spot

Be careful with gerunds and infinitives – the *Cambridge Learner Corpus* shows that exam candidates often make mistakes with these.

I look forward **to hearing** from you.

NOT I look forward to ~~hear~~ from you.

Correct the mistakes that candidates have made with gerund and infinitive forms in these sentences.
a I should give up to swim every morning.
b Do you want go out with me?
c I'm used to sleep in a tent.
d There's no point play today.
e I suggest you to go to the sports centre.
f I really enjoy to read about the old tennis stars.
g I recommend you going there.
h I hope hearing from you soon.
i I am interested to receive documentation about the courses.
j I agree with you to find a job.

---

7 Read through this email and put the verbs in brackets in the correct form. Give your reasons.

Send Chat Attach Address Fonts Colors Save As Draft

To: Jill Campbell
Cc:
Subject: Trip to Mont Blanc

Dear Jill,
I've just got back from (**1**) .... (climb) Mont Blanc in the Alps and I must (**2**) .... (tell) you what a great time I had. On (**3**) .... (arrive) in Chamonix we were introduced to our guides. We were then kitted out with ice-axes, crampons and climbing boots and were sent straight out into two days' (**4**) .... (train) in and around the Le Tour glacier. The guides used this time (**5**) .... (assess) our ability (**6**) .... (make) the ascent and (**7**) .... (teach) us the basics of (**8**) .... (mountaineer), such as how (**9**) .... (use) an ice-axe and how best (**10**) .... (work) in a team.
    The first day consisted of (**11**) .... (climb) for five hours from the Nid d'Aigle to the Gouter Hut. I thought I'd be too cold (**12**) .... (sleep) but in fact that wasn't a problem at all! Day 2 started at 2 am with a four and a half hour walk to the summit. (**13**) .... (reach) the summit was only a third of the day's work. The descent route included (**14**) .... (jump) across gaps in the ice and took seven hours.
    I'm really looking forward to (**15**) .... (see) you next weekend so I can (**16**) .... (tell) you all the details.
Love, Sue

8 Complete the second sentence so that it has a similar meaning to the first sentence, using the word given. Do not change the word given. You must use between two and five words, including the word given.

1 The newspapers said that Pete had pushed the other player.
   ACCUSED
   The newspapers .... the other player.

2 The pitch isn't dry enough to play on.
   TOO
   The pitch .... play on.

3 It wasn't easy for me to learn how to paraglide.
   DIFFICULTY
   I .... how to paraglide.

4 'I wouldn't go diving by yourself, if I were you,' the instructor said.
   ADVISED
   The instructor .... diving by myself.

5 I prefer to go on walking holidays than lie on a crowded beach.
   RATHER
   I .... walking holidays than lie on a crowded beach.

7.2

Speaking

1 Discuss these questions with a partner.

  a Which sports would you consider to be extreme or dangerous? Why?

  b Have you ever tried or watched a dangerous sport? What was it?

Exam spot

Paper 4 Part 3 consists of six questions and five short extracts linked by a theme. You need to match each extract to one of six options, A–F. There is one extra option that you do not need.

Listening

2 Listen to this extract, where a woman is talking about a sport she has recently taken up. As you listen, try to work out what the sport is. What clues did you hear?

3 **1 09** Now you're going to hear the first speaker again and also four other people talking about dangerous sports. For questions 1–5, choose from the list of statements A–F what each speaker states. There is one extra letter which you do not need to use.

Speaker 1	1
Speaker 2	2
Speaker 3	3
Speaker 4	4
Speaker 5	5

  A I like to set myself challenges.

  B I've always enjoyed taking risks.

  C It's not as dangerous as some ordinary sports.

  D Knowing I might be killed makes it more enjoyable.

  E It puts some excitement in my life.

  F I wanted to prove to everyone that I could do it.

4 What dangerous sports do the speakers mention? Are they popular in your country?

Vocabulary

Collocations – sports

5 Match the sports (A) with the correct verb (B) and the place where the sport takes place (C).

A		B	C	
aerobics	snowboarding	do	pitch	course
martial arts	golf	play	court	track
swimming	running	go	stadium	studio
athletics	football		gym	pool
basketball	gymnastics		piste	

6 Decide which is the correct word in each sentence and explain the meaning of the other word to your partner.

  a Sally had only done three *marathons / laps* of the stadium before she fell.

  b The *spectators / defenders* all cheered when their team won.

  c The football *umpire / referee* sent two players off during the game.

  d In the French Open tennis final they had only completed two *sets / penalties* before rain stopped play.

  e A midfield player scored a *goal / shot* just before half-time.

Expressions with *do*

7 Speaker 5 in the Listening said 'I did my best'. Here are some other expressions with *do*. Complete the sentences below, putting *do* into the correct tense.

do damage	do business with someone
do a good job	do something for a living
do without	do someone a favour

  a I've always found that they are a very good company to ....

  b What does your father .... ?

  c The engineers .... on building the new stadium.

  d The fire .... a lot of .... to the sports hall.

  e I'd forgotten my wallet, so Mark .... and lent me some money.

  f The players always .... for the team and that's why they win.

  g One thing I can't .... is my bicycle – I use it all the time.

8 Ask and answer the following questions with a partner.

a What couldn't you do without?

b What do you do / would you like to do for a living?

c When was the last time you did someone a favour?

d Do you always do your best? Why? / Why not?

Word formation

9 Use the word in brackets to form a word that fits in the gap.

With some personal fitness trainers charging as much as £150 an hour, it's not surprising that only the rich and **(1)** .... (FAME) can afford the kind of one-to-one that will **(2)** .... (SURE) they work out enough to stay in shape. However, the idea that they are only for the elite is about to be shattered by *Get Motivated*, a new London-based company that charges just £25 for an hour with a **(3)** .... (FULL) qualified trainer. I decided to put this scheme to the test and asked *Get Motivated* to send a personal trainer to my home for a **(4)** .... (TRAIN) session. When 23-year-old Stephanie arrived, I was initially **(5)** .... (CERTAIN) about her as she seemed so young, but what followed was a very **(6)** .... (DEMAND) hour. Stephanie grew up in Australia and has a degree in Human **(7)** .... (MOVE) Studies and a diploma in **(8)** .... (EDUCATE) – the minimum **(9)** .... (QUALIFY) *Get Motivated* requires. Stephanie says that what appeals most to her about the GM scheme is that it gives her the **(10)** .... (FREE) to design her own sessions for clients.

Do you think it would be useful to have a personal trainer? Why? / Why not?

Speaking

Exam spot

Paper 5 Part 3 is a 'shared task', where you must have a discussion with the other candidate and then try to decide together on a solution to the task. It is acceptable to 'agree to disagree', however! You will have a total of three minutes for this task. Remember you need to give your partner a chance to talk and you will have to come to a decision at the end of your discussion.

10 Look at the five pictures of sports facilities. Imagine that your town is going to build one of them. First, talk about how popular/useful these sports facilities would be. Then decide which one would be best for the people in your town.

Below are some useful phrases.

Being polite
OK, where shall we start?
What do you think?

Hesitating
Well, um, I'm not sure …
Well, let me see …

Asking for repetition
I'm sorry, could you say that again?
Could you repeat that, please?

Making things clear
What I mean is, ...
What I'm trying to say is, ...

Giving a different view
Well, it is true that ..., but ...
Of course, ...

Concluding
So, let's come to a decision.
Right, what we've decided is that ...

Exam folder 4

Paper 3 Part 1
Multiple choice cloze

In this part of the Use of English paper you must choose one word or phrase from a set of four (A, B, C or D) to fill a gap in the text. There are twelve gaps and an example. The text always has a title, which will give you some help in telling you what it is about before you start reading. Below are some examples of the type of words that are tested in this part of Paper 3.

Expressions

1 I .... the conclusion, after failing to win any matches, that I would do better to give up playing tennis altogether.
   A reached   **B** got   **C** did   **D** came
   A is the right answer. The expression is to reach a/the conclusion. You can come to a conclusion.

Verb/Adjective + preposition

2 The man was .... with burglary at the police station.
   A accused   **B** charged   **C** investigated   **D** arrested
   B is the right answer. Investigated and arrested are followed by for; accused is followed by of.

Phrasal verbs

3 Susie fell .... with her best friend last week.
   A for   **B** out   **C** apart   **D** through
   B is the right answer. To fall out means to no longer be friends. The other phrasal verbs here, fall for, fall apart and fall through all exist but mean something different.

Linking words

4 I really like skiing, ... my friend prefers snowboarding.
   A once   **B** provided   **C** whereas   **D** or
   C is the right answer. Whereas means but. Provided, or and once are used in a different type of clause.

Vocabulary

5 The .... of the party welcomed us at the door.
   A guest   **B** companion   **C** household   **D** host
   D is the right answer. All the other words are connected with people, but are used differently.

EXAM ADVICE

- Always read the text all the way through before you try to fill in any gaps.

- Make sure you read each sentence carefully so that you don't miss any important words.

- Always put down an answer even if you're not completely sure that it's correct.

- Make sure you transfer your answers to the answer sheet correctly.

For questions 1–12, read the text below and decide which answer (A, B, C or D) best fits each gap. There is an example at the beginning (0).

Example:

0 **A** dates   **B** calls   **C** looks   **D** stands

0 | A̲ B C D

The History of Football

Football or soccer, which is so popular all over the world, **(0)** .... back to the Middle Ages. At that **(1)** .... it was very different from the game we play today. Any number of players could **(2)** .... part and the matches usually developed into a free-for-all. In its modern **(3)** .... , football is less than two hundred years old.

In 1846 the first rules to govern the game were drawn up at Cambridge University. The number of players was **(4)** .... to 11 per side, which made things much more orderly than before. Later, in 1863, the Football Association was **(5)** .... up to help promote the game in Britain.

The game is played on a grass or artificial **(6)** .... with a goal net at each end. The **(7)** .... is to move the ball around the field, **(8)** .... the feet or head, until a player is in a **(9)** .... to put the ball into the net and score a goal.

Professional football is not only the most popular **(10)** .... sport in the world, **(11)** .... also more people actually play football themselves than any other team sport. In 1904 FIFA, the world **(12)** .... of football, was founded. It organises the World Cup tournament every four years.

1	**A** season	**B** time	**C** term	**D** stage
2	**A** play	**B** make	**C** take	**D** do
3	**A** form	**B** shape	**C** fashion	**D** pattern
4	**A** limited	**B** checked	**C** counted	**D** defined
5	**A** put	**B** set	**C** born	**D** called
6	**A** court	**B** pitch	**C** course	**D** track
7	**A** objective	**B** reason	**C** focus	**D** purpose
8	**A** by	**B** to	**C** of	**D** with
9	**A** place	**B** point	**C** position	**D** spot
10	**A** witness	**B** audience	**C** spectator	**D** viewer
11	**A** because	**B** but	**C** while	**D** so
12	**A** association	**B** band	**C** collection	**D** group

Speaking

1 Student A: Look at photos 1 and 2. They show children playing. Compare the photographs and say which of the activities the children would enjoy more. Student B: give your opinion.

2 Student B: Look at photos 3 and 4. They show teenagers at home. Compare the photographs and say what the photos tell you about modern teenagers. Student A: give your opinion.

Reading

3 Below is an extract from an autobiography. Read it quickly and then say whether you think the writer had a happy or unhappy childhood.

GROWING UP

I lived in the same house in Westpark Grove for my whole childhood. There was no major landmark to help you find your way around in my neighbourhood. Every street looked almost identical, like a soap opera set. Our two-storey house was set a few metres back from the road and was a perfectly hideous pink colour, which my parents seemed to like. The only feature we had that no-one else had was a huge garage, over the door of which my dad had painted the words GARAGE ENTRANCE in large black letters. Anyone silly enough to park in front of the driveway should beware. You didn't want to get on the wrong side of my dad, believe me!

We had three bedrooms and I used to share mine with my sister Lucy, who is two years older than me. We had a bunk bed – I slept on top – a wardrobe and a desk. Our brother Tom, who is a year younger than I am, had a room the size of a broom cupboard at the very back of the house, overlooking the garden. The three of us used to have terrible fights with each other in those days. We always worried that my mum would find out about the fights. We used to slip handwritten notes under the bedroom doors, asking, 'Are you going to tell Mum?' There were boxes to tick for 'yes' or 'no'.

We all had chores to do before and after school and Mum would check our efforts when she got home from work each evening. It seems hard now but we were used to doing them. Meanwhile, the neighbourhood kids would be playing in the street outside. Sometimes we would go out and play with them, but we kept an eye open for Mum, who disapproved of us playing outside. She thought we should be inside doing useful things, like homework and housework. There was a big supermarket just on the edge of town, but my mum and I would struggle the six kilometres into town by bus every Saturday to the weekly market in the centre of town. <u>It</u> was

line 32

better and cheaper than a supermarket, she said. We would then come home <u>laden down with</u> what seemed like a mountain of plastic bags and sink gratefully onto the sofa in the living room when we got in. Dad thought that getting the car out for shopping was a waste of time.

line 34

My first best friend was Sarah. We got on really well and she was good at keeping secrets. I can't remember a single occasion when we fell out. I used to sleep over at her house and we'd have midnight feasts of chocolate. We spent all our spare time together – like sisters. I used to hang around the local shops with her, if there was nothing decent showing at the local cinema. I wanted to be a pop star or be in films when I grew up and poor long-suffering Sarah was very good about listening to me singing all the latest pop songs and showing off my dancing to practise my stage technique. I think it helped having a critical audience as when I finally started at drama school, I felt quite confident and <u>this</u> showed.

line 49

She had an elder brother called Pete and he had a motorbike. One day he gave me a lift home from school and I felt so proud! He was great at Maths and didn't mind helping me. I often moaned to Sarah on my mobile so much about Maths homework that in the end she'd get round Pete to email me the answers to any equations.

In the summer, Sarah and I and the rest of our class went to school camp. It was on an island off the coast. It seemed so adventurous to spend the night sleeping in a tent miles from anywhere. Sarah was more sensible than I was and often kept me from getting into trouble with the narrow-minded Mrs Dodd, our teacher. Once I thought it'd be a good idea to go swimming in the sea just before sunrise. I'd forgotten that Mrs Dodd would be coming round to wake us up and would see immediately if anyone wasn't in bed. Sarah covered for me, though, and put a pillow under the sheets so Mrs Dodd would think I was there. We actually got away with it, too! Great times.

Part 1 of Paper 1 is a text with eight multiple choice questions, where you have to choose the answer to a question or finish a sentence from four given alternatives. You should read the text and the questions carefully, because this part of the exam tests detailed understanding. It is helpful to underline the words in the text which contain the answers to the questions.

4 Read the first paragraph more carefully and answer question 1. Then look at the explanation below – were you right?

1 What does the writer say about her father in the first paragraph?
  A He was very proud of his garage.
  B He could get angry if you annoyed him.
  C He disliked his neighbours.
  D He was quite a selfish person.

> The answer is B. – *Anyone silly enough to park in front of the driveway should beware. You didn't want to get on the wrong side of my dad, believe me.*
>
> A, C and D are all likely, but there is nothing in the text which says this.

Now read the notes and answer questions 2–4.

> There will often be a question which asks you what the writer is 'suggesting' or 'implying'. This is called an inference question and you have to decide from various clues in the text what the writer means to say.

2 In the second paragraph, what does the writer suggest about her family?
  A There was a large age difference between the girls and Tom.
  B They were afraid their mother would tell their father about the fights.
  C Some members of the family got on with each other better than others.
  D They had only limited living space while they were growing up.

> Sometimes a 'reference' question is included, which tests your understanding of words such as *it* and *this*. You must read the lines before and after the word carefully before deciding what it is referring to.

3 What does 'It' refer to in line 32?
  A the supermarket
  B the centre of town
  C the bus
  D the weekly market

> There is often an item of vocabulary such as a word or phrase which is unusual or idiomatic, or one that is used by the writer in a special way. You should work out the meaning by looking at the context around the word or phrase itself.

4 What does 'laden down with' mean in line 34?
  A having bought
  B carrying
  C having chosen
  D borrowing

Now do the next four questions, underlining the word or phrase in the text which gives you the answer.

5 What impression do you get of the writer's mother from the third paragraph?
  A She demanded high standards of her children.
  B She didn't like the other children in the neighbourhood.
  C She was unkind to her own children.
  D She had very little money to spend on food.

6 What does the writer say about her friend Sarah in the fourth paragraph?
  A She lived in a nicer house than the writer did.
  B She was a very easy-going person.
  C She and the writer sometimes had arguments.
  D She had the same ambitions as the writer.

7 What does the writer mean by 'this' in line 49?
  A her confidence
  B her technique
  C her dancing
  D her audience

8 What happened when the writer went swimming in the sea one morning?
  A Sarah told the teacher what had happened.
  B The writer's absence went unnoticed.
  C Mrs Dodd didn't come into the tent that morning.
  D The writer managed to get back to bed in time.

5 In pairs, discuss the following questions.
  a What do you think about the writer's childhood? Was it similar to yours? Why? / Why not?
  b Do you think children should help their parents with housework? Why? / Why not?
  c How much time do you spend at home rather than doing activities outside the home?
  d Do you think that children grow up too quickly nowadays? Why? / Why not?

used to and would

1 Read examples a–c and then match them with uses 1–3.

 a The three of us used to have terrible fights. (*used to* + verb)

 b Sometimes we would go out and play. (*would* + verb)

 c We were used to doing them. (*be/get used to* + *-ing* verb)

 1 To talk about something in the past that doesn't happen now. This could be something permanent.

 2 To mean 'to be/get accustomed to'.

 3 To talk about a repeated action in the past which doesn't happen now. Note that the action must be repeated and this form is normally used for narrative.

 Look at the following sentences and decide what the difference is between them.

 I'm used to living away from home.
 I'm getting used to living away from home.

> **Corpus spot**
>
> The *Cambridge Learner Corpus* shows that exam candidates often make mistakes with *used to*.
>
> I **used to** live in London.
> NOT I ~~use to~~ live in London.

2 Correct the following sentences, if necessary.

 a Britain would have a large manufacturing industry.

 b People used to work very long hours in the past.

 c People are now used to working harder for less money.

 d It takes a long time to get used to do a new job.

 e My grandmother was used to work very long hours when she was a girl.

 f When I worked for the BBC, I would often have to travel abroad.

 g When I was a child, I use to go to the zoo with my parents.

G → page 169

3 Discuss the following situations using *would*, *used to*, *get used to* or *be used to*.

 a What did you used to do in the holidays when you were a child?

 b Have you ever had any problems getting used to doing something?

 c What did you used to do in the past that you don't do now?

 d What kind of food are you used to eating?

Vocabulary

Collocations

4 Look at this example from 8.1.

 *She was good at **keeping secrets**.*

 Choose the correct collocation in a–g.

 a My father's new car can *have / do* 200 kph.

 b I don't like people who *break / keep* their promises.

 c We're *doing / having* a holiday in South Africa this year.

 d Max *made / took* a fortune from computer software.

 e The music from the festival *made / kept* me awake for ages last night.

 f This ice cream *gets / tastes* really good.

 g Lily *spends / keeps* too much time at her friend's house.

Phrasal verbs with *get*

5 In the text in 8.1 the writer says, 'We got away with it, too.' Complete the sentences using the phrases in the box.

> the flu washing the floor the tennis team some work
> the angry neighbour not paying

 a The two boys got away from .... as quickly as they could.

 b Susie needs to get down to .... because she has exams soon.

 c Tom got out of ...., which put him in a good mood.

 d I'm just getting over .... after being in bed for a week.

 e He was delighted when he got into .... at the weekend.

 f You won't get away with .... taxes.

6 In pairs, look at a–f in 5 again and decide what each phrasal verb means. Then talk about the following questions.

   a What sort of things do you try to get away with not doing?
   b Did you get to go anywhere interesting last weekend?
   c Do you need to get down to some work soon?
   d Have you ever had a bad dose of flu? How long did it take you to get over it?
   e Have you ever got into a sports team?

Word formation

7 For questions 1–10, read the text below. Use the word given in capitals at the end of some of the lines to form a word that fits in the gap in the same line.

HOW YOUR FRIENDS AND THEIR FRIENDS CAN AFFECT YOUR MOOD

Recent research shows that our moods are more **(0)** _STRONGLY_ influenced	**STRONG**
by friends than we tend to think. Not only that, but the moods of friends	
of friends affect us too – even up to three degrees of **(1)** .... Indeed, it is	**SEPARATE**
becoming clear that a whole range of things are transmitted through **(2)**	**SOCIETY**
networks of friends in ways that are not entirely understood, from **(3)**	**HAPPY**
to a **(4)** .... for certain types of music to what you watch on TV.	**PREFER**

Your **(5)** .... to be happy increases with the number of happy friends you	**ABLE**
have. However, it does depend on the nature of your **(6)** .... to them. For	**RELATION**
example, if a good friend who lives within a couple of kilometres of you suddenly	
becomes happy, that increases the chances of you becoming happy by more	
than 60 per cent. Surprisingly, one of your parents at home with you becoming	
happy doesn't make such a big **(7)** .... That's less than 10%.	**DIFFERENT**

Psychologists have shown that people **(8)** .... copy the facial expressions,	**CONSCIOUS**
manner of speech, body language and general **(9)** .... of people around them,	**BEHAVE**
often with **(10)** .... speed and accuracy, despite being unaware they are doing	**REMARK**
it. This causes them to actually experience the emotions associated with what	
they are copying.	

Speaking

8 How important are your friends to you? Discuss the following questions with a partner.

   a Do you think you make friends easily? Why? / Why not?
   b How long have you known your best friend?
   c Have you ever fallen out with a friend?
   d What is the most important quality to you in a friend?
   e Do you sometimes get on with your friends better than with your family? Why? / Why not?
   f Do you usually do the same things as your friends? Why? / Why not?
   g Do you copy your friends' clothes or manner of speech?

DO YOU NEED MORE PRACTICE?
CD-ROM UNITS 7–8

Writing folder 4

Essays

In Part 2 of Paper 2, you may be asked to write an essay giving your opinion on a topic or issue. The essay normally follows on from a class discussion and the target reader is the teacher. You must write between 120 and 180 words.

1 **Read the following essay question and then look at the plan which follows.**

You have had a class discussion on jobs and salaries. Now your teacher has asked you to write an essay, giving your opinion on the following statement:

Compared to people in other jobs, sportspeople are paid too much for what they do.

Write your **essay**.

Essay plan
Paragraph 1 – a general introduction
Paragraph 2 – an argument either for or against, possibly with an example from your own experience
Paragraph 3 – another argument either for or against
Paragraph 4 – the conclusion and your personal opinion

Below are four paragraphs. In pairs, put them in order so they follow the essay plan above.

A
On the other hand, it is important to say that a sportsperson's career does not last very long and he or she will only earn a high salary for a limited period of time – possibly as little as ten years. It is also the case that injury can cut short a career. Therefore it is reasonable that they receive higher than normal salaries.

C
To sum up, I agree that sometimes sportspeople are paid too much. However, perhaps the problem is really that people in more important jobs are paid too little.

B
First of all, I'd like to say that playing sport for a living is not essential to society. Nurses do an essential job but they earn very little compared to many sportspeople. Also, a football player, for example, will only be playing for a few hours a day while a nurse could work up to twelve hours a day.

D
The topic of sportspeople's earnings is one which often causes a great deal of discussion, especially in newspapers and on the television. Many people have strong feelings on the subject, and so do I.

2 **Read this essay question.**

Your teacher has asked you to write an essay, saying whether you agree or disagree with the following statement.

Everyone should have the opportunity to take up a sport.

Read the student's answer and divide it into paragraphs.

Sport is generally believed to be very good for the body **and** to be very good for the mind. In this essay I shall consider different aspects of this topic. I'd like to begin by saying that, on the whole, the people in my country really enjoy sport. **But** nowadays they tend to watch it rather than take part themselves. In the past, schoolchildren would spend at least two hours a week playing football or basketball. **And** they used to play on a Saturday **and** also spend some time after school playing games with their friends. Today, schoolchildren get a lot of homework to do and **so** they have to spend more time on their computers rather than doing exercise. **And** not everyone is keen on competitive sports or going outside to do sport in the cold or wet. **So** I believe there should be opportunities for people who want to do more individual exercise like yoga or aerobics. In conclusion I'd like to say that I think that everyone should have a free choice to do a sport which suits them best.

3 Why do you think that some of the words in the essay in 2 are in bold?

If you use some of the words and phrases in the box below, you will impress the examiners more than if you just use *and*, *but* or *so*. Decide which word or phrase you could use from the box instead of the words in bold in the essay. Think about other changes you may need to make in order to use some of these linkers.

Addition
in addition
moreover
as well as

Contrast
nevertheless
in contrast
on the other hand
however

Result
as a result
therefore
consequently

---

4 Using the expression *not only ... (but) also* in the right place will also impress the examiners.

EXAMPLE: *Elisa not only plays volleyball, (but) she also does fencing.*

Where could you put the expression *not only ... but also* in the essay in 2?

5 In pairs, think about the following essay task and make some notes using the questions below.

Your teacher has asked you to write an essay discussing the following statement.

Stress can be reduced by playing sport.

- Do you have any personal experience of this? Think of an example.
- Can playing sport when you feel stressed be bad for your health?
- Are there other things to help reduce stress which are better than sport?
- How do you feel about the statement – do you agree completely or just partly, or do you disagree totally?
- Any conclusions – in general / personally?

Now organise your notes into:

- an introduction
- some reasons / arguments / personal experience
- a conclusion

Make sure you use appropriate linking words.

Useful expressions

To begin
First of all, …
In my opinion, …
I'd like to begin by saying that …
Many people think/believe/say that …

To finish
In conclusion, …
To sum up, …

To give an example
For example, …
A good illustration of this is …
For instance, …

EXAM ADVICE

- Read the question carefully.
- If the question asks for your experience, don't forget to give an example.
- Remember to organise your essay. It shouldn't be a string of sentences but should present a logical answer to the question.
- Don't forget to use paragraphs (three or four is about right, but five would be acceptable).
- Check your spelling, grammar and punctuation.
- Use linking words.
- Check you have really answered the question.
- Count your words or make sure you know how many lines of your handwriting make 120–180 words. It doesn't matter if you are a little over 180 but it does matter if your essay is too short.

Modals 2: Speculation and deduction

1 Look at the advert opposite. What do you think it is selling? Discuss your ideas with a partner, using some of these openers.

Well, it could be advertising …
Or perhaps it might be for …

I think it must be a …
It can't be for … because …

Look at page 85 to find out if you guessed correctly.

2 The modal verbs in the first pair of examples above indicate that the speaker is unsure about something. It is also possible to use *may*, though less common. However, *can* is not used in this way.

Is the speaker unsure in the second pair of examples? Which words tell you?

Now look at this example. Is the speaker unsure?

It couldn't possibly be an advert for chocolate.

Does the meaning change if the full stop is replaced by a question mark? Say the sentence and the question aloud to your partner. The question would sound better with extra words at the end. Which words?

G → page 170

3 Now read the text about a TV advert and underline examples of the modals used in 1.

4 Explain the meaning of these words from the text.

a voice-over
b jingle
c celebrity
d verdict
e brand
f cunning

Why is the title of Bob's article appropriate?

The best ad missed the boat at Cannes

This is the title of an article by Bob Garfield, an American expert on advertising. He was writing about the International Advertising Film Festival, which takes place some time after the main film festival in Cannes.

For Bob, the best ad of the year was from Delvico Bates, Barcelona, for *Esencial* hand cream. The ad shows a woman riding her bike, which has a very squeaky chain. The woman gets off the bike, opens her jar of *Esencial* and rubs some of the cream onto the chain. Then she rides away – but the squeak remains. Why? Because, as the voice-over says, '*Esencial* moisturises, but it has no grease.'

Why is this ad so good? It can't be for its special effects, because there aren't any. Might it be the music? No, there isn't even a jingle. Could it be that the woman is a celebrity? No. Bob's verdict: 'It's a vivid demonstration of brand non-attributes. Inspired. Cunning. Brilliant.' In other words, by showing failure in a different context, the quality of the product is reinforced – grease is good for bike chains, but not for the skin.

So surely this ad must have won at Cannes? No. The simple truth is that it couldn't win, because the agency failed to enter it in time for the festival deadline!

5 In the final paragraph, it says *So surely this ad must have won at Cannes?* Here, the modal is referring to a past action. Say whether the speaker is sure or unsure in sentences a–c below.

a Their latest TV commercial must have cost a fortune to produce.

b There's one commercial showing a man sitting in an armchair on a mountain peak. That couldn't have actually happened – it must be done by special effects.

c Advertising has come a long way in the last forty years. Audiences of the 1960s might have been totally overwhelmed by an action-packed commercial of today!

G → page 170

6 Read this text and think of the word which best fits each gap. Use only one word in each gap. There is an example at the beginning (0).

DAVID OGILVY THE KING OF MADISON AVENUE

David Ogilvy, originally from Scotland, has often **(0)** _BEEN_ called 'The Father of Advertising'. He believed that you should see **(1)** .... single aim or idea through with passion and 'Go the whole hog!' A larger **(2)** .... life figure, he showed endless enthusiasm **(3)** .... the things that really interested him. The role he played best, and indeed defined, was that **(4)** .... the British gentleman in New York. When he set **(5)** .... the advertising agency Ogilvy and Mather there in 1948, he drove a Rolls-Royce, wore a full-length cape and used **(6)** .... attend parties in a Scottish kilt, **(7)** .... sure to pause at the top of the stairs to give fellow guests 'the full effect'.

Starting from a two-room office, Ogilvy hired bright young staff and developed the advertising agency into a huge empire, transforming **(8)** .... into the most famous ad man in the world in **(9)** .... process. He was a complete workaholic and disapproved of the culture of long lunches in advertising. He was a rather moral individual as **(10)** .... , who walked away from cigarette advertising long before his competitors. He campaigned **(11)** .... billboards, which in his view made the world look ugly, and **(12)** .... never accept any marketing strategy that deceived the public. He told copywriters to just 'tell the truth, and make the truth interesting'.

Vocabulary
Collocations

7 Look at the adjectives below. Which ones collocate with each of the nouns on the right? List the phrases that are possible, for example *huge variety*. Use some in the role play in 8.

huge	variety
high	message
low	idea
deep	budget
shallow	market
narrow	character
wide	picture
	view
	voice

8 Role play: XK trainers. Get into small groups and read your instructions (A or B). Then spend a few minutes listing useful vocabulary, using a dictionary if necessary. When groups A and B are both ready, have a face-to-face discussion.

Metallic mesh upper for strength and breathability.

Inflatable cushioning to fit perfectly around foot.

Self tying, no need for laces.

Shock absorbing gel pumped into undersole to absorb impact.

Group A: Advertising agency
A leading manufacturer of sports shoes, XK, is about to launch their new trainer. Your agency hopes to get the contract for the TV commercial and you need to prepare your ideas. As there is a big budget for this, you should use famous people and exotic locations! Prepare to meet XK.

Group B turn to page 85.

9.2

Listening

1 Briefly describe a TV commercial to your partner, using some of the expressions below. Explain your feelings about it.

There's one commercial that is for …
The thing I really like about it is …
What I can't stand is …

2 **1 10** You are going to hear two people talking about some TV commercials. In Part 1, which of these aspects are mentioned by the speakers? Tick the ones you hear.

a a puzzling beginning
b a storyline with flashbacks
c a dramatic ending
d a setting that is out of the ordinary
e a surprising location
f a well-known personality
g a powerful slogan
h an extravagant production

3 **1 11** Listen to Part 2, where one particular advert is discussed. Answer the questions below by writing W for woman or M for man in the boxes.

1 Who didn't like the advert?   [1]
2 Who was surprised by part of the advert?   [2]
3 Who agrees that Ray was an effective character?   [3]
4 Who liked the music in the advert?   [4]

Exam spot

In Paper 4 Part 4, you have to answer seven multiple-choice questions about a conversation or monologue. The questions will focus mainly on people's feelings or opinions.

4 Answer this practice question as you listen to Part 2 again.

What do the speakers agree is important in a successful advert?
A a strong storyline that people will find entertaining
B attractive characters that people will identify with
C an unpredictable element that will be memorable

5 **1 12** You will hear a man talking about making successful TV commercials. For questions 1–4, choose the best answer (A, B or C). To help you, there will be a pause on the recording between questions.

1 According to the speaker, what is the key factor when making a TV commercial?
A the type of location
B the choice of actors
C the depth of storyline

2 When developing the script, the speaker believes it is vital to
A time the overall message.
B feature the product by name.
C use a lot of beautiful language.

3 According to the speaker, if the same advertising company produces several commercials for a product,
A it could create a sense of boredom with the brand.
B it may attract new clients with similar advertising needs.
C it can be beneficial to include a familiar element in the series.

4 Before booking air time for a TV commercial, the speaker recommends
A targeting a product to a suitable channel.
B finding out accurate viewing figures.
C giving priority to cost over timing.

G rammar extra

Order of adjectives

The woman talks about a *graceful silver vehicle*. Which of the two adjectives is used to give an opinion? Can the order of these adjectives be changed?

Underline the adjectives used in slogans a–d and then identify them according to the types below. What is the rule for opinion adjectives?

a The classic British motorbike
b The sensational new CD from Jack Johnson
c Our popular full-length navy cotton nightshirt
d Bite-sized biscuits with a delicious creamy filling

OPINION

DESCRIPTION: SIZE SHAPE AGE COLOUR NATIONALITY MATERIAL

Descriptive adjectives are usually in the order above. It is quite unusual to have four adjectives in a row (as in example c). More commonly, any additional descriptive information is given in a separate phrase (as in example d).

Decide whether the following adjectives are in the correct order. Reorder them where necessary.

a a black huge dog
b an awful old woollen coat
c the Italian famous singer
d a red large apple
e an elaborate wooden square box
f a sophisticated new novel by a Scottish tremendous author

Vocabulary

Expressions for discussing ideas

6 There are a number of verbs in English that may signal an opinion or idea. Look at this example from the recording.

*I **reckon** I know pretty much what the magic ingredients are.*

In British English, *I reckon* is informal in register and would not be used in formal speech or writing. Which of these verbs are also informal?

admit   bet   doubt   expect   guess
suggest   suppose   stress

7 Put the phrases below into these groups. You heard some of them in the recordings. Use them in the next Speaking section.

Introducing an idea or opinion
Giving a different point of view
Adding to an idea

I suppose	Not only that, but
On the other hand	True enough, though
It seems to me that	What's more

Speaking

8 Look at the four photographs. Identify what product each billboard is advertising and discuss how effective it is at selling the product. Then decide which two adverts are the most effective, giving reasons for your choice.

- Spend some time looking at the photographs and note down useful vocabulary for each one. Remember that when you do the task, you will have to give an opinion about them rather than describe them.
- Think about how to structure the discussion so that you and your partner have equal opportunities to take part. Use some of the phrases from Unit 7 to achieve this. Remember also to use expressions from exercises 6 and 7.
- Try to speak together for about three minutes. Make sure you allow enough time within this to decide on the two adverts so that the task is completed. Give clear reasons for your choice.

Exam folder 5

Paper 4 Part 2 Sentence completion

> In this part of the Listening paper you hear either a monologue or a conversation. The task is to complete a set of sentences. You have 45 seconds to read the questions for this part. Use the time before the recording starts to predict what you might hear, underlining key words and phrases.

1 Look at these examples of Part 2 sentences and find words and phrases in the recording script below that relate to the underlined words and phrases. Can you predict what the missing words are?

As an example of making a scientific claim, the speaker talks about an advertisement for **1** ....

The most important message in the advertisement for the car is to do with **2** ....

When targeting teenagers in advertisements, products are often linked to **3** .... which others would find unacceptable.

Advertisements aimed at parents may include young children or **4** .... *and* .... , as they connect with their role as carers.

Recording script

1 To support the suggestion that one product is better than its competitors, the existence of actual proof is often mentioned. In one case, involving the promotion of .... , reference was made to an unnamed university research project, which analysed shades of white.

2 It must be true that there are more advertisements focusing on our love of driving than on anything else. While the messages of freedom and mobility are always important, it is above all the aspect of .... that is stressed in this particular one. We are supposed to believe that this car will take us to new places in society and change our role for ever.

3 Advertisers adopt different strategies as far as young people between the ages of 15 and 19 are concerned. For this population, it is not about conforming but about the complete opposite of that. Indeed, products for this age group are frequently connected with **3** ...., the kind that older people such as parents might well disapprove of.

4 Turning to mothers and fathers as consumers, advertisements targeting these people often reinforce the experience of bringing up a family. An advert that links its product to young children or even, interestingly enough, to .... , will probably succeed because these images appeal directly to motherly or, perhaps less commonly, fatherly instincts!

2 🔊 13 Now listen to the recording and write one or two words in gaps 1–4.

3 Transfer your answers to this sample answer sheet. Be careful with spelling.

Part 2 (Remember to write in CAPITAL LETTERS or numbers)	Do not write below here
9	9 1 0 u
10	10 1 0 u
11	11 1 0 u
12	12 1 0 u
13	13

4 Read this advice before you do the exam task in 5.

EXAM ADVICE

- Use the time before the recording starts to read the questions carefully.
- Look at the words either side of the gap to predict what you might hear.
- Write down the actual words that you hear – don't waste time trying to rephrase the information.
- Don't include extra information – you only need to write one, two or three words at most.
- Don't panic if you miss a question at the first listening – listen out for the answer at the second listening.
- Always write something, even if you're not sure that it's the correct answer.
- At the end of the test, write your answers clearly in capital letters on the answer sheet.
- Check your spelling – although minor errors are accepted, you may lose marks for incorrect spelling.

5 1 14 You will hear part of a talk about advertising jingles. For questions 1–10, complete the sentences.

THE COMMERCIAL JINGLE

One example of the contents of a basic jingle is a ⬚ **1**

The first modern jingle in 1926 advertised a ⬚ **2**

The rules on radio advertising in the 1930s forbade the use of ⬚ **3** of goods during peak listening periods.

The programme about a family began with a jingle for a ⬚ **4** , which was the first of its kind in the USA.

In the 1950s, jingles were often created by ⬚ **5**

When the jingle became less popular, advertisers started to use ⬚ **6**

From the late 1980s, commercials have had to reflect a complete ⬚ **7**

Payments from advertisers have covered earnings lost due to ⬚ **8** of music.

According to some psychologists, music that has a ⬚ **9** to the listener is easier to remember.

An 'ear worm' is up to ⬚ **10** long.

I can't get this tune out of my head!

SPAC

Speaking

1 The pictures show people in imaginary future situations away from the Earth. Compare the people and say whether you think these situations could happen in the future.

Reading

2 Skim the article on space travel for its general meaning, ignoring the missing sentences. Why do NASA and the SFF have different priorities?

CHEAP ACCESS TO SPACE

'Cheap' is an important word in space technology nowadays and re-usable rockets will be a key way of controlling costs. They will deliver things, bring stuff back to Earth and then go up again, perhaps with machinery for a space factory, or even carrying tourists. In the future, these space vehicles will be orbiting the Earth as efficiently as air freight carriers. There could be a billion-dollar market in taking packages from one side of the planet to the other in an hour.

NASA, the government-owned space program, once aimed to develop a re-usable rocket. **1** [   ] It plans to launch a manned expedition to an asteroid by 2025 and since this will require different technology, it is more likely that people outside the NASA program will develop re-usable rocket design.

Rick Tumlinson, co-founder of the Space Frontier Foundation (SFF), has spent the past two decades pushing for human exploration and settlement of the solar system. *Space News* magazine described him as one of the 100 most influential people in the space industry. Tumlinson has always maintained that businesses should get involved, and views NASA as a bit of a dinosaur. **2** [   ] '25 years after the Wright brothers flew a plane for the first time, people could buy a commercial plane ticket, but 25 years after landing on the Moon, we sat around watching old astronauts on TV talking about the good old days.'

Using his high profile, Tumlinson is going to try to prove a point. Space is our destiny, he says, so why not get on with it? He and his colleagues encourage any business that shares this aim. **3** [   ] For example, in December 2010, SpaceX (Space Exploration Technologies) launched their re-usable space capsule *Dragon*. After circling the planet twice, it returned with parachutes, landing as planned in the Pacific Ocean. Tumlinson immediately congratulated the company on successfully completing the world's first commercial orbital space flight and recovery, saying, 'This flight will go down in history as a turning point for the opening of space to regular people.'

While it was a significant technical achievement for SpaceX as a company, the flight was also highly significant for the American taxpayer. With the retirement of the Space Shuttle, the United States has an urgent need for commercial manned space flight. Until that happens, NASA will be totally dependent on the Russian Soyuz to carry astronauts to and from the International Space Station, at a price of over $50 million per seat. **4** [   ] They submitted their proposal to NASA just days after *Dragon* returned to Earth.

Tumlinson is also a strong supporter of commercial involvement in transportation to the International Space Station. At one point, the SFF ran a survey on the internet called 'Cheap Access to Space', where it asked American taxpayers for their opinions on the US space program and future priorities for space transportation. **5** [   ] That is simply not the purpose for which it was designed. NASA is 'elitist and exclusive', whereas the SFF believes in opportunities for everyone: 'a future of endlessly expanding new choices'.

The SFF wants to see 'irreversible human settlement' in space as soon as possible and maintains that this is only going to happen through free enterprise. It is inappropriate for government-sponsored astronauts to be constructing buildings and driving trucks. **6** [   ] SpaceX's achievements to date demonstrate a willingness to make this happen.

Once space transportation becomes affordable, mass space travel will be possible. Many people believe that by 2025 space tourism will have become a viable industry. However, US government officials don't really see a future for space tourism. **7** [   ] David Ashford, Managing Director of the British company Bristol Spaceplanes Limited, once said that space tourism would begin ten years after people stopped laughing at the concept. People have already stopped laughing.

Exam spot

In Paper 1 Part 2, remember that there is an extra sentence that isn't needed. After you have chosen your answers, check that the extra option doesn't fit anywhere in the text.

3 Seven sentences have been removed from the article. Choose from the sentences A–H the one which fits each gap. There is one extra sentence, which you do not need to use.

Work through the text, using the underlined phrases in sentence A to help you decide whether it fits in any of the gaps. Discuss your ideas with a partner.

Then underline the words and phrases in sentences B–H that link to the text and decide on your answers.

A   At the same time, the SFF accepts that NASA's missions could bring other scientific benefits.

B   More than one such firm has developed impressive solutions for getting into space and back cheaply.

C   Commercial activity such as this is what the private sector should be doing.

D   However, the USA's priorities have changed in the 21st century.

E   Here again, private companies may well prove them wrong in the very near future.

F   The SFF's own view has always been that it is impossible for NASA to offer an 'open frontier'.

G   In an early article he wrote about the government-owned space program, he made the following observation.

H   SpaceX is prepared to meet this need – and at less than half the cost.

Vocabulary

Word formation

4 Go through the text again to find words related to a–j (i and j are in sentences A–H). An example is given. Which word contains both a prefix and a suffix?

a   use   *re-usable*   f   appropriate
b   settle   g   willing
c   commerce   h   afford
d   achieve   i   science
e   end   j   impress

5 The use of the negative prefixes *il-*, *im-*, *in-* and *ir-* depends on the first letter of the word they join, as in *inappropriate*. Look back at Exam folder 2 for guidance. Add a prefix to form negative adjectives in a–f.

a   legal   d   moral
b   experienced   e   regular
c   responsible   f   patient

6 Use four of the negative adjectives to complete a–d.

a   Someone who wants something to happen as soon as possible is ....

b   A young adult who has no knowledge of working life is ....

c   Driving a car without a licence is ....

d   Friends who only see each other occasionally meet at .... intervals.

Speaking

7 Discuss these questions, using some of the words from this unit.

a   Do you think you will ever take a holiday in space? Why? / Why not?

b   What benefits and drawbacks might the commercial development of space bring?

c   Should governments spend tax-payers' money on space travel?

d   Why are there so many satellites orbiting the Earth? Will this technology become more important, in your view?

10.2

Review of future tenses

1 Look at sentences a–e from the article on space and identify the future forms listed 1–4 below. What other tense is used in sentences f and g to refer to the future?

1 *going to* future
2 future simple
3 future continuous
4 future perfect

a They will deliver things, bring stuff back to Earth and then go up again.
b This is only going to happen through free enterprise.
c In the future, these space vehicles will be orbiting the Earth as efficiently as air freight carriers.
d Many people believe that by 2025 space tourism will have become a viable industry.
e Tumlinson is going to try to prove a point.
f It plans to launch a manned expedition to an asteroid by 2025.
g However, this situation is due to change.

2 Which of the sentences a–g mention the following?

1 a prediction about the future
2 a planned event that is expected to happen soon
3 an event that has not yet happened but will happen within a certain period of time
4 an intention to do something

3 How are predictions about the future expressed in these two examples?

a Private companies may well prove them wrong.
b There could be a billion-dollar market in taking packages from one side of the planet to the other in an hour.

4 Why is *would* used in this example instead of *will*?

David Ashford once said that space tourism would begin ten years after people stopped laughing at the concept.

 → page 170

5 Choose the correct option in italics in these sentences and explain why it is correct.

a Within the next twenty years, the cost of space travel *will be falling* / *will fall* dramatically.
b In the near future, it's likely that adventure holidays *won't be* / *aren't going to be* limited to remote places on Earth.
c People *will* / *may* one day have the opportunity to go to distant planets, but first we need to discover a way of travelling faster than the speed of light.
d Our 7-day trip is due to depart on 1st December, 2025 and *will carry* / *will have carried* you 100 km into space.
e I've decided I *am going to book* / *will book* a trip into space as soon as I can afford it.
f The Americans always said they *would fly* / *will fly* to Mars.
g Sooner or later people *will live* / *will be living* in space.
h The International Space Station *will have been* / *will be* manned for 14 years in November.

6 What will we wear in the future? Read these exam candidates' ideas and complete the summary, using the future perfect of the verbs in the box. You may need to use the passive form. One verb isn't needed.

A new technology will change fabrics so they will change their colour during the day. People will be even more concerned with pollution and harmful UV rays, so their clothes will have built-in protective filters to help them keep healthy.

You may think that people will wear silver clothes like in science-fiction movies but I think everyone will wear very colourful balloons. They will use a special gas inside the balloons to make them fly.

become	fill	include	manage	rise	take

One person predicts that pollution
(1) .... to a dangerous level, but optimistically suggests that manufacturers
(2) .... some form of protection against this in their clothes. The other writes about people flying in their clothes, explaining that these 'balloons' (3) .... with gas to lift them off the ground. Neither feels that clothes (4) .... a uniform colour such as the silver of so many futuristic films. In fact, one person believes that a development in technology (5) .... place to create materials that can change colour while they are being worn.

What are your own ideas about future clothes?

Listening

7 ▶1 15 You are going to hear three people talking about the future. Decide whether each speaker has a positive or a negative view of what life for human beings might be like.

Speaker 1 ....
Speaker 2 ....
Speaker 3 ....

Which speaker is closest to your own ideas about the future? Why?

Vocabulary

Phrases with *at*

8 Speaker 2 used the preposition *at* in three different ways:

I'm reading one of his sci-fi ones at the moment.
They live for at least three hundred years.
There will always be some country at war with another.

Choose the correct phrase for each of these sentences and explain the meaning of the incorrect options.

1 Hurry up, we'll be locked inside the building unless we leave ....
A at first **B** at once **C** at last

2 Jordi is looking forward to the move but, ... , I know he'll miss his friends here.
A at least **B** at present **C** at the same time

3 For the first time in ten years, this war-torn country is now ...., thanks to the skills of the negotiators on both sides.
A at peace **B** at war **C** at rest

4 Journalists often get scientific facts slightly wrong, but this article is inaccurate reporting ....
A at his laziest **B** at its worst **C** at their best

Notice, as in the last example, that *at* is commonly used with a pronoun and a superlative.

Writing folder 5

Articles

1 Look at these titles of articles about the future. Which article would you most like to read? Why?

2 Match the titles to the opening paragraphs A–D. Do all four paragraphs fit their titles well? Why? / Why not?

Aliens are coming …

3 – 2 – 1 Lift off!

Is anybody there?

A lifelong ambition

A

Imagine being launched in a rocket towards that final frontier. Strapped into your seat in a shiny silver capsule, you feel the power of the engines as they carry you up and away. And soon you are orbiting around the Earth, covering vast distances and looking down on the planet you call home.

C

Our planet is going to be invaded – not by little green men but by a revolutionary new form of transport! Next week sees the launch of a worldwide advertising campaign, for a vehicle that could completely change our life on Earth.

B

I want to go up into space. I think it may be possible for ordinary people to go up into space soon. I read something about space travel. I want to be one of the first to go. I hope I can go up into space.

D

On some nights, I open my window and <u>watch</u> the stars. It's a <u>nice</u> thing to do. Sometimes I stay there for ages, wondering what the universe holds. It makes me feel <u>small</u>. Space is a <u>big</u> place. There are <u>a lot of</u> galaxies apart from our own – so there must be other life?

3 Look again at paragraph D. How could it be improved? Choose words and phrases from the pairs below to replace the words underlined. In each pair, both a and b fit the text correctly, so the final choice is up to you!

D

> On some nights, I open my window and <u>watch</u> the stars. It's a <u>nice</u> thing to do. Sometimes I stay there for ages, wondering what the universe holds. It makes me feel <u>small</u>. Space is a <u>big</u> place. There are <u>a lot of</u> galaxies apart from our own – so there must be other life?

a	b
stare at	gaze at
wonderful	brilliant
unimportant	humble
vast	huge
so many	an enormous number of

What parts of speech are the words in a–d below? Insert all these words into paragraph D where they fit best.

a cloudless   beautiful   twinkling
b forms of
c very   such
d truly   surely

Read through the paragraph once more. Could any sentences be joined together? Write out a final version.

4 Paragraph B is a poor attempt at an opening paragraph. Why? Rewrite it, making the following improvements, along with any others of your own.

- Order the ideas more clearly.
- Join any short sentences together.
- Include a first sentence that links back to the title.
- Replace any repeated words, e.g. *want: wish, hope*.
- Use a variety of sentence openers.
- Add suitable words to describe and emphasise.

Exam spot

An article is not an essay! It is written for a wider audience and will appear in a certain type of magazine. Read the exam question carefully to find out where the article may be published and who will read it. Choose a suitable style and use a range of language to make your article interesting to read.

5 Now look at this exam question.

You see this notice in an in-flight magazine and decide to enter the competition.

GALAXY TRAVEL COMPETITION

What forms of transport will we be using in 50 years' time?

Where will we take our holidays?

Write us an article, giving us your views on both of these questions. Science fiction writer John T. Price will choose the most original article, which will receive a prize of $1,000 and be published in our magazine next year.

Write your article in 120–180 words.

6 Answer these questions about the writing task.

a Which **two** topics do you need to write about?
b What is meant by 'forms'?
c Should the style be serious or lively?
d How many paragraphs should you write?

7 Plan your article before you start writing. Make content notes for each paragraph and think of a suitable title. Look back over Units 9 and 10 for relevant vocabulary and grammar. Then write your article in 120–180 words. Don't be afraid to use your imagination!

Like mother, like daughter

Speaking

1 Look at these photos of famous people and their children. Do you think the children resemble their mother or father? What similarities or differences can you see?

Exam spot

In Paper 5 Part 1, the examiner will ask you to give some personal information about yourself. This is to help you to relax before you do the rest of the Speaking test. The questions could be about where you come from, your family, your studies or work, your hobbies or your future plans.

2 With a partner try to find out as much as you can about each other. When you ask about each other's family, also ask these questions:

Who do you most look like in your family? Do you sound like anyone in the family when you answer the telephone? Who do you take after in character?

For extra practice take it in turns to think of a famous person but don't tell your partner who it is. Your partner has to ask you personal questions to try to find out your identity. Try not to make it too easy!

Exam spot

Remember that a wrong answer often repeats the same vocabulary you hear in the recording, and although it might be true, doesn't actually answer the question, so read through the questions very carefully before you listen. You will have one minute to do this.

Listening

3 🔈1 16 You will hear an interview with the daughter of a Hollywood film star. For questions 1–7, choose the best answer (A, B or C).

1 For her 14th birthday, Hannah
A took some friends to see a Harrison Ford film at the cinema.
B went to watch the making of a film.
C was given whatever she wanted.

2 How did Hannah's mother feel when Hannah said she wanted to be an actress?
A She wasn't keen on her doing it.
B She wasn't discouraging.
C She didn't think she was serious about it.

3 What does Hannah say about the comparison with her mother?
A They have the same shaped eyes.
B They are both tall.
C Their noses are similar.

4 Hannah and her mother both think that
A they look identical.
B they look a bit alike.
C people are completely wrong.

5 How did Hannah feel about her mother's attitude to acting?

A She was a bit upset.

B She was angry.

C She understood.

6 Why was Hannah encouraged to train to be an accountant?

A Her mother had had a bad experience with money.

B Hannah needed to learn the importance of saving.

C Her mother considered it a useful profession.

7 How does Hannah's mother sound?

A very demanding

B slightly foreign

C like her daughter

4 Now listen to the interview again. What adjective or adjectives does Hannah use to describe:

a her childhood in Hollywood?

b how her mother had felt when she first arrived in Hollywood?

c part of her nose?

d her mother talking about acting?

e the quality they both possess?

f her mother's attitude to money?

g her mother's voice?

Speaking

5 Find out who in your class has the same number of brothers and sisters as you, then form the following groups, where each person in the group is:

- an only child
- the youngest of two or more children
- the oldest of two or more children
- the middle child
- part of large family (five or more children)

Talk to the others in your group about what your family is like, how you feel about the size of your family and what effect, if any, it has had on you. Talk about your place in the family, and whether it's best to be the eldest, youngest, only one, middle child and so on.

6 Are there any special characteristics that run in your family? Is there anything you all like/dislike? Think about things such as: hair colour, height, occupation, the possibility of having twins, the need for glasses, etc.

Grammar extra

You've heard already the expression *to look like* + a noun phrase, which means *to resemble* or *to take after physically*.

EXAMPLE: *She looks like her mother.*

Now look at these two questions.
A What's he/she like?   B What does he/she like?

Decide which of the words below can be used to answer the questions.

tall   swimming   friendly   hamburgers   watching TV   photography   amusing

Vocabulary

Adjectives describing personality

1 Use one of the adjectives in the box to answer questions a–n.

> aggressive bad-tempered bossy
> cheerful competitive impatient
> jealous lazy loyal optimistic
> stubborn unpopular
> unreliable witty

How do you describe a person who:
a uses words in a clever and funny way?
b is usually happy?
c always believes good things will happen?
d always wants what you have?
e always tells you what to do?
f is not liked by other people?
g never turns up on time?
h refuses to change their plans or ideas?
i is always in a hurry to get things done?
j becomes angry or annoyed easily?
k behaves in an angry and violent way towards others?
l wants to be more successful than others?
m will always support you even when others don't?
n never wants to do any work?

2 Which of the adjectives above are positive, and which are negative? What are their opposites? Remember you can extend your vocabulary by thinking of adjectives with opposite meanings. Use a negative prefix if necessary.

In pairs, say which of the adjectives in 1 you would use to describe:

a yourself
b your parents
c your brothers/sisters
d your neighbours
e your best friend
f your worst enemy

Phrasal verbs and expressions with *take*

3 In the interview Hannah talks about her grandparents not wanting her mother to 'take up acting'. Complete these sentences using one of the words or phrases in the box.

> account of after charge for granted
> off out seriously turns

a I took .... $300 from the bank yesterday.
b No one ever seems to take me .... – they always think I'm joking.
c My sister and I always take .... loading the dishwasher.
d I hate the way my best friend always takes me .... and thinks I'm always available.
e I take .... my uncle Fred when it comes to height and weight.
f My grandmother always takes .... of what happens in her kitchen.
g My father's business really took .... after he had a new website designed.
h Lisa took .... her sister's untidiness when she decided not to move into a flat with her.

Collocations – adverb or adjective?

> Normally adverbs are used with verbs.
> EXAMPLE: *Hannah acts beautifully.*
> This tells you how she acted.
>
> However, with certain verbs it is sometimes necessary to use adjectives. These verbs are usually connected with our senses – *look, sound, taste, feel* and *smell*. Other verbs include *be, appear* and *seem*, and *become*.
> EXAMPLES: *Hannah is **beautiful**.   Hannah looks **beautiful**.*

4 With a partner discuss what you would say in these situations.

EXAMPLE: You're eating a lemon.
        It tastes sour.

a You're listening to a love song. It sounds …
b You're walking by the sea. It smells …
c You're walking home late at night. It feels …
d You're eating spaghetti. It tastes …
e You're looking through a travel brochure. It looks …
f You're wearing a designer suit. It feels …

5 Some of these verbs can have two meanings. Look at the underlined verbs and explain the differences.

A The actor <u>looked</u> angry when she read the bad review.
B The actor <u>looked</u> at her co-star angrily at one point in the film.

A I <u>feel</u> fine.
B I <u>felt</u> the water carefully to see if it was hot enough.

> In A examples, *looked* and *feel* are states, meaning 'seemed' and 'am'. In the B examples, *looked* and *felt* are both actions. If the verb means 'be' or 'seem', then an adjective is used after it. If the verb is used for an action, it can be followed by an object and/or an adverb, but it can also stand on its own.

Complete these sentences using an adverb or an adjective.

a The food tasted ....
b I felt the soft fur on the rabbit very ....
c I didn't feel very .... when the bus was late again.
d Ann looked .... to see if there was any traffic, before crossing the road.
e Noises can sound quite .... at night.
f Your coat looks ....
g He looked at her .... when she entered the room.
h The rabbit appeared .... out of the hat.

Past and present participles

Corpus spot

Be careful with *-ed* and *-ing* adjectives – the *Cambridge Learner Corpus* shows that exam candidates often make mistakes with these.

My friend was very **excited** about going to Hollywood on holiday.
NOT My friend was very ~~exciting~~ about going to Hollywood on holiday.

In our home we want to do many things otherwise we feel very **bored**.
NOT In our home we want to do many things otherwise we feel very ~~boring~~.

6 When Hannah is talking about her mother and her attitude to acting, she says her mother became quite embarrassed. Hannah means that her mother became a bit red or maybe blushed and wasn't sure what to say. What would it mean if Hannah had said 'my mother became quite embarrassing'?

Can you finish these sentences, which explain what the grammatical rule is?

1 To talk about how we feel about something, we use ....

2 To talk about the person or thing that is causing the feeling, we use ....

G → page 170

Speaking

7 In pairs, talk about how you feel when the situations in a–g happen.

Use some of these adjectives.

bored/boring
fascinated/fascinating
depressed/depressing
amused/amusing
pleased/pleasing
moved/moving
irritated/irritating
shocked/shocking
gripped/gripping

EXAMPLE:
There are only soap operas to watch when you and your family sit down to watch TV. *I'm bored by soap operas. They're not very amusing but my mother is fascinated by them.*

a Your brother/sister keeps borrowing your stuff without asking.
b You see a sad film with your mother.
c People keep telling you that you look like your mother/father.
d Your father has decided to move the family to another city.
e People think your mother/father is actually your sister/brother.
f A long lost relative has left your family a huge sum of money.
g You find out that your cousin is coming to live with you.

Exam folder 6

Paper 4 Part 1 Short extracts

In this part of the Listening paper you will hear eight unconnected short recordings of about 30 seconds each. There will be either one or two speakers. For each question, you have to decide which is the correct answer from three possible options. Both the question and the options are recorded, which gives you time to think about the recording that is coming up. Each recording is repeated.

You should make the best use of the time available. Read through each question as you hear it and underline any key words. Think about what to listen out for during the pause before each recording starts. After you have listened once, choose the option that you think is correct. As you listen for the second time, check that the other two options are definitely wrong.

If you do not know the answer to a question, keep calm and move on to the next one. At the end of the Listening test, you will have time to transfer your answers to an answer sheet. For any questions you haven't been able to answer, make a guess – there is a one in three chance of your being right!

1 **Look through these questions and underline the key words.**

You will hear people talking in eight different situations.
For questions **1–8**, choose the best answer (**A**, **B** or **C**).

1 You hear this advertisement on the radio for a new magazine.
Who is the magazine aimed at?
A gardeners
B cooks
C climbers

2 As you leave the cinema, you overhear this conversation.
What is the man's opinion of the film?
A It is longer than necessary.
B It has a weak storyline.
C Its actors are disappointing.

3 You hear a woman describing a music festival.
What did she like best about it apart from the music?
A the wide selection of food stalls
B the amount of space at the location
C the various free activities on offer

4 You hear two friends discussing a skiing holiday they have just been on. What did they both dislike?
A the amount of snow
B the times of the flights
C the facilities of the hotel

5 You overhear this conversation in a hotel.
Why has the woman come down to reception?
A to ask for another room
B to order some food
C to complain about the service

6 You hear this radio report about a football match.
What happened at the match?
A Some fans ran onto the pitch.
B A player was badly injured.
C The referee stopped the match.

7 You hear part of an interview on the radio.
Why did the man give up his job?
A to recover from stress
B to reduce his expenses
C to move somewhere quiet

8 You overhear this woman talking about an evening course.
What does she enjoy most?
A doing maths
B watching films
C having coffee

2 ♪1 17 Now listen and answer the eight questions. Remember that each recording is repeated. When you have finished, check your answers.

3 Fill in this extract from the answer sheet for Part 1 with your answers.

Part 1			
1	A ▭	B ▭	C ▭
2	A ▭	B ▭	C ▭
3	A ▭	B ▭	C ▭
4	A ▭	B ▭	C ▭
5	A ▭	B ▭	C ▭
6	A ▭	B ▭	C ▭
7	A ▭	B ▭	C ▭
8	A ▭	B ▭	C ▭

EXAM ADVICE

- Think about possible contents for each question as you listen.
- Choose your answers at the first listening.
- Check your answers at the second listening.
- Keep calm and make a guess if necessary.
- Remember to transfer your answers to the answer sheet at the end of the Listening test.

A great idea

Speaking

1   Student A: Look at photos 1 and 2.
Compare the photos and say why
electricity is important in modern life.
Which electrical appliance couldn't
you live without?

Student B: Look at photos 3 and 4.
Compare the photos and say what the
advantages and disadvantages are of
each method of transport. Which method
of transport do you prefer and why?

Reading

Exam spot

In Paper 1 Part 3 you need to match words or phrases in
the question with words of similar meaning in the text.

2   You are going to read a magazine article about items that were invented or discovered by accident.
You will have to decide which question is mentioned in each section. First of all, skim the text for
general meaning. Then look at the first question below. The key words which you will need to find a
paraphrase for in the text are underlined.

Which section mentions the need to change people's attitude when <u>buying goods</u>? | 1 |

The answer is in section E and the part that contains the answer is underlined. The key words are
purchase and *groceries*.

Now answer questions 2–15 in the same way. Underline the part of the text in which you find the
answer to the question.

Which section mentions

an idea which was the result of a complaint?	2
the need to find a cheaper way of doing something?	3
someone who didn't believe their discovery was important?	4
an idea which resulted from someone not being able to find what they wanted easily?	5
an idea which people made fun of initially?	6
a misunderstanding of how to use something?	7
a decision to keep on trying to make an idea better?	8
an idea which resulted from the addition of another substance?	9
the need for a new method of storage?	10
the need to manufacture something in large amounts for it to be worthwhile?	11
an idea which was a copy of something found in nature?	12
an idea which was an instant success with some people?	13
an idea which arose from an attempt to improve on an already well-known item?	14
a change that some people believed was for the worse?	15

5 Complete these sentences with information of your own, using passive forms of the verbs in brackets. Try to vary the tenses you use.

a The film .... (direct)
b This wonderful story .... (set)
c All of the costumes .... (design)
d The main character .... (play)
e The supporting cast .... (choose)
f Most of the music .... (compose)
g A subtitled version .... (show)
h The screenplay .... (nominate)

6 Now read this exam question.

You have seen this announcement on your college noticeboard.

> **We want your reviews**
> # NOW!
> Have you enjoyed a particular programme on TV recently? Or is there one that you just can't stand? Either way, why not write a review for the college website? Include plenty of information about the programme and give us your opinions on it, good or bad.
>
> **Email your review to Sam at the Student Office: sam@unitel.ac**

Write your **review**.

7 Which programme will you write about? List as many nouns as you can related to each type of programme below.

comedy: *jokes,*
documentary: *photography,*
game show: *quiz,*
reality show: *celebrities,*
soap opera: *drama,*

8 Make a paragraph plan before you start writing. Remember to name the programme at the start. Use some of the language in 2 and include a recommendation, unless your review is negative. Write your review in 120–180 words.

Grammar

1 For questions 1–12, read the film review below and think of the word which best fits each gap. Use only one word in each gap.

The best film I have seen is *LA Confidential*, starring Kim Basinger and Kevin Spacey. It was set (1) .... 1950s Los Angeles, and (2) .... the budget wasn't particularly extravagant, the film had very powerful images and seemed totally authentic. (3) .... example, the costumes looked just like what people (4) .... have worn; the cars seemed to (5) .... exactly what people (6) .... to drive around in. (7) .... of the actors played their parts extremely well, and Kim Basinger in particular gave (8) .... truly outstanding performance. The film was absolutely gripping, largely (9) .... the storyline was so carefully put together. There were several ingredients: (10) .... only the obvious (11) .... like murder and blackmail, but also corruption, Hollywood lifestyles and some moving family histories. (12) .... is an impressive film. See it!

Topic review

2 Read these sentences and say which are true for you, giving more details. Don't be afraid to use your imagination!

a I used to be different from how I am now.
b Next weekend I'm going to do something dangerous!
c I look like a famous film star.
d It must have been difficult looking after me when I was younger.
e I can't stand losing when I play sport.
f I'd like to invent something useful, like the Post-it Note.
g At home, I was always made to finish my food.
h By this time next year I'll have passed *Cambridge First*.
i I really enjoy watching adverts on TV.
j I find it hard to believe that the Earth has been visited by aliens.

Vocabulary

3 Two common verbs are used in these sentences. Decide what they are and fill the gaps, using a suitable verb form.

a We're .... used to living in a village now.
b Jane .... after her grandmother when it comes to looks.
c Don't try and .... out of doing the chores!
d Bill is still at home .... over a cold.
e You should .... turns to go on the trampoline.
f I finally .... a letter from the company last week, offering me a refund.
g Susie gets really annoyed when Jack doesn't .... her suggestions seriously.
h I should really .... account of other people's feelings more.

4 Decide which is the odd one out in these sets and say why.

a disturbing, terrifying, cunning, appalling
b voice-over, jingle, slogan, campaign
c martial arts, snowboarding, aerobics, gymnastics
d fancy, detest, loathe, hate
e deep, wide, huge, shallow
f pitch, sports centre, court, track
g intend, pretend, expect, hope
h extravagant, economical, affordable, cheap

Phrasal verbs

5   Complete sentences a–h with phrasal verbs formed from the verbs given. There is one extra verb in each set.

ON | get   keep   look   pass   switch |

a The property market is .... on favourably by investors.
b It must be really hard to .... on in advertising – it's such a competitive business.
c Sally never gave up hope and .... on trying to get her novel published.
d How about .... on the lights for this court – it's too dark to see the ball!

OFF | break   make   put   take   work |

e Sales of electric cars could really .... off given the current price of petrol.
f I'm going to use the exercise bike in the gym later, to .... off that huge lunch!
g Jenny .... me off seeing that film; she said it was very shocking.
h He .... off a piece of the freshly baked bread and chewed it with great pleasure.

Here is the complete advertisement from exercise 1 on page 60. It is for Samsung's 3D LED television, advertised in 2010.

Writing

6   Read paragraphs A–C and decide what type of writing each one is:

1 letter   **2** story   **3** article   **4** essay

A
To sum up, people should work fewer hours in the future, in my opinion. By doing this, unemployment could be reduced and working parents would be able to spend more time with their children. Moreover, life would be less stressful, which must be a benefit to society in the end.

B
She suddenly noticed something shiny on the sand just in front of her. It was a small metal object, about the same size as a mobile phone, but unlike anything she had ever seen before. Without a second thought, she picked it up and put it in her pocket, planning to take the strange thing home to show her brother. That was Maria's first big mistake.

C
Have you ever thought of joining a gym? I recently did and it changed my life. I used to come home from my job and just sit watching TV, but now I work out every evening. My friends say my personality has changed. Before, I would be rather aggressive whenever my day had been bad, but now they say I'm much better tempered.

Which paragraph is an opening and which is a conclusion?

Introducing the world's first 3D LED TV.
A new dimension in television.
Featuring Samsung's LED backlighting technology.
SAMSUNG
TURN ON TOMORROW
www.samsung.com/3D

9.1 exercise 8
Group B: XK Trainers
You are suspicious of advertising agencies, because two recent advertising campaigns failed. One used a famous basketball player, who was accused of taking bribes the same week the adverts appeared. Another, filmed at great cost in Antarctica, did not attract the public. Decide on the style you are now looking for.

Speaking

1 Look at this pair of photographs, which show two different classrooms in Britain. Talk to a partner about the differences and say which school is closer to your own learning experience.

2 Now talk to each other about your early schooldays. You should each describe:

  a a school you attended (size, location, atmosphere)
  b a teacher you remember well
  c something at school that you particularly enjoyed
  d someone at school that you found really annoying

  Report your partner's answers to the class.

  X told me / said that he/she …
  X spoke about / talked about his/her …
  X thinks/feels/remembers that he/she …
  X claims / believes strongly / is convinced that …

  Which tenses did you use to report what you heard?

3 Write David's confession below as reported speech, being careful to use suitable past tenses.

  EXAMPLE: *David said that it wasn't Simon's fault. …*

It isn't Simon's fault! I want to describe what really happened. I was inside the classroom during break and I saw a group of my friends outside. I went over to the window and tried to get their attention. I waved at them but they didn't see me, so I hammered on the window. I know glass is breakable but I just didn't think. When my hand went through, I panicked. I wasn't hurt and I wanted to avoid getting into trouble, so I put Simon's bag over the hole and left the room. I'm sorry I haven't told anyone the truth until now.'

Listening

4 You are going to hear a radio interview with two work colleagues, Sandra Wilson and Mike Tripp, who also used to attend the same school.

  First, read the reported statements a–h below.

  a Sandra explained that she had disliked Mike because of his attitude to school.
  b Sandra accused Mike of deliberately forgetting certain things he had done at school.
  c Mike explained that he had known at the time how irritating he was.
  d Mike wished he had worked harder at school.
  e Mike said that he had left the science exam because he couldn't answer the questions.
  f Mike felt that his father had expected him to do well when he left school.
  g Mike admitted that the school careers teachers had been quite helpful.
  h Mike mentioned that his father had helped him financially in starting his business.

  2 02 Now listen to the recording and tick the statements that are true. Compare your answers and listen again to check.

Vocabulary

Word formation

5 What words in the same word family as the noun *education* do you know? Use a dictionary if necessary to complete the definitions below. Two are adjectives.

  a .... : [*often passive*] to teach someone at a school, college or university
  b Someone who is .... has learned a lot at school or in college and has a good level of knowledge.
  c .... : providing education or relating to education

Collocations

6 Match the two adjectives from 5 to their noun collocates a–d. Which adjective is the more useful to learn, in your opinion? Why?

    a qualifications
    b person
    c opportunities
    d standards

7 Read these sentences written by past exam candidates and compare their experience of school and learning with your own.

    a There is no motivation in studying something you are not interested in.
    b Dad let me go to the cinema with my friends, as a reward for getting such good results in maths.
    c Although discipline is essential, I think the methods being used today are as awful as the old ones.
    d The school rules in my country are more strict than in other countries.

8 Opposite are some short descriptions of the first jobs some famous people had. Work out which job was done by each person.

9 In the descriptions there are several words commonly found in letters of application, which will be dealt with in the next Writing folder. Underline any words you think may be useful. Check their meaning in an English–English dictionary and look for further examples of their use.

A His parents divorced when he was 12 and his mother was left to bring up four children single-handed. All four kids had jobs – his three sisters worked for different local restaurants, while he cut grass and did a paper round. It probably took him a year to earn what he can now make in a single day.

Agatha Christie

B He became an apprentice on a cargo ship at the age of 17 and his very first experience was gained on a voyage to Rio de Janeiro. Altogether he spent five years at sea. He devoted his spare time to his hobby, which was ultimately to become a full-time career, but only once he was 35.

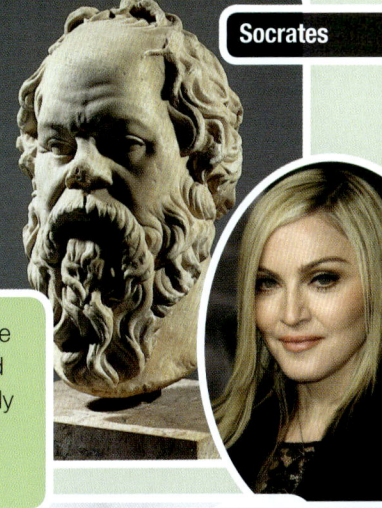
Socrates

Madonna

C On leaving school at 17, the only jobs available were in the local fish factory. The smell was appalling and working on the filleting machine made her constantly want to throw up. She escaped to London in the end and found employment as a waitress.

D He inherited the family sculpting business but showed little interest in it. He had no talent for stonework whatsoever and so, not surprisingly, the business went downhill fast. Instead, it was his determination to solve the twin mysteries of life and death that led him to be considered the wisest man alive.

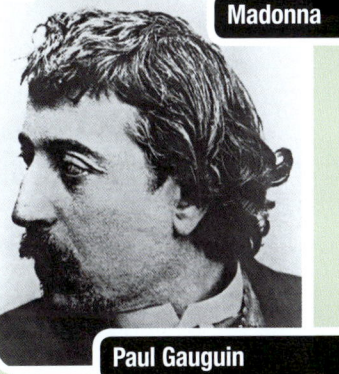
Paul Gauguin

E She worked long hours at a hamburger restaurant and was so poor that she had to search through the dustbins after work for any thrown-out food. She also sold ice cream and was a coat-check girl at the Russian Tea Rooms in New York.

Annie Lennox

F Initially, she took a position as an unpaid assistant in a chemist's shop, and later qualified in pharmacy. Her duties gave her a sound knowledge of poisons, that would subsequently be extremely relevant.

Tom Cruise

Reporting

1 Look at quotes a–c and explain why the tenses underlined have been used in reporting them.

a 'I can't remember much about my first school; my mother will, though.'
Greg claimed that he <u>couldn't</u> remember much about his first school, but thought that his mother <u>would</u>.

b 'When Jack moved to secondary school he became less motivated.'
His mother said that Jack <u>had become</u> less motivated when he had moved to secondary school.

c 'Girls are now doing better than boys at school.'
The expert said girls <u>are</u> now doing better than boys at school.

G → page 171

2 Match the quotes a–d with the reported statements 1–4.

a 'I visited my old school recently and it was much smaller than I remembered.'
b 'Perhaps we should educate parents about how they can help their children.'
c 'We belong to an anti-learning culture.'
d 'I'll make more of an effort.'

1 She complained that society doesn't encourage education.
2 He promised to work harder.
3 She explained that she had been back and had found it very different.
4 He suggested showing parents what to do.

Corpus spot

Be careful when using reporting verbs – the *Cambridge Learner Corpus* that shows exam candidates often make mistakes in the structures that follow them. Here are two of the most common mistakes.

My father suggested **that I should read** this wonderful story.
NOT My father ~~suggested me to read~~ this wonderful story.

We explained **the situation** to her, so she let us in.
NOT We ~~explained her the situation~~, so she let us in.

3 Decide which structures can be used after the following reporting verbs, giving examples. Two are done for you.

accuse *She accused him of cheating.*
admit *He admitted (to) being wrong. He admitted (that) he was wrong.*

apologise	deny	promise	suggest
argue	explain	refuse	urge
claim	insist	say	warn

Listening

Exam spot

In Paper 4 Part 3 the six options may be presented as sentences which summarise what each speaker says. Identify key words in the sentences to help you predict content.

4 You will hear five different callers to a radio phone-in giving their views about educational performance in Britain. First, read A–F and underline the key words.

A Changes in society explain why boys and girls have different career ambitions.
B The recently improved academic performance of girls should be recognised.
C Boys can miss out on the influence of men while they are growing up.
D Limited educational opportunities are affecting some children's development.
E Parents tend to raise boys and girls differently from a young age.
F A different approach is needed to the early stages of learning.

5 **2 03** Listen to Speaker 1. Complete this summary using present tenses. Then match the content to one of the options A–F.

The first speaker claimed that there (**1**) .... too many women teachers in British schools and argued that boys (**2**) .... men as role models. He also suggested boys (**3**) .... more by broken marriages than girls.

6 **2 04** Now listen to Speakers 2–5 and note down the main points each person makes. Then report their views by writing summaries similar to the one in 5. Match your summaries to A–F and write your choices below.

Speaker **2**   Speaker **3**   Speaker **4**   Speaker **5**

7 As you listen again, listen out for words or phrases that mean the same as a–h. The number of the extract is given in brackets.

  a are usually (1)
  b make good progress (2)
  c misbehaving (2)
  d earners (3)
  e accepted (3)
  f referring to (4)
  g make longer (4)
  h be pleased about (5)

8 Discuss these questions.

  • Are girls doing better at school than boys in your country? Why? / Why not?

  • Whose responsibility is it to achieve good school results – yours, your parents' or your teachers'?

  • How should the problem of educational underachievement be tackled?

  • Is it essential to be university-educated in today's world? What are the alternatives to university in your country?

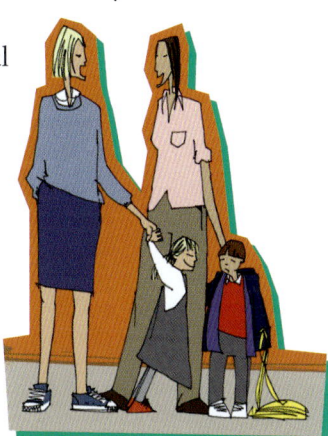

Grammar extra

Reported questions usually involve changes in word order. Look at the questions below and how they have been reported. Then report questions a–e.

What's the answer to number 14?
He asked what the answer to number 14 was.
Where are the scissors?
He asked where the scissors were.
When did this term start?
She asked when this term had started.
Are there enough books to go round?
He asked if there were enough books to go round.
Should I repeat the question?
She asked whether she should repeat the question.

  a Why are girls gaining more university places?
    He asked …
  b In what ways was the situation different twenty years ago?
    He asked …
  c Will things get better in the future?
    He asked …
  d Should British children spend more time at nursery school?
    He asked …
  e Why haven't we faced up to this problem?
    He asked …

---

9 Complete the second sentence so that it has a similar meaning to the first sentence, using the word given. Do not change the word given. You must use between two and five words, including the word given.

1 'You put that frog on my chair, didn't you, Charlie?' said Sally.
  OF
  Sally ....
  a frog on her chair.

2 'Stop misbehaving or you'll be sent to the head for punishment,' the teacher said to Johnny.
  WARNED
  The teacher ....
  or he would be sent to the head for punishment.

3 At the interview, Kate was asked how well she had done in her exams.
  DID
  The interviewer asked Kate, 'How well
  .... in your
  exams?'

4 'Please try to stay awake during the lesson,' the teacher told them.
  URGED
  The teacher ....
  asleep during the lesson.

5 Susan denied wasting her time at school when she was younger.
  NOT
  Susan said ....
  her time at school when she was younger.

6 'Have you tidied up in the science lab?' the chemistry teacher asked them.
  TIDIED
  The chemistry teacher wanted to know
  .... in the
  science lab.

7 'I'm sorry, I've forgotten my homework,' Nicholas said.
  APOLOGISED
  Nicholas .... his
  homework.

8 Stephen told me he would see me the next day at the lecture.
  SEE
  'I .... at the
  lecture,' Stephen said.

Exam folder 7

Paper 4 Part 3 Multiple matching

In this part of the Listening paper you hear five short extracts which are all related to each other in some way. It may be that the speakers are all talking about the same subject or experiences. Another possible link may be function or feeling or job. You need to match each of the five extracts to one of six options. You hear the extracts twice, and it is very important that you take the opportunity to check your answers carefully during the second listening. One mistake could affect two answers.

1   **2 05** You will hear the first speaker talking about his experience of education. Look at the statements A–F and decide which one is true for the first speaker.

A I really enjoyed meeting new people.
B My attitude to studying had been wrong.
C It taught me how to cope with money.
D I'm not sure what I want to do now.
E I realised I worked better in a freer environment.
F I had to work harder than I expected.

The answer for Speaker 1 is B. Now look at the recording script. The part containing the answer is underlined.

EXAM ADVICE

- Don't sit looking out of the window while you're waiting for the recording to start. Read the questions carefully.
- Try to predict what each person might say.

Recording script

Speaker 1: When I started my last year at school, <u>I didn't take it seriously enough. I should've chosen subjects which were useful rather than ones I liked or that sounded easy.</u> By the time the exams came, I'd given up and I did very badly. I knew I'd have to work hard but I wasn't able to catch up with my friends. Because I failed at science, I can't be a teacher, which is what I really want to do. I'm doing a part-time job in order to make ends meet and next year I'll be starting evening classes to get better qualifications.

Look carefully at the options.

A I really enjoyed meeting new people.
  – *He doesn't mention new friends.*
B My attitude to studying was wrong.
  – *Right answer.*
C It taught me how to cope with money. – *Money is mentioned (to make ends meet) but nothing is said about learning what to do with money.*
D I'm not sure what I want to do now.
  – *He's going to study, so this isn't the answer.*
E I realised I worked better in a freer environment. – *This isn't mentioned at all.*
F I had to work harder than I expected.
  – *This isn't the answer, as he knew he had to work hard.*

King's College, Cambridge

2　**2 06** Listen to the other speakers and for questions 2–5, choose from the list A–F
in 1, which each speaker states. (Remember that B has already been used.) Use the
letters only once. There is one extra letter which you do not need to use.

Speaker 2　☐ **2**
Speaker 3　☐ **3**
Speaker 4　☐ **4**
Speaker 5　☐ **5**

3　Now look at the recording script for Speakers 2–5 and underline the parts which
give you the answers.

Recording script

Speaker 2:　I left school and moved to a college to take my final exams. It was
the best decision I could have made. At the college nobody seemed
to care about homework and this really motivated me. I had to plan
my work myself – there was no one to make you do it and no one to
check up on what you'd done. I was still dependent on my parents for
money – but that was OK. I learned a lot about real life there – things
like getting on with people and organising your time – which has been
really useful now I'm working.

Speaker 3:　When I left school I didn't have a particular career in mind so I
decided to do Environmental Studies at university, mainly because I'd
enjoyed geography at school. I didn't really like the course at university
and I did think about leaving, but instead I changed courses, which
was easier than I expected. I think university was useful in that I learnt
how to live alone and how to budget, and as I'm an underpaid teacher
now, that really helps.

Speaker 4:　I had no difficulty choosing what I was going to do – my parents
are both doctors and ever since I was small I also wanted to do that.
They really encouraged me and I did well at school and got into a
good medical school fairly easily. It was surprisingly tough at medical
school, but I had some good friends and we pulled through together.
I think the doubts only began to set in when I graduated and got my
first job in a hospital. I began to wonder if I'd missed out because
I'd been so focused on becoming a doctor. So now I'm doing some
voluntary work in Africa, which I'm really enjoying.

Speaker 5:　I decided to take a year off after doing my last year at school. I'd had
enough of revising and sitting in a library, so I decided to go off to
Australia for nine months and earn a bit of money. I've got relatives
there who put me up when I first arrived and found me a job. It wasn't
doing anything particularly interesting, but the great part was that I
was getting to know people who were completely different to the ones
I'd known back home. I really recommend taking a year out, but you
need to have a firm plan or it could end up a waste of time.

Career moves

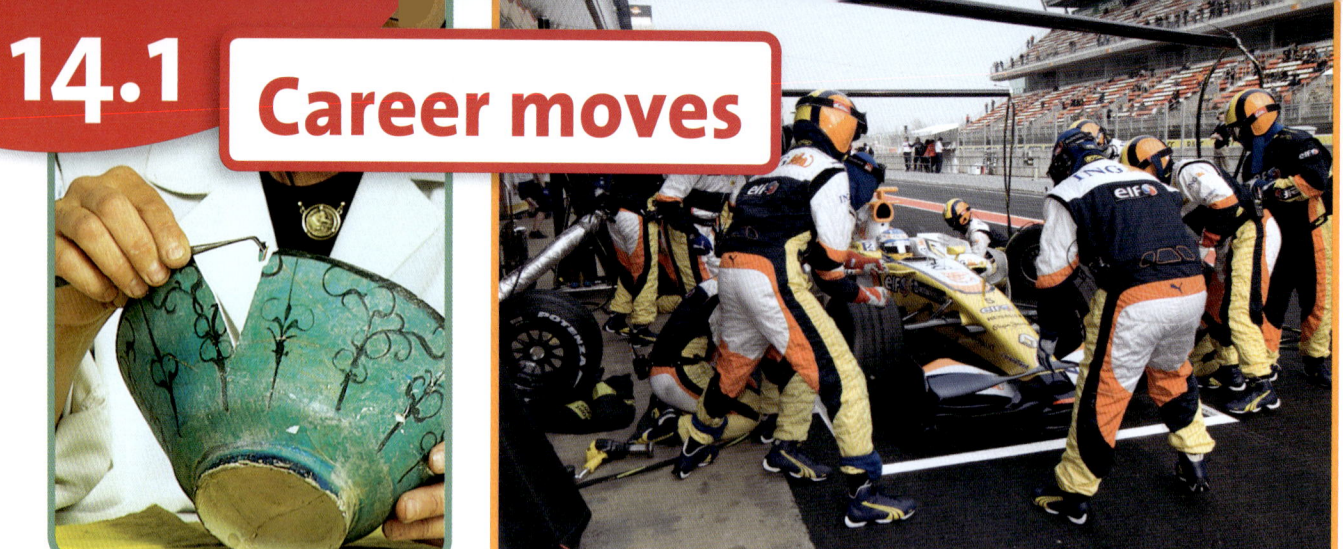

Speaking

1 Identify the jobs in the photos and say what skills are important in each one. Which job would you prefer and why?

2 Check you know the meaning of these words and then choose four to complete the quotes below.

> adventurous   concerned   flexible
> redundant   secure   self-confident

a
> A career used to be for life. Once you had left school, you found a job and worked your way up the career ladder. Today, the job market is far less .... , and no one knows what tomorrow may bring.

b
> You have to be ready to accept change, in short be totally .... , if you are going to stay in the job market. There's a positive side to this – instead of feeling that you have to stay in the job you've been trained to do, you can be more .... and try different things.

c
> Women are more willing to take career risks, partly because they are less .... with status, but also because they like to experiment. It's just a question of saying: I think I can do this. And then giving it a go.

Reading

Exam spot

In Paper 1 Part 3, you don't need to read the texts word by word. Read the questions first, to know what to look for. Then scan the texts for the information you need. Always allow time to check your answers.

3 You are going to read a magazine article about five women who have recently changed careers. For questions 1–15, choose from the women (A–E).

Which woman

reduced her working hours in order to study?	1
took part in competitions in her early teens?	2
spends a lot of time outdoors?	3
felt grateful that her employers trusted her?	4
would like to start her own business?	5
began her studies in a new location?	6
had a medical background originally?	7
travelled in her previous job?	8
chose to be made redundant?	9
is satisfied with her new lack of routine?	10
took a long time to get on top of the job?	11
visited another continent during a career break?	12
found her first job very tiring?	13
had financial support from her parents?	14
intends to expand her range of products?	15

4 Now answer these questions about the women.
   a Why do you think Amanda felt increasingly *dissatisfied* with her life at the age of 29?
   b What sort of things would Dani have been *inexperienced* at doing on the farm?
   c How might Rachel's new life seem *uncertain* to some people?

Meet five women who have changed careers

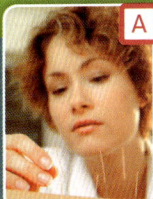

A Amanda, 33

I had been working in sales for six years when I suffered an ankle injury that was to change my whole life. It didn't heal and someone suggested acupuncture, a traditional Chinese treatment for pain. I was so impressed by the treatment that I found out about classes. I had reached a point in my life where things had to change. In many ways I had it all: a company car, foreign business trips, my own house, a secure job. But at 29, I felt increasingly dissatisfied and wanted to be more adventurous. So I persuaded my boss to let me work a four-day week and did classes on the remaining day. It took four difficult years to qualify, as I was studying 25 hours a week on top of my job. It's been worth it though, and I get on well with the people I work for now. As for the BMW, I don't miss it at all!

B Dani, 30

I trained as a doctor but I knew all along it wasn't right for me and I found working in a hospital exhausting. My parents had run their dairy farm for thirty years and needed a long holiday, so we decided that I'd look after things for six months while they visited my brother in Australia. It gave me the career break I'd been looking for, except that I never went back. Mum and Dad have emigrated, so now I'm in charge for good, which is fine by me. At the beginning, I was quite inexperienced, though it felt natural to be back on the farm and didn't take me long to master everything. I've learned to be flexible – to fit in with the weather! Being in the open air is the best thing of all. I've just started selling my own cheese and by this time next year, I'll have launched my own ice cream.

C Sue, 34

I'd never seen myself as academic. Hairdressing seemed glamorous and I wanted a car, so I went to work in a salon as an apprentice. I wasn't concerned about the poor pay – I had fun! Then, all of a sudden, my husband's job moved to London. This forced me to reconsider my own life and I decided to take English and Law at night school there. I was spending 45 hours a week cutting hair and working for exams as well. I lost ten kilos in weight, but for all the stress of studying, I knew I was doing the right thing. After leaving college I went into market research. My confidence has always been low and it was three years before I felt I could cope effectively in the role. But it was worth it – my present earnings would have been unimaginable back in the salon.

D Rachel, 28

I worked for three investment banks in London, earning £60,000 a year in my last job. If I'd added up the hours I spent at my desk, it would have been huge – sometimes I was there until midnight. To begin with, I had lots of energy and I got a real buzz from the work, helped by the fact that everyone was willing to give me so much responsibility. Eventually, third time around, it got to me. At the time, the bank needed to reduce its staff and was offering a good leaving package, so I jumped at it. I spent six months getting to know Latin America, where I'd never been. Now I'm working freelance, editing articles for financial magazines. I've set up the spare room as an office and I hope to pick up enough work. People who need certainty and structure would find my new life difficult, but all in all, I feel I've made the right decision.

E Eleanor, 25

I'd always loved skating and what I wanted above all was to be an ice dancer. Mum and Dad found classes for me but the rink was in another town so it took up a lot of their time driving me there. I'm so grateful to them for that, not to mention the huge sums they've invested in my training. I started competing at 14 and turned professional at 16. I've done a lot of great shows, but I chose to hang up my skates long before most ice-dancers do. For the last six months, I've been working for a sportswear firm to gain experience in business and marketing and my dream is to set up a company before long, producing boots, skates and costumes for the ice.

Vocabulary

Word formation

5 Choose suitable negative prefixes for these words. Then match them to the short definitions a–e.

> honest organised patient responsible successful

a not planned well
b easily annoyed
c not achieving what was intended
d likely to lie or do something illegal
e not thinking about the possible bad results of your action

G rammar extra

There are a number of expressions with *all* in the article. Say how *all* is used in a–h.

a I *had it all* (A)
b I don't miss it *at all*! (A)
c *all along* (B)
d *the best thing of all* (B)
e *all of a sudden* (C)
f *for all* the stress (C)
g *all in all* (D)
h *above all* (E)

Sometimes, *all* is confused with *whole*. In this example, it is not possible to use *all*.
... an ankle injury that was to change my whole life.

Now complete these sentences using *all* or *whole*. Where it is possible to use either, write both alternatives. Add any words necessary.

1 The firm acknowledged .... 279 applications the same day.
2 The recession had affected .... car industry, causing many redundancies.
3 .... world depends on electronic communications nowadays.
4 Accountants have a powerful voice in .... companies.
5 We had been staring at figures on screen .... day and .... us were fed up.
6 There are disadvantages to .... these jobs.

What rules can you make about the use of *all* and *whole* on the basis of these examples?

G → page 172

Perfect tenses

1 Explain the differences in meaning in these sentences and identify the tenses used.

   a I have never sent an email.
   b I never sent an email in my last job.
   c I had never sent an email until I started working here.
   d I will have sent over 500 emails by the end of this week!

2 Read these examples of perfect tenses from 14.1.

   a I had been working in sales for six years.
   b I've set up the spare room as an office.
   c I'd always loved skating.
   d By this time next year, I'll have launched my own ice cream.
   e It gave me the career break I'd been looking for.
   f My confidence has always been low.
   g If I'd added up the hours …
   h I've been working for a sportswear firm to gain experience.

Now look at the different uses of perfect tenses, 1–7, and find examples of them in sentences a–h. Some uses have more than one example.

1 talking about a recent event or situation which has been completed
2 talking about an event or situation which started in the past but is still true
3 emphasising the duration of a recent event or situation
4 talking about an event or situation that happened earlier than the past time being described in the sentence or paragraph
5 emphasising the duration of an event or situation which took place earlier than the past time being described
6 used in a conditional structure
7 talking about an event that will happen within a specified future time

Which perfect tense has not been exemplified in a–h? Give an example of this tense.

G → page 172

3 Choose the correct tense.

   a What I *have been showing / had been showing* you today is only part of our huge range of products.
   b Last week, the company *was voted / has been voted* top supplier for the third time.
   c Since she started college, Sara *was studying / has been studying* every night, including weekends.
   d On Friday, I *have been working / will have been working* in the department for exactly a year.
   e The end of year results were not as bad as the directors *had feared / have feared*.
   f By May, eight new designs *have been launched / will have been launched*, increasing our sales potential.
   g Our sales director *has made / made* some appalling decisions recently and frankly, we'd be better off without him!
   h They *have been waiting / had been waiting* for the fax all day but when it came through the final page was missing.

Corpus spot

Correct any mistakes with tenses in these sentences written by exam candidates. Two sentences are correct.
a I felt very sorry after I've seen your report.
b Some months ago he has directed a movie.
c Their fans want to know what has been happening to them.
d For thousands of years our civilisation is making progress.
e When I left your house in Ljubljana, I've decided to visit the lakes.
f Some friends of mine have been working there last summer.
g If I hadn't met you, I wouldn't have been able to find my way home.
h The Astrid Hotel is closed since last year.

Listening

4 **2 07** You are going to hear five people talking about their skills and work experience which make them suitable for the following jobs. Note down the skills, qualities and experience mentioned by each person.

Speaker 1: office administrator
Speaker 2: interpreter
Speaker 3: shop assistant
Speaker 4: first-aid worker
Speaker 5: cook

What other skills and qualifications would be useful in each job?

5   Now read the role play instructions for Student A or B.

Student A

You are about to attend an interview for a job at an international sports event in Canada, next summer. The job will be one of the five listed in exercise 4. You don't know exactly which one it will be yet, but you really want to get a job. Spend a few minutes thinking about relevant experience and qualifications.

Remember to be enthusiastic at the interview and explain why you think you would be suitable.

Student B

You are going to interview someone for a job at a major international sports event in Canada. Tell the interviewee what the job involves (choose one of the five listed in exercise 4). Then ask the interviewee about relevant experience (including knowledge of English), qualifications, general commitment and suitability for the job you have in mind.

Then decide on a scale of 0–5 (5 being the most positive) how your interviewee has performed, according to these criteria:

Experience Qualifications Commitment
Inter-personal skills   Enthusiasm

6   Skim the article below to decide who it is aimed at. Then put the verbs in brackets into the correct perfect tense.

How to survive in business today

The current stripping away of management layers and large-scale staff redundancies **(1)** .... (shrink) companies radically. In some ways, this harsh new reality **(2)** .... (bring) bosses and workers closer together. At the same time, many new small businesses **(3)** .... (set up) in the last few years and a staggering 60 per cent of the population now work in small groups of five or less. Alongside these trends, the need to apply psychology in the workplace **(4)** .... (grow) constantly. 'Jobs for life' **(5)** .... (cease) to exist, and in contrast, survival skills at work **(6)** .... (become) absolutely essential. Here are some top tips on how to survive in the office.

- Fax or email people at night – it will look as though you **(7)** .... (put in) extra hours.
- Try to remember people's names – recent studies **(8)** .... (show) that this simple gesture makes people think more highly of you.
- Spend money on smart clothes – a survey by Hays Personnel Services **(9)** .... (find) that 42% of men and 52% of women think well-dressed people have a career advantage.
- Become known as a safe pair of hands rather than a high-flying genius – in ten years' time, you **(10)** .... (give) the top job while your flashy colleagues **(11)** .... (claim) unemployment benefit for at least five years.
- Be concise in meetings – if you **(12)** .... (ramble on) at length, the chances are that you won't have got your message across.

Writing folder 7

Applications

1 Give the adjectives related to these nouns, using your dictionary if necessary.

motivation ....
commitment ....
determination ....
cheerfulness ....
enthusiasm ....
energy ....
organisation ....
talent ....
skill ....
confidence ....

2 Read this advertisement. Decide which skills would be essential for the job, choosing from the nouns above and adding ideas of your own.

WANTED

Friendly, English-speaking people to work as restaurant and bar staff on our Mediterranean cruise ships

Tell us about
- why you would like to work for us
- any relevant experience you may have
- personal qualities that would be useful on board.

Contact Cool Blue Cruises, PO Box 500, Southampton SO4 5TR, quoting reference PM44.

---

3 Now read these two letters of application. Has each applicant covered all the necessary points? Who would stand a better chance of getting the job?

Dear Sir or Madam

I have just seen your advertisement for jobs on board your cruise ships (reference PM44) and I would like to apply. I am a 20-year-old Swede with determination and commitment. I have often thought of spending time at sea and your job seems the perfect opportunity.

Although I have no on-board experience, I have been working as a waiter in a local restaurant for the last 18 months and I have also had some experience of bar work. My knowledge of English is quite good, as I have been attending classes for the last six years. I would like to add that I have visited many parts of the Mediterranean myself and could talk to guests confidently during the voyage.

As for other personal qualities which might be useful on board a ship, I am an organised and easy-going person, so sharing a cabin with other crew members would not be a problem.

I am sure I would make a success of this job and I hope you will consider my application.

Yours faithfully

Pernilla Axelsson

Dear Mr or Mrs

I saw the job you advertised and I want to give it a go. I love the idea of going on a cruise and I'm just the person you need. I never thought of working on a ship but it sounds fine.

By the way, I've worked in a bar, though I didn't enjoy it that much. I wouldn't mind being a waiter on your ship though. Do the staff eat the same food as the guests? I've heard it's very good.

You ask about me. Well, I tell good jokes. I'm always cheerful and I think you would have to be, stuck on a ship for so long.

Write to me soon.

Harry

4 Make improvements to the second letter, rewriting it according to these guidelines.

  a Change the opening and closing formulae. Make sure the style is formal throughout.

  b Rewrite the first sentence to make it clear which job is being applied for. Remember to use the present perfect!

  c Edit the first and second paragraphs to make them sound more positive. Build up the information about previous experience, including some reference to learning English.

  d Write a new third paragraph on personal qualities, using some of the adjectives and nouns in exercise 1.

  e Try to write around 180 words in all.

Exam spot

If you choose to write a letter of application in Part 2 of Paper 2, you do not need to write any addresses. Remember to cover all the points in the question and try to sound positive about yourself. You should use a formal style, with an appropriate opening and closing formula.

5 Now look at this exam question. Underline the parts of the task that you need to cover. Remember to plan your answer before you start writing.

You see the following advertisement in an international magazine.

Can you answer YES to these questions?

★ *Do you speak English confidently?*

★ *Do you enjoy visiting new places?*

★ *Do you get on well with people?*

If so, we would be interested in hearing from you! We are looking for energetic and cheerful guides to lead our 15-day coach tours round Europe. Tell us why you would be suitable.

Apply to: Europewide Coach Tours, PO Box 23, London W1X 6TY, stating where you saw our advertisement.

Write a **letter of application** in 120–180 words. Do not include any postal addresses.

15.1 Too many people?

Speaking

1   Have you ever visited a place that is famous for being beautiful or interesting and been disappointed when you arrived? What sort of problems do tourists cause?

Student A: Look at photos 1 and 2. Compare the photos and say what you think tourists will feel when they visit these places.

Student B: Look at photos 3 and 4. Compare the photos and say what you think the local people feel about the tourists who visit these places.

Listening

2   **2 08** You will hear a woman talking about problems faced by the Grand Canyon National Park Service. Complete the sentences.

The Grand Canyon is located in the [____ 1] part of Arizona.

The canyon is [____ 2] deep from top to bottom.

The Grand Canyon National Park was opened in [____ 3]

[____ 4] people a year visit the Grand Canyon National Park.

The park provides visitors with [____ 5] to help solve the problem of parking.

In the summer the park is affected by [____ 6], brought by southwesterly winds.

The park also suffers from a lack of [____ 7] and this sometimes has to be brought in by truck.

The temperature of the Colorado river is now [____ 8] all year round.

Some types of [____ 9] have now totally disappeared.

The Grand Canyon is often said to be one of the [____ 10] in the world.

Vocabulary

Topic set – the natural world

3   It is a good idea to learn words in meaning categories and check you know the differences in meaning. In the recording, you heard the following words that are all connected with water. Do you know what they mean?

dam   floods   rapids
reservoir   river

In pairs, write a sentence which explains the difference between each of the two words below.

a   pond / lake
b   stream / river
c   canal / river
d   waterfall / rapids

Word formation

4   Make nouns, adverbs and verbs from these adjectives.

long   weak   deep   strong
wide   short   warm

5 For questions 1–10, read the text below. Use the word given in capitals at the end of some of the lines to form a word that fits in the gap in the same line. There is an example at the beginning (0).

POLLUTING THE ENVIRONMENT

Oil on beaches, vehicle exhaust fumes, litter and many other waste **(0)** __PRODUCTS__ are called pollutants, because they pollute our environment. Pollutants can affect our health and harm animals and plants. Releasing **(1)** .... waste from factories and power stations is one of the main ways in which we pollute our **(2)** .... These waste substances are the **(3)** .... results of modern living.

Pollution itself is not new – a hundred years ago factories sent out great clouds of **(4)** .... smoke and, **(5)** .... , pollution has now spread to the land, air and water of every corner on Earth. Our **(6)** .... have much to learn about pollution, but we do know more about how to control it. The use of solar energy, instead of coal and gas, will help in the fight as it is very much cleaner than fossil fuels. We can also achieve some **(7)** .... in pollution by recycling waste and using biodegradable materials which eventually break down in the soil and **(8)** ....

The use of cars which run on **(9)** .... instead of petrol is also a key feature in the fight against pollution. It is up to everyone to be as **(10)** .... as they can with the Earth's limited resources.

0 PRODUCE	**6** SCIENCE
1 CHEMIST	**7** REDUCE
2 SURROUND	**8** APPEAR
3 WANT	**9** ELECTRIC
4 POISON	**10** ECONOMIC
5 FORTUNATE	

Speaking

6 How environmentally friendly are you?

a How can people recycle household rubbish?

b What could your town do to reduce pollution?

c What do you think about wearing second-hand clothes?

d What can be done to stop people dropping litter on the streets of your town?

e Are you economical about using water and electricity? Why? / Why not?

f How would you feel if you had to walk or cycle everywhere?

g What's your opinion of people who wear real fur coats?

7 **2 09** You need to be able to say numbers correctly. Practise saying the following numbers and then listen to the recording to check your pronunciation.

Measurement	'0'
13 km	'0' can be pronounced
30 cm	in different ways in
0.5 km	English.
2.5 m	Telephone number:
153 kilos	012-323-66778
1m 53 cm	Football score: 3–0
½	Tennis score: 40–0
¼	Science and
⅔	temperature: 0 degrees
	Celsius

Dates
1st May 1899
3rd August 2000
12th February 2004
6th September 2016
25th December 1990
the 15th century
4/5/11

Telephone numbers
01256-311399
00-44-324-667012

Maths
$2 + 6 = 8$
$3 - 2 = 1$
$4 \times 4 = 16$
$10 \div 2 = 5$
20%
3°
$\sqrt{16}$

Money
10p
£1.45
$50
€20.30

8 Now ask and answer the following questions.

a What's your date of birth?

b What's your telephone number?

c What's your address?

d How tall are you?

e How much did you weigh when you were born?

f When did man first walk on the moon?

g What's the average temperature in summer where you live? In winter?

h What's the population of your country?

i How many people are there in a football team?

j In which century was your school or college built?

k What was the score of the last sports match you saw?

Countable and uncountable nouns

Many English nouns can be countable and uncountable according to their different meanings. For example:

You really should take more exercise. (uncountable)
I do my exercises every morning. (countable)

1 Decide which words in the following pairs are countable.

Which words can be both countable and uncountable? What is the difference in meaning?

a	information	note
b	spaghetti	meal
c	recommendation	advice
d	travel	journey
e	job	work
f	money	coin
g	lightning	storm
h	weather	temperature
i	English	verb
j	vehicle	traffic
k	seat	furniture
l	hair	hairstyle
m	luggage	suitcase
n	mountain	scenery
o	land	country

Corpus spot

Be careful with uncountable nouns – the *Cambridge Learner Corpus* shows that exam candidates often make mistakes with these.

I have a lot of **homework** tonight.
NOT I have a lot of ~~homeworks~~ tonight.

These uncountable nouns are the ones which candidates make most mistakes with.

- information
- advice
- transport
- homework
- knowledge
- furniture
- work
- equipment
- research
- damage

Using determiners with countable and uncountable nouns
With **plural countables or uncountables**, e.g. *coins* or *money*, we use
plenty of, a lot of, lots of

With **uncountables**, e.g. money, we use
much, little
a great/good deal of, a large/small amount of

With **plural countables**, e.g. *coins*, we use
many, (a) few, several
a great/good/small number of

All verbs, determiners and pronouns referring to **uncountable** nouns are singular:
*A **great deal** of research **has been done** into the pollution produced by cars in cities. Unfortunately, very **little** of **it is taken** seriously by politicians.*

2 Use the information above to correct the following sentences where necessary.

a How much of the tourists actually realises the problems they cause?

b Little of the soils can be used for cultivation now the trees have been cut down.

c A large number of equipment are needed to camp at the bottom of the Canyon.

d Only few luggages can be carried on the back of a donkey down the dirt tracks.

e A large amount of rainforest are being cut down every year.

f The amount of traffic are causing too many congestions in major cities.

g Much governments believes that nuclear power are the key to future energy problems.

h The Park Ranger gave me several good advices about camping in the national park.

i Little people nowadays wear fur coats.

3 Both these pairs of sentences are correct, but there is a difference in meaning. What is it?

I make few mistakes with English grammar.
I make a few mistakes with English grammar.

I have little time to watch the TV at the weekend.
I have a little time to watch the TV at the weekend.

 G → page 172

Grammar extra

some and any and no

Look at the following sentences and decide what the rule is for using *some* and *any* and *no*.

a At lunchtime the Prime Minister announced some of the government's plans for reducing congestion in cities.

b I haven't been able to see any stars in the sky recently because of light pollution.

c Would you like me to give you some information on ways you can cut down on using water?

d Have you any idea of the amount of food that is wasted each day in the developed world?

e No amount of persuasion will make some people use public transport rather than private cars.

f Have you got any/some change for the parking meter?

g Any of the students could have answered the question.

G → page 172

Vocabulary

Expressions of quantity

4 Expressions like *a piece of* or *a bit of* are often used to limit an uncountable noun. However, these words aren't very precise and it is better to use the right expression.

EXAMPLE: *In a shop you ask for **a loaf of** bread; at home you ask for **a slice of** bread.*

Which of the words on the left are used with the uncountable nouns on the right?

shower	clothing
slice	lightning
item	rain
glass	cake
clap	string
pane	people
ball	glass
flash	chocolate
crowd	water
bar	thunder

5 Using the information in this unit, complete the following sentences.

a Would you like .... chocolate to take on your trip?
– Yes, could you put in a couple of .... ?

b Did you have .... bad weather over the weekend?
– Yes, heavy rain and enormous .... of lightning.

c .... of the football hooligans spent Saturday night smashing all the .... of glass in the local school.

d I used to have short .... , but I've decided to grow it.

e Could you give me .... about travelling in India?

f My bank always refuses to change ....
that I bring back from abroad.

g You can only take one small .... on board the flight and all other items of .... must be checked in.

6 For questions 1–12, read the text below and think of the word which best fits each gap. Use only one word in each gap. There is an example at the beginning (0).

The Pyramids

On (**0**) .....*THE*..... great rocky plain of Giza in Egypt, stand (**1**) .... of the world's most remarkable buildings – three pyramids. There are quite a (**2**) .... other pyramids in Egypt, but these three are the largest and most famous. They were erected more than 4,000 years (**3**) .... and, while other great monuments have fallen into ruins, these pyramids have stood the test of time.

As the Egyptians believed (**4**) .... life after death, each ruler had a great (**5**) .... of his treasure buried with him. (**6**) .... the pyramids are enormous, the rooms inside are very small, because the pyramids themselves consist chiefly of solid stone. The largest, the Great Pyramid at Giza, was built by King Khufu in about 2500BC and is still mostly intact. Its original height was almost 147 metres, and it weighed more (**7**) .... seven billion kilograms.

The pyramids were made out (**8**) .... huge blocks of stone (**9**) .... were quarried, trimmed to a fairly regular shape, transported to the construction site and then piled on top of (**10**) .... another with astonishing precision. It used to be believed that over 100,000 men (**11**) .... been needed to build the pyramids, but now scientists think that the true figure (**12**) .... nearer 10,000.

Exam folder 8

Paper 4 Part 4 Multiple choice

In this part of the Listening paper there are seven questions. Each question has three options (A, B or C). You must choose the correct option. The questions follow the order of the information in the conversation. You will hear the recording twice and you have one minute to read through the questions before you listen.

EXAM ADVICE

- Read the questions carefully in the time you are given before the recording begins and try to predict what you might hear. It is very important to use this time well.

- Remember that each question is similar to what you will hear. This will be helpful if you lose your place in the recording.

- You might hear each option A, B or C mentioned in some way but only one of them will correctly answer the question.

- You can write notes on the question paper as you listen for the first time.

- Remember to put your answers on your answer sheet. At the end of the test there will be a pause of 5 minutes on the recording for you to copy all your answers onto your answer sheet.

- Always choose an answer, even if you are unsure about it.

1 You will hear a girl called Lisa Greene giving a talk to her classmates about her stay at an ecolodge, an environmentally friendly hotel in Costa Rica, Central America. For questions 1–7, choose the best answer (A, B or C).

Look at question 1.

1 How did Lisa feel about her journey to Costa Rica?

A She was relieved when she eventually arrived.

B She was worried about missing her flight connections.

C She was surprised that it took so long to get there.

Here are some things to think about before you listen to the recording:

- Read the question carefully. It's asking about how she *felt*.

- You need to ask yourself the following questions:
  A How did she feel when she arrived – had the journey been a bad one?
  B Did she feel anxious about missing her flight connections?
  C Does she make any comment about the length of the journey being surprising?

2 [10] Now listen to the first part of the recording. The recording will be stopped when you hear the following words:

... travelling by myself for the first time.

2 Decide on the correct answer for question 1. Which sentence in the talk tells you?

Remember that a wrong answer often repeats the vocabulary you hear in the recording, and might be true but doesn't actually answer the question.

Here is the part of the recording script for question 1. Underline the sentence with the right answer.

Lisa: OK, everyone … um, as you know, last year I entered and, amazingly, won an essay competition in a magazine. I had to write about recycling and why it is a good thing for the planet. The prize was a trip to stay in an environmentally friendly hotel, called an ecolodge, in Costa Rica for one week.

So, the journey. I flew to Costa Rica from London and then had to take a small plane to an airport very near the ecolodge. I was then picked up at the local airport by the ecolodge manager in an electric car. It all took a bit longer than I was expecting but then I hadn't travelled outside of Europe before and I was only used to short journeys. Anyway, I was so excited I didn't care about having to change planes or travelling by myself for the first time.

Now, look at the other two possible answers in question 1. Why are they not correct?

3 **2 11** Read through questions 2–7 and try to predict what you might hear. Then continue listening to the rest of the talk and answer questions 2–7.

2 What does Lisa say about the animals and birds she saw from the observation gallery?
  A It was great to see some of the larger animals.
  B Some of the birds were very friendly.
  C She enjoyed feeding the monkeys fruit.

3 What did Lisa fail to understand at first about her accommodation?
  A the lack of hot water
  B the lights switching off automatically
  C the air conditioning being out of order

4 What does Lisa say about walking in the forest?
  A The noises you hear can be quite frightening.
  B You need a guide as it's easy to get lost.
  C It's important you have a good level of fitness.

5 Lisa says that one of the best parts of her trip was swimming
  A in the sea.
  B in a natural pool.
  C in the ecolodge swimming pool.

6 Lisa says that the main purpose of the conservation centre is to
  A train local people in building methods.
  B inform tourists about the area.
  C provide food for the ecolodge.

7 Lisa's classmates will be able to get a copy of the magazine
  A in November.
  B in January.
  C in February.

Listening

1 Make a list of what you normally eat in a day for breakfast, lunch and dinner. Compare your list with a partner.

2 What do you think people eat in Japan, Alaska and California?

Kunu (Alaska)

Akiko (Japan)

Gayle (California)

3 🔊 2 12 Now you are going to hear these three women talking about the food they normally have for breakfast, lunch and dinner. Listen and make brief notes.

Whose diet would you like to try?

4 Would you eat any of the following? Why? / Why not?

- a very red apple?
- a green banana?
- a soft biscuit?
- blue bread?
- flat lemonade?
- very red meat?

Reading

5 You are going to read an article about the taste of food. Seven sentences have been removed from the article. Choose from the sentences A–H the one which fits each gap (1–7). There is one extra sentence which you do not need to use.

How sound and colour influence the taste of food

The sound diners hear while they are eating food can change the way they think it tastes, scientists have discovered. In fact, researchers have also found that changing the colour of a food can influence the flavour experienced by consumers. Food manufacturers are now hoping to exploit the findings in an attempt to make their foods more appealing.

Previously it was thought that the sense of taste and smell were the only human senses that played a role in experiencing flavour. Professor Charles Spence, a sensory psychologist at Oxford University, is a leading expert in his field. [1] For example, listening to waves hitting the sea shore can make diners detect seafood flavours, while the sound of chickens clucking brings out the taste of eggs.

Professor Spence has also discovered that simply changing the colour of a food can influence the way it tastes. [2] He said: 'This colour has strong associations with very ripe fruit. Another example is the colour orange, which has such strong flavour associations that just changing the amount of orange on the packaging can make the flavour seem more acidic.'

For some foods sound is incredibly important, particularly if the food makes a sound itself when it is consumed. With carbonated drinks, for example, a lot of the fizzy flavour comes from the sound of bubbles popping. Scientists have found that boosting certain high frequency sounds when volunteers bite into crisps and biscuits could make them appear to taste crunchier. [3]

A One of these firms has unveiled a new centre for research and development and its experts have used brain scanning equipment to identify the parts of the brain that are stimulated by frozen foods.

B He found that by changing a drink from yellow to a deep red, it is possible to make it taste up to 12 per cent sweeter than it really is.

C Indeed, much research has been done on all four of these.

D In that setting, everything appeared to be a normal colour.

E They seemed to become softer once the sounds were lowered.

F By melting, it changes its physical characteristics and creates contrasts that continually keep your senses interested.

G He believes that it is possible to change the flavour of food simply by exciting people's sense of hearing.

H If they are too green, that is also undesirable as people think they don't taste ripe even though they are.

Many companies are now employing neuroscientists to help them develop their products. **4** ☐ They have found that the change in texture that, for example, ice cream undergoes in the mouth as it melts, is part of what makes it so enjoyable.

Flavour is not just as simple as the way something tastes, as all the other senses come into play and some can dominate the way the brain interprets a food. Ice cream activates a part of the brain which is just behind the eyes and is where emotions are processed. **5** ☐

Another study has found that the colour of food has a significant effect on people's appetites. Test subjects were placed in a room with special coloured lighting installed, and then given a steak and French fries to eat. **6** ☐ However, when it was revealed that the steak was blue and the fries were green, some participants became ill.

Recently, one firm held a special taste conference in Brussels to demonstrate how the colour of tomatoes can effect how consumers enjoy them. Ian Puddephat, a leading scientist, said: 'Amazingly, we have found that there is such a thing as tomatoes that are too red. **7** ☐ How they feel is also particularly important for consumers. Some prefer a firm skin, while others want something that is softer and more associated with ripe juiciness.'

So next time you are in a restaurant or a supermarket, or just sitting down at home to eat something, think about whether your choices have been influenced by sound or colour. You may be surprised!

6 In groups, discuss these questions.

a What do you think about the scientists' findings?
b Do you trust the food industry to provide you with safe, healthy food?
c Do you think you have a healthy diet?
d Are you, or could you become, a vegetarian?
e Is there anything you can't stand or aren't allowed to eat?

Vocabulary

Collocations – food

7 Choose the correct adjective or adverb to complete each sentence.

EXAMPLE: *This tastes like ⟨canned⟩ / dairy soup – I much prefer soup that is freshly made.*

a Silvio's on a diet – he has to give up all *bitter / rich* foods for a month.
b When I opened the fridge, I realised the milk had gone *rotten / off*.
c The meat that the local supermarket sells is often *tough / rich*.
d I always buy yellow lemons because I know they are *strong / ripe*.
e I like curry, as long as it tastes quite *mild / weak*.
f The last apple in the bowl had to be thrown away because it was *juicy / rotten*.
g The coffee in the café was a bit *bad / weak* for my taste, with too much milk in it.
h When I opened the pack of meat, I realised from the smell that it had gone *bitter / bad*.

Speaking

8 Your college is thinking of opening a new relaxation area for students. There is only a certain amount of money available for the project. In pairs, decide which two things would be the most popular to include. Then change partners and explain your previous choices.

The article

1 Look at these nouns from the listening in 16.1:

waiter   noodles   fish   cheese   lunch

Which of these nouns are

- singular countable?
- plural?
- uncountable?

Which of them take

- *a/an* (the indefinite article)?
- *the* (the definite article)?
- nothing?

2 Match sentences a–j with rules 1–11. Some sentences match more than one rule. The rules can be used more than once.

a He's a waiter.
b The Earth is egg-shaped.
c The United States exports wheat.
d The British love curry.
e He's the best chef in Bangkok.
f I usually go to a restaurant that overlooks the River Thames.
g The Rocky Mountains are great for skiing.
h I hate fast food.
i There's a restaurant next to our house – it's the restaurant with a red sign.
j Football always makes me hungry.

  1 *the* is used with rivers, oceans, seas, mountain ranges
  2 no article is used with most streets, villages, towns, cities, countries, lakes, single mountains
  3 *the* is used with national groups
  4 *a/an* is used with jobs
  5 no article is used with sports
  6 *the* is used when there is only one of something
  7 *the* is used for countries in the plural, e.g. The Netherlands
  8 *the* is used with superlatives
  9 no article is used when a noun is used generally
  10 *a/an* is used when something is mentioned for the first time
  11 *the* is used when a noun has already been mentioned

3 Read through this article and decide whether to use *a/an*, *the* or nothing in the gaps. Some gaps can have more than one answer.

'I'll have what he's having.' That's what
(1) .... diners sometimes tell **(2)** .... waiters when another customer is served
(3) .... meal that looks delicious. Wouldn't it be simpler if you could see every dish on **(4)** .... menu before making up your mind? In **(5)** .... Japan, that's exactly what diners can do. There, **(6)** .... restaurant displays of real-looking fake food, called *sanpuru*, serve as **(7)** .... three-dimensional menu.

At one time, restaurants in Japan used to display real food to advertise **(8)** .... restaurant's specialities, and to allow customers to 'preview' their meal. **(9)** .... displays also meant that **(10)** .... foreigners unable to read **(11)** .... Japanese menu could figure out **(12)** .... best thing to order. In the 1930s **(13)** .... first fake foods were made from **(14)** .... wax. Eventually such fake foods replaced **(15)** .... real foods. Today *sanpuru* are made from vinyl, **(16)** .... kind of plastic.

4 Decide whether you need to use an article or not in these sentences.

a I went to .... hospital to see a friend who was ill.

b I went to .... hospital when I was knocked off my bike.

c I go to .... library once a week.

d She always goes to .... bed early.

e I often get hay fever in .... summer.

f The shops in my town always close for .... lunch.

g My father used to go to work by .... bike.

h When are you going on .... holiday?

i Tom never gets to .... work on time.

j He earns £800 .... week.

k I'll visit you in .... October.

l I can't play .... football very well.

m George Washington once held .... office of US President.

n My uncle goes to .... prison to teach the prisoners computer skills.

o I've played .... flute ever since I was a child.

G → page 172

Possession

1 When we are talking about people we use *'s* or *s'*:
my sister's boyfriend, the visitors' cars
In the first example there is only one sister, so the apostrophe is before the *s*. In the second example, the apostrophe is after the *s* because there is more than one visitor.

2 *'s* is also used when we are talking about time or distance:
a month's holiday, a kilometre's walk

3 We usually use *of* when we are talking about objects or position:
the back of the room, the film of the book
also for when a container has something in it:
a bottle of milk, a box of chocolates

4 Quite often we use a noun to describe another noun when it describes either the kind, use or place:
a pear tree, a coffee cup, a shop window

5 Correct the following sentences where necessary.

a The father of my husband works in an Italian restaurant.

b I looked through the restaurant's window but couldn't see anyone.

c He was sitting at the front of the terrace.

d I bought a magazine of cookery.

e I'm sure we all always look forward to pay day.

f Most waiters get tips to help supplement their day's pay.

g The boss of my company is having a big party to celebrate his birthday.

h Can I have a coffee cup and a piece of that delicious cake, please?

Corpus spot

The *Cambridge Learner Corpus* shows that exam candidates often have problems with expressions of time. A common problem is whether or not to use an article or preposition.

I received your letter **last week**.
NOT I received your letter ~~the~~ last week.

In the afternoon we're going to have tea in the Plaka.
NOT ~~At~~ the afternoon we're going to have tea in the Plaka.

Correct the mistakes candidates have made in the following sentences.

a I am coming at 24th June.

b So cycling at the rush hour is nearly as fast as driving a car.

c Young people have a nice time in the weekend.

d We had to wait long time for lunch.

e During evening she made a cake.

f At the first day of my holidays, I was afraid because I was alone.

g In afternoon we could go for a burger.

h I played tennis during seven years.

i The man is coming in Tuesday morning.

j I should arrive on 3 am in London.

Writing folder 8

Transactional letters and emails 2

This question is compulsory – all candidates have to answer it. 'Transactional' means that the letter or email will require further action by its reader, usually in the form of a written response. The letter or email must be based on the information given in the question.

1 When you write a letter or email it is important that you keep in the same style all the way through. Read through this informal letter and, with a partner, decide which is the best alternative, a or b, in 1–10 below. The first one has been done for you.

1 **a** I am writing to thank you
   b Thanks a lot
2 **a** to discuss the
   b to talk about the
3 **a** found it very useful
   b thought it was extremely productive
4 **a** come up with
   b propose
5 **a** We all appreciate your
   b Thanks a million for
6 **a** I feel sure everyone will have an enjoyable time
   b It's certain to be a great night
7 **a** go down well
   b prove very popular
8 **a** that's all for now
   b I will contact you again at some point
9 **a** See you soon
   b I look forward to seeing you in the near future
10 **a** Yours faithfully
   b Best wishes

Dear Pete,

(1) __*Thanks a lot*__ for coming along (2) .... plans for the new student café on campus. I really think we all (3) .... and I hope that we can (4) .... some ideas for interesting menus. (5) .... asking your friend Marco Brown, the TV chef, to open the café on Saturday. (6) .... when we open, and I think the café will (7) .... with the students. Anyway, (8) .... (9) .... (10) .... ,

George

2 Look at this exam question.

You have received an invitation and map from your friend Anna. You want to go to her party but you need to find out some information. Read the invitation and look at the map, and look at the notes you have made. Then write an email to Anna, using all your notes. You must use grammatically correct sentences with accurate spelling and punctuation in a style appropriate for the situation.

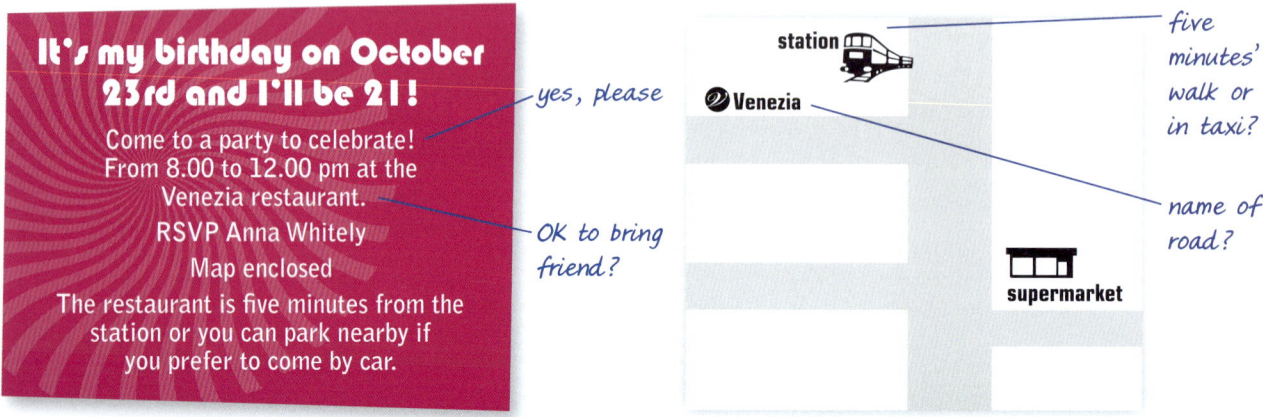

It's my birthday on October 23rd and I'll be 21!

Come to a party to celebrate! From 8.00 to 12.00 pm at the Venezia restaurant. RSVP Anna Whitely Map enclosed The restaurant is five minutes from the station or you can park nearby if you prefer to come by car.

yes, please

OK to bring friend?

station

Venezia

supermarket

five minutes' walk or in taxi?

name of road?

3 This is the email that Anna received. It would receive very low marks in the exam. Discuss with a partner what the main problems with this answer are. Then work together to rewrite it in a more appropriate way.

Dear Anna,
I'm writing with reference to the invitation you sent me on September 4th. I'm really greatful you asked to me and I'm pleased to come.
I am extremely greatful if you could tell me name of road restaurant is in. I will have friend staying with me. She is nice. I bring her.
I look forward to see you in near future.
Kisses

Corpus spot

Here are some of the most frequent spelling mistakes made by exam candidates. Correct each word.
a accommodation
b advertisment
c wich
d belive
e becouse
f beggining
g confortable
h bycicle
i convinient
j embarrasing
k expecially
l recived
m beatiful
n comunicate
o sincerly

4 Read the advertisement and the notes you have made. Then write an email in 120–150 words to your friend Chris. You must persuade Chris and your other friends to come with you on the weekend.

activity holidays
Spring weekend breaks in Scotland

fully qualified

On our weekend breaks our instructors will teach you how to climb or sail. You can also go swimming in the nearby lake. For those of you who prefer walking, there are plenty of places in the area. The nearby town has many facilities, including an interesting museum, a heated indoor swimming pool and good supermarkets.

heated

Accommodation for four in comfortable wood cabins, situated in the forest.

Only £150

between four

no food

5 Write an email. You must use grammatically correct sentences with accurate spelling and punctuation in a style appropriate for the situation.

Remember, you want your friend to go with you so you need to be persuasive. Make sure you read both the advertisement and your notes carefully. Make sure you balance any negative points with some positive ones. You need to sound enthusiastic and make this friend feel he/she is really wanted on this holiday.

EXAMPLE: *I know you've always wanted to learn to climb and that's one of the reasons why I think you would enjoy this holiday. Don't worry about Scotland being cold, as the accommodation is heated and very comfortable.*

Collectors and creators

Speaking

Exam spot

In Paper 5 Part 2, the long turn, you must listen carefully while the other candidate is speaking, as you will have to make a brief comment afterwards. Try to include a new idea when you do this.

1   Here are two pairs of photographs showing various hobbies. Look at the first pair with another student. Decide who will be Student A and who Student B. Then read your instructions. Student A can also refer to the notes below.

   Student A

   Compare the pictures, describing the possible benefits and problems of collecting the things shown.

   Shells – beautiful, many different kinds. Free! Need access to good beaches.

   Football badges – lots available. You can wear them. Don't take up a lot of space. Old ones may be expensive.

   Student B

   When Student A has finished, say which hobby you would find more interesting, and why.

   Now carry out the speaking task. Student A should try to keep talking for about a minute and then Student B should talk for a maximum of 20 seconds. Time yourselves.

2   Look at the second pair of photographs and change roles. Student A should listen carefully to what Student B says. Remember to keep talking for up to a minute.

   Student B

   Compare the pictures, describing the main differences between these two hobbies. (about 1 minute)

   Student A

   Say which hobby appeals to you more, and why. (20 seconds)

   Did Student B manage to talk for a full minute? Suggest other ideas if necessary.

3   How many hobbies can you think of which involve collecting or making something? Work in two teams: the collectors and the creators. See who can produce the longer list! Then, in pairs, decide on the four most interesting hobbies from the two lists, giving your reasons why. You can agree to disagree!

Listening

4   **2 13** You are going to hear eight short extracts to do with hobbies. For questions 1–8 choose the best answer (A, B or C). You will hear each extract twice. Compare your answers with another student.

1   You hear a woman talking about making jewellery. What metal does she normally use?
   A gold
   B silver
   C copper

2   You overhear this conversation in a café. What sort of postcards is the woman keen to collect?
   A ones that are in good condition
   B ones from the 1930s
   C ones with a printed message

3   You hear a woman talking on the radio. Why were the wooden objects she describes unusual?
   A They were painted with beautiful designs.
   B They were made from different types of wood.
   C They were carved from a single piece.

4   You will hear a man talking on the radio. How does he spend his weekends?
   A pretending to be a soldier
   B doing a history course
   C producing different plays

5   You hear part of a radio programme. Which kind of beads does the girl have most of?
   A glass
   B wooden
   C plastic

6   You overhear a man talking on the phone. Who is he talking to?
   A an assistant in a shop selling kits
   B a journalist working for a magazine
   C a member of staff at a factory

7   You hear a girl being interviewed about her hobby. Why does she paint pebbles?
   A to remind her of her holidays
   B to improve her art technique
   C to make some pocket money

8   You hear this radio interview. Who suggested the boy took up slot-car racing?
   A his father
   B his friend
   C his cousin

5   In pairs, decide which of these hobbies would interest you least, explaining why. Report your views to the class.

Vocabulary

Phrasal verbs and expressions with *look*

6   In listening extracts 2, 3 and 6, *look* was used as in a–d below. Five more uses are given in e–j. Check their meanings before answering questions 1–10 below.

a look for
b be on the lookout
c the look of
d Now look here!
e look after
f look at
g look into
h Look out!
i look up to
j look forward to

1   Who might you ask to **look at**
   A your wrist?   **B** a broken pipe?
   C faulty brakes?

2   What might you be planning to do if you are **looking for**
   A a needle?   **B** a saucepan?   **C** a dictionary?

3   Who might **be on the lookout** for
   A a missing yacht?   **B** murder clues?
   C tax savings?

4   Describe **the look of**
   A leather.   **B** thick mud.   **C** concrete.

5   Who **looks after**
   A patients?   **B** rose bushes?   **C** local residents?

6   Continue the statement **Now look here** …, as if you are arguing with
   A a bank manager.   **B** a young child.
   C a journalist.

7   What might someone discover if they **looked into**
   A a rejected proposal?   **B** an old murder case?
   C the possibility of working abroad?

8   Why might someone shout **Look out!** at you, if you were
   A driving?   **B** swimming in the sea?
   C walking under a ladder?

9   Who might these people **look up to**?
   A a six-year-old boy   **B** a first-year student
   C a trainee cook

10   What might these people be **looking forward to** doing?
   A someone who is running a marathon
   B someone who has been at sea for two months
   C someone who rarely has any time off

Relative clauses

1 Look at the pair of sentences a and b, then answer questions 1 and 2 for each of them.

  a The children who were tired went straight to bed.
  b The children, who were tired, went straight to bed.

  1 Were all the children tired?
  2 Did all the children go to bed?

  Which sentence contains a defining relative clause? Which has a non-defining clause in it?

G → page 173

  Explain the difference in meaning between c and d.

  c It was getting late, so we decided to stay at the first hotel which had a pool.
  d It was getting late, so we decided to stay at the first hotel, which had a pool.

2 Here are two examples of relative clauses from the listening extracts. Which sentence has a defining relative clause and which has a non-defining one?

  a Jamie Eagle, who is the outright winner of today's slot-car racing, is with me now.
  b I'm on the lookout for older ones that have text on the picture.

  Identify the relative clause in each of these examples, underline the relative pronoun used, and decide whether the clause is defining (D) or non-defining (N).

  c Looking at the stamps, they're older than you say, which is brilliant.
  d I knew someone once who had an absolute passion for making things out of wood.
  e It was my cousin who's to blame.
  f Jenny Braintree, whose bedroom I'm sitting in right now, has a rather unusual hobby.
  g I'm trying to paint a scene from every country in the world, most of which I haven't been to.
  h The group that puts on these events was only formed about four months ago.

3 What relative pronoun has been left out in this example? Insert it in the correct place.

Here are those cards I bought for you in Oxford.

> Omission of the relative pronoun is quite common in spoken English, but can only be done when it is the object of a defining relative clause. So, for example, you could not leave out the word *that* in example *h*.

Decide what relative pronouns have been left out of these sentences and underline the defining clause in each.

  a The picture I wanted to buy had already been sold.
  b She was the teacher I really looked up to.
  c The thing I can't stand about Harry is his odd socks!
  d That boy you met at John's party plays tennis.
  e The hotel we stayed at had luxurious bathrooms.

4 The last example could be rewritten like this:

The hotel where we stayed had luxurious bathrooms.

> You can use *where*, *when* and *why* in defining relative clauses after nouns to do with place, time and reason. Again, in spoken English, *when* and *why* are sometimes omitted. Here are two examples from 17.1.
>
> *2003 was the year my passion for jewellery making began.*
>
> *That's not the reason she's mad at me though.*
>
> In non-defining relative clauses, these words cannot be omitted.

Insert *where*, *when* or another *wh-* word into these non-defining relative clauses.

  a The writer Iain Banks was born in Fife, Scotland, ... he still lives.
  b The earthquake happened shortly before dawn, ... most people were asleep.
  c Aidan, ... lives in our road, plays the double bass.
  d They sent an information booklet, ... was really helpful.

Relative pronouns

who or whom?

5   In informal English, it is always safe to use *who* as both subject and object. However, in formal written English, *whom* is the object form, often used with a preposition.

   Rewrite sentences a–c using *whom*, adding commas where necessary and making any other changes.

   EXAMPLE: The man they had given all their money to took a one-way flight to Rio.
   The man *to whom they had given all their money took a one-way flight to Rio.*

   a   The collector I have bought many rare film posters from lives in Paris.
   The collector ....

   b   The weird millionaire that my sister worked for expected her to clean his collection of antiques every day.
   The weird millionaire ....

   c   I went riding with Wetherby and he was always the perfect gentleman.
   Wetherby ....

whose

6   You use *whose* to add information about a person or thing just mentioned. Join the two sentences in a–d, using *whose*.

   EXAMPLE: Johnson is going to sail around the world alone. His yacht is sponsored by a leading British firm.
   Johnson, whose yacht is sponsored by a leading British firm, is going to sail around the world alone.

   a   The singer has always been a fan of modern British painters. His art collection is now worth millions.

   b   Maria works in a bank in central London. Her hobbies include skydiving and collecting antiques.

   c   The hot air balloon was designed by the Montgolfier brothers. Its first flight was made in 1783.

   d   The number of collectors has doubled over the last decade. Collectors form an increasingly large part of the buyers at local auctions.

 → page 173

Vocabulary

Word formation

7   What nouns are related to these adjectives?

   a delightful   c exceptional   e remarkable
   b elegant   d massive   f substantial

8   Confident and effective use of a range of adjectives in Papers 2 and 5 will impress the examiners. Put the adjectives in 7 into the groups below.

   emphasising attractiveness
   emphasising extent
   emphasising rarity

9   For questions 1–12, read the text and think of the word which best fits each gap. Use only one word in each gap. There is an example at the beginning (0).

A PASSION FOR BOTTLES

Hobbies (0) *can* so easily take over your life, can't they? They make substantial demands on your time and, even (1) .... seriously, they sometimes invade your living space. One crazy friend (2) .... mine is haunted by the desire to collect bottles. This passion, (3) .... started quite by chance, has now reached an absurd stage. For my friend, (4) .... massive collection currently stands at 3,429 bottles, has had to rebuild his house to accommodate his obsession. Admittedly, there are some remarkable items, such (5) .... two elegant examples in Murano glass, an exceptional hand-painted wine bottle (6) .... the 1920s, and about fifty delightful perfume bottles in (7) .... colour, shape and size you could imagine. However, the vast majority of his bottles are very ordinary and (8) .... to have been taken away for recycling long (9) .... The reason he has hung on to them for all of this time is (10) .... at all clear. Just think, (11) .... only my friend had chosen bottle tops, his collection (12) .... only fill three drawers at most!

10 Underline the six adjectives from 7 in the text. Choose another noun from the box that collocates with each adjective (some nouns can be used with more than one adjective). Write sentences using your adjective–noun combinations.

   | amount   challenge   memory |
   | painting   scale   woman |

   EXAMPLE: *My brother has a massive amount of information about model trains.*

Exam folder 9

Paper 1 Part 2 Gapped text

This part of the Reading paper requires you to read a text from which seven sentences have been removed, and then choose the correct sentences to fill the gaps. There is always one extra sentence which you don't need.

There are fewer questions in this part than in Part 3 but, as in Part 1, each question is 'double-weighted', that is, it is worth two marks instead of one. Part 2 is a difficult task and you must allow enough time for it.

Complete the exam task below using the steps in the Advice box. Try to keep to the suggested timings.

EXAM ADVICE

- Read the text quickly, in order to get an idea of what it is about. (3 minutes)
- Underline key words in the text to predict what each gap might contain. Look for linking and reference words too. (5 minutes)
- Scan the missing sentences for matching information and note down likely answers. (5 minutes)
- Read through the whole text with your answers in place to check that it all makes sense. (3 minutes)
- Make sure that the extra sentence does not fit anywhere. (2 minutes)

You are going to read a magazine article about building an unusual bridge. Seven sentences have been removed from the article. Choose from the sentences A–H the one which fits each gap (1–7). There is one extra sentence which you do not need to use.

Building the Meccano bridge in Liverpool

Meccano is an educational toy that encourages children to construct models out of metal. Anything from a robot to a bridge or a plane can be made using this toy, whose basic parts consist of long strips and flat plates of metal, together with the nuts and bolts that are needed to put them together.

The idea for Meccano began in a small shop in Liverpool in 1898, when Franck Hornby invented a construction game for his children using screws and nuts. This gave rise to the Meccano system at the very beginning of the 20th century. **1**⬚ Some 66 years later, the factory here closed and production was moved to France, and later, also to China.

It was no accident therefore that Liverpool was chosen as the place where a lifesize bridge made solely from pieces of Meccano would be built. The project formed part of a TV series called 'James May's Toy Stories', which featured ambitious constructions out of some of Britain's best-loved toys. **2**⬚

If the total length of Meccano used in the bridge was laid end to end, it would stretch over 5 kilometres. Around 100,000 individual pieces were needed and it took 11 weeks to build the bridge. **3**⬚

For the earlier stage, Liverpool University was approached by the television company and asked to run a bridge design competition. **4**⬚ The winning proposal was drawn up by three of their most talented students, whose ideas were then taken forward by a structural engineering consultant and turned into professional drawings.

Engineering students at Liverpool University were largely responsible for the bridge's construction, assisted by members of the North East Meccano Guild. **5**⬚ They also organise regular museum visits and were eager to participate in the bridge-building project.

The Meccano bridge spans a canal and is in two sections. These are connected by a series of pulleys and work together. **6**⬚ The other rolls out vertically and both sections meet over the middle of the canal to form a level platform.

At the public opening of the bridge, TV presenter James May had to walk the whole way across the bridge. **7**⬚ However, there was no need for concern, as the bridge supported his weight without problems. His successful crossing was of course filmed for the TV programme.

A   Five teams from the School of Architecture took part in this and some excellent work was produced.

B   One of the first places where it was made was the British city of Liverpool.

C   He admitted to feeling nervous as a big crowd encouraged him to take his first steps.

D   That was the amount of time needed once the preliminary planning and design work had been done.

E   One of the pair looks a bit like a canal lock gate and swings out horizontally.

F   This canal extension runs from Liverpool to Leeds and the new bridge sits 5 metres above it.

G   Other programmes included the building of a real house from Lego and a lifesize 'model' plane.

H   This is a club where fans of the product get together to share ideas.

Reading

1 Look at the illustration and decide what it shows. Which part of the world might this be?

2 You are going to read an extract from *The Old Man and the Sea* by Ernest Hemingway. First, read these brief reviews. What do you learn about the book from them?

> Not only the finest short story that Hemingway has ever written, but one of the finest written by anyone.

> Every word is meaningful and there is not a word too many.

> The writing is as tight, and at the same time as cleverly played out, as the line on which the old man plays the fish.

3 Now read the first paragraph of the text quickly. Where is the old man? Is anyone with him? What are the weather conditions like?

The old man rubbed the cramped hand against his trousers and tried to ease the fingers. But the hand would not open. Maybe it will open with the sun, he thought. He looked across the sea and knew how alone he was now. The clouds were building up for the trade wind and he looked ahead and saw a flight of wild ducks against the sky over the water, and he knew that no man was ever alone on the sea.

He thought of how some men feared being out of sight of land in a small boat and knew they were right in months of sudden bad weather. But now they were in hurricane months and, when there are no hurricanes, the weather of these months is the best of all the year. If there is a hurricane you always see the signs of it in the sky for days ahead, if you are at sea. They do not see it ashore because they do not know what to look for, he thought. But we have no hurricane coming now. He looked at the sky and saw the white cumulus clouds built like friendly piles of ice cream and high above were the thin feathers of the cirrus against the high September sky. 'Better weather for me than for you, fish,' he said.

His left hand was still cramped, but he was unknotting it slowly. I hate a cramp, he thought. It is a treachery of one's own body and it humiliates oneself especially when one is alone. If the boy were here he could rub it for me and loosen it down from the forearm, he thought. But it will loosen up. Then, with his right hand he felt the difference in the pull of the line. As he leaned against the line and slapped his left hand hard and fast against his thigh he saw it slanting slowly upward. 'He's coming up,' he said. 'Come on, hand. Please come on.'   line 21

The line rose slowly and steadily and then the surface of the ocean bulged ahead of the boat and the fish came out. He came out unendingly and water poured from his sides. He was bright in the sun and his head and back were dark purple and in the sun the stripes on his sides showed wide and a light lavender. His sword was as long as a baseball bat and he rose full-length from the water and then re-entered it, smoothly, like a diver and the old man saw the great blade of his tail go under and the line started to race out.

He is a great fish and I must convince him, he thought. I must never let him learn his strength nor what he could do if he made his run. If I were him I would put in everything now and go until something broke. But, thank God, they are not as intelligent as we who kill them; although they are more noble and more able.

The old man had seen many great fish. He had seen many that weighed more than a thousand pounds and he had caught two of that size in his life, but never alone. Now alone, and out of sight of land, he was fast to the biggest fish he had   line 36
ever seen and bigger than he had ever heard of, and his left hand was still as tight as the gripped claws of an eagle.

It will uncramp though, he thought. Surely it will uncramp to help my right hand. There are three things that are brothers: the fish and my two hands. It must uncramp. It is unworthy of it to be cramped. The fish had slowed again and was going at his usual pace.

I wonder why he jumped, the old man thought. He jumped almost as though to show me how big he was. I know now, anyway, he thought. I wish I could show him what sort of man I am. But then he would see my cramped hand. Let him think I am more man than I am and I will be so.

4 Work through the questions below in pairs. Read the text carefully to identify the parts that relate to each question. Choose your answers together, deciding why the other options are wrong.

1 How did the old man feel about being out at sea?
A He enjoyed it because he had time to himself.
B He didn't mind as there were creatures around him.
C He realised how dangerous his work was.
D He wasn't happy at being out of sight of land.

2 Why was he sure the weather would stay fair?
A It was not the right time of year for hurricanes.
B Bad weather had not been forecast ashore.
C He could see no trace of an approaching hurricane.
D There are more fish during good weather.

3 What does 'it' refer to in line 21?
A his boat
B the line
C his hand
D the fish

4 What does the old man worry about after seeing the fish?
A The fish might swim too fast to be caught.
B He isn't as clever as the fish.
C He doesn't have enough line.
D The fish is too powerful for his boat.

5 What does the writer mean when he says the old man was 'fast to the biggest fish he had ever seen' in lines 36–37?
A He was joined to the fish by his line.
B He was attracted by such a big fish.
C He was chasing the fish in his boat.
D He was surprised to see the fish's size.

6 The old man didn't want the fish to see that he was
A alone in the boat.
B so small.
C too tired.
D in some difficulty.

Vocabulary
Phrasal verbs with *come* and *go*

5 The extract described the fish *coming up* and *going under*. Make phrasal verbs with *come* and *go* to use in a suitable form in a–h.

	across
	ahead
	by
come	off
go	out
	through
	up
	up with

a The novelist has .... a remarkable plot for his latest book.

b It's risky to spend much time writing until a publisher has decided to .... with your proposal and issued a contract.

c Sales of all his titles .... after an extensive lecture tour.

d Time .... slowly while I was on my own and I managed to do a great deal of reading.

e When J. K. Rowling's latest novel .... , there were large queues at bookshops around the world.

f I .... an exceptional detective novel the other day when I was browsing the library shelves.

g Towards the end of his life, Hemingway .... a period of severe depression.

h I used to love science fiction but I've really .... it recently.

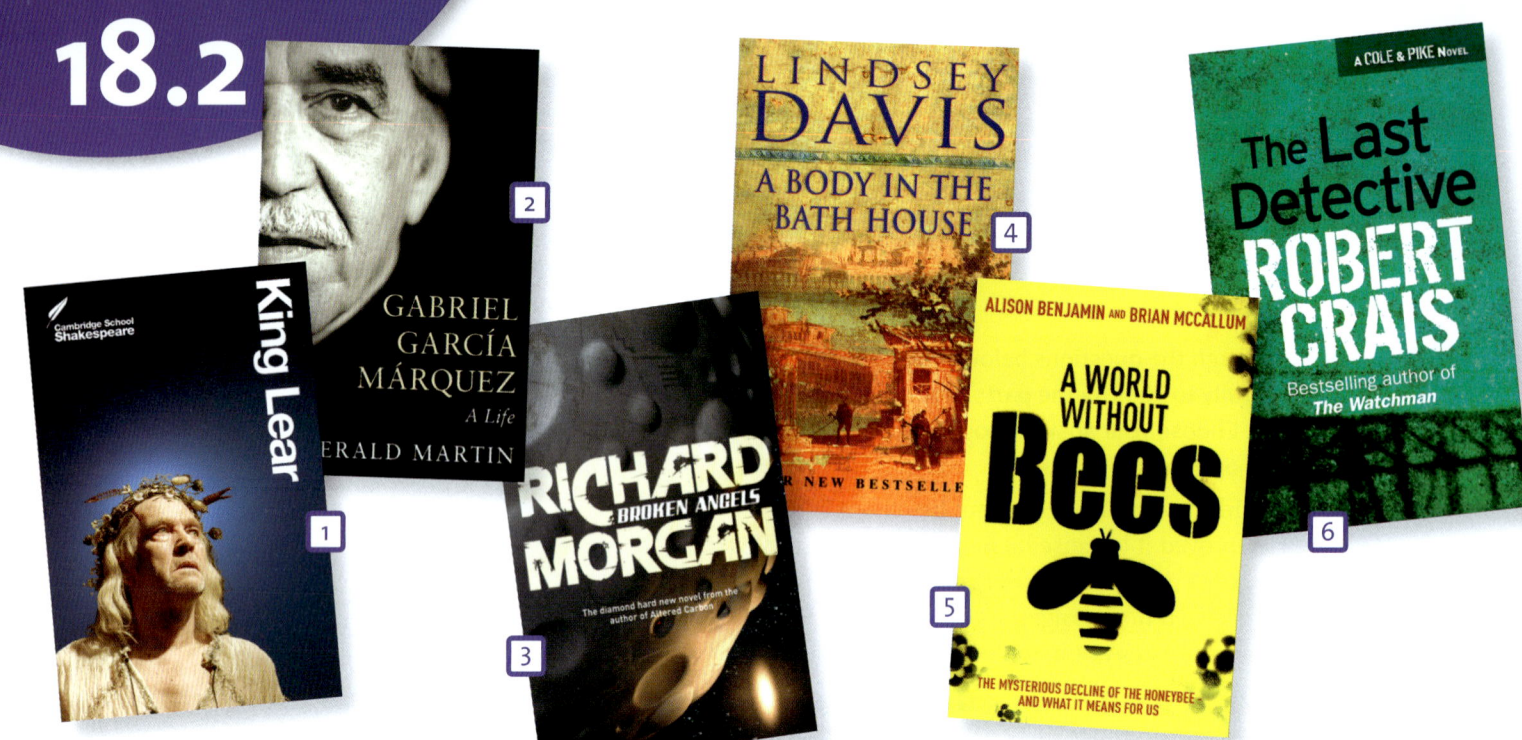

Listening

1 Identify the books shown, choosing from these types.

science fiction   biography   short stories
crime novel   non-fiction   historical novel   play

2 **2 14** You will hear five people talking about books
they have read recently. Match the books shown
above to the five speakers. There is one extra which
you do not need.

Speaker 1   ☐ 1
Speaker 2   ☐ 2
Speaker 3   ☐ 3
Speaker 4   ☐ 4
Speaker 5   ☐ 5

enough, too, very, so, such

> **Corpus spot**
>
> Be careful with word order when using *enough* – the
> *Cambridge Learner Corpus* shows that candidates often make
> mistakes with this.
>
> We were **lucky enough** to meet some famous writers.
> NOT We were ~~enough lucky~~ to meet some famous writers.

3 Read this article about the role of the book today,
ignoring the missing words. Does the writer believe
that the book has a future? Why? / Why not?

For questions 1–12, think of the word which best fits
each gap. Use only one word in each group. There is
an example at the beginning (0).

The book in the 21st century

How many times in (**0**) __THE__ last hundred years or
so have people talked of the imminent death of the
book? Films were an early threat, because they were
so effective at telling stories in a visual way. Next
there was radio, (**1**) .... swept into the mid-
twentieth century and provided such alternatives to
books (**2**) .... drama, documentaries and
discussions. When television arrived, many people
believed that it (**3**) .... finish the book off.
Nowadays, (**4**) .... the threat from TV, the
book in print form is thought to be endangered by
computers and the Internet, and by other technological
attractions, too. If that is so, surely there are now
enough reasons (**5**) .... the book ought to be
dead, (**6**) .... at least very badly injured.

However, this is (**7**) .... the case. Firstly,
we have more leisure time than we (**8**) ....
to, and people are generally living longer. This means
there is more time available to read and do other
things we enjoy. As (**9**) .... as this, there
is the strength of the book as a tradition. We are all
too dismissive of traditions in our modern world, but
they can have a very strong pull on us. Added to this,
the book is such a practical tool: it doesn't cost too
(**10**) .... , it is usually small enough to carry
around, and it can easily (**11**) .... revisited.
We will never go without books, even if they are
starting to be read increasingly in e-book form rather
(**12**) .... in print.

4 Find all the examples of the following words in the article in 3 and study the ways in which they are used. There are 12 examples in all. Then match the examples to the statements a–k. There is one extra statement which you do not need.

enough

a used before an uncountable noun or a countable noun in its plural form to say that there is as much of something as is needed

b used after an adjective or adverb to say that someone or something has as much of a quality as is needed

c used after an adverb in certain expressions

too

d used in front of an adjective or adverb to say that there is more of something than is acceptable or desirable

e used after a piece of information, to emphasise its importance

very

f used to give emphasis to an adjective or adverb

so

g used to emphasise an adjective or adverb

h used to indicate that an amount is approximate

i used to refer back to something that has already been mentioned

such

j used to give an example of something

k used to emphasise an adjective in a noun group

Now compare some of these examples. What are the differences in usage between the two words in brackets?

b and d (enough/too)
d and f (too/very)
f and g (very/so)
g and k (so/such)

G → page 173

5 Insert *enough* into each of these sentences in the correct place.

a Surely you've had time to finish the exercise?

b The room wasn't large to hold everyone.

c There weren't books to go round, so we had to share.

d I had had of other people's problems, so I left work early.

e The course was cancelled as not people had enrolled for it.

f – 'How much money do you have on you?' – 'I've got to pay for the cinema and buy us supper after.'

g 'But that's quite about me! What about you?'

h 'Funnily, I'm reading one of his books at the moment, too.'

6 Complete the second sentence so that it has a similar meaning to the first sentence, using the word given. Do not change the word given. You must use between two and five words, including the word given.

1 The weather was too cold for us to go out.
   SUCH
   It was .... didn't go out.

2 I'm sorry there's not enough time to explain.
   TOO
   I'm sorry there's .... you an explanation.

3 Why not turn professional, as you are such a good swimmer?
   SO
   You swim .... turn professional.

4 Barry really knows how to get other people involved.
   VERY
   Barry .... other people involved.

5 I make all my clothes by hand, so it's very time-consuming.
   SUCH
   It .... time because my clothes are all hand-made.

6 Provided this is the case, your money will be refunded.
   SO
   If .... will be given.

DO YOU NEED MORE PRACTICE? CD-ROM UNITS 17–18

Writing folder 9

The set book

Exam spot

In question 5 of Paper 2, there is a choice of two tasks, at least one of which will be an essay. The other task might be an article, report, review or letter. Although your answer must make reference to the book or short story you have read, you should avoid giving a lengthy description of what happens in the book. This is not asked for and may well be seen as irrelevant to the question that has been asked. If some of your answer in irrelevant, a low mark will be awarded. Remember to read the question carefully, decide exactly what is required, and plan your answer before you start writing.

1 Read this essay and correct the 20 spelling and punctuation errors.

The book 'Marcovaldo', by Italo Calvino, is actually a series of twenty short storys, all conteining the same charakter, Marcovaldo. He lives with his large family in an unamed city in Northern Italy. Each story is set, in a diffrent season: there are five stories about living in the city in summer, and so on.

Many aspects of modern life are described, such as advertiseing and pollution of the enviroment, but the book is not completly true to life. This is perhaps it's greatest strength. It has a unique mixtur of realistic events and bizare ones, which often take the reader by suprise.

One particluar story features the publicity campains of rival soap powder manufacturers. Marcovaldos' children and their frends collect hundreds of free cartons of washing powder, which they hope to sell to people in the neigbourhood. In the end, they have to get rid of everything quickly and so throw the cartons into the River. The story closes with a memmorable description of soap bubbles being blown over the city, their whiteness competing with the black factory smoke. Black wins.

2 Does the essay in 1 answer the following question? How could it be improved?

How true to life is *Marcovaldo*?

Write an essay, discussing this question.

3 Now think about *The Old Man and the Sea*. How true to life is it? Look again at the extract on page 116 and think about how it could be used to illustrate an essay. Then read the notes. What else could you mention from the extract to support the view that this book is very true to life? Think about where the scene takes place and what is described apart from the old man.

Introduce book briefly and give my opinion on how true to life it is (= very!)

Mention part where old man gets fish on his line (mustn't describe story in detail here)

Discuss character of old man – believable – strong, has great determination in spite of age, but has physical problems (mention writer's focus on hand in this scene)

Add something else here?

Include a conclusion

4 The notes talk about the old man's *determination*. Here are some other nouns that are useful to the set book question. Sort them into the two basic categories below, using a dictionary if necessary. Do any apply to both characters and events?

> adventure atmosphere attitude climate
> determination episode impact incident
> mood personality qualities reputation
> risk surroundings sympathy temper

Characters	Events

5 Say which of the adjectives below collocate with the nouns in 4. For example, you can talk about *great determination* but not *small determination*.

> concluding deep enormous final great
> massive minor remarkable serious
> shallow substantial unimportant vast
> weak

6 Remember to address the topic of the question in your opening paragraph. Notice how this has been done in the opening paragraph for the question below.

> How likeable is the main character in *The Old Man and the Sea*? Write an essay explaining your views.

In 'The Old Man and the Sea', the old man, who is the main character, shows great determination. Although he is old and suffers a lot of physical pain, he is mentally strong. For this reason, he is extremely likeable and the reader has deep sympathy with him from the start. When he goes through the final episode of seeing the fish he has successfully caught being torn apart by sharks, we feel enormous sadness for him.

7 Now write a similar opening paragraph for the following question, using the extract in Unit 18 as the part of the book you will refer to. Include some of the adjective–noun collocations in your answer.

> Several memorable events take place in *The Old Man and the Sea*. Write an essay, saying which part of the book you find the most memorable and why.

8 Now write a complete essay about a character or a memorable event in the book of your choice, using vocabulary from 4 and 5. Write 120–180 words.

Topic review

1 Together with a partner read these sentences and discuss which are true for you, giving more details. Try to use as much of the vocabulary and language from the units you have just studied as you can.

a Although I like to read at night, sometimes I'm just too tired to stay awake.

b I have never considered being a vegetarian.

c My cooking is so bad that no one will eat it.

d I'd rather have an interesting job than a large salary.

e There was one subject that I did at school that I just couldn't stand.

f My teachers told me that I would do well after I left school.

g I think that more men have hobbies than women.

h I don't have enough time to read books.

i I admit that I could have worked harder at school.

j I don't do enough to save the planet.

Vocabulary

2 For questions 1–12, read the text below and decide which answer (A, B, C or D) best fits each gap. There is an example at the beginning (0).

Example:

0 **A** made   **B** done   **C** got   **D** had

0	A	B	C	D
	<u>_</u>	_	_	_

Kitchen Star

Peter White has (**0**) .... such a great success of his new restaurant Tastes that he has just received a second star. The fourteen-table restaurant is fully booked every evening this year, and two receptionists are on full-time duty to ensure the business (**1**) .... smoothly. Not only is he fulfilling a lifelong ambition, he is also (**2**) .... more than he ever dreamt possible – he's just bought a new Ferrari to add to his (**3**) ....

However, life hasn't always been so easy for Peter. He (**4**) .... in Northern Ireland, in a family which, although poor, always (**5**) .... on eating well and they never went without. After doing a (**6**) .... at catering college, and (**7**) .... his exams with distinction, he moved to London to work in one of the city's (**8**) .... restaurants. On his first day, Peter remembers two things – the smell of baking bread and the chef throwing a pan of sauce at him because he hadn't (**9**) .... it enough! Peter (**10**) .... that he doesn't treat his own (**11**) .... in such a manner, (**12**) .... he does admit to shouting and regular outbursts of anger!

1 **A** runs	**B** happens	**C** flows	**D** moves
2 **A** taking	**B** gaining	**C** winning	**D** earning
3 **A** collection	**B** store	**C** set	**D** group
4 **A** brought up	**B** put up	**C** grew up	**D** showed up
5 **A** promised	**B** insisted	**C** accepted	**D** maintained
6 **A** training	**B** work	**C** course	**D** lecture
7 **A** passing	**B** succeeding	**C** graduating	**D** qualifying
8 **A** head	**B** peak	**C** top	**D** lead
9 **A** stirred	**B** chopped	**C** grated	**D** turned
10 **A** tells	**B** claims	**C** denies	**D** speaks
11 **A** crew	**B** troop	**C** staff	**D** band
12 **A** despite	**B** because	**C** even	**D** although

Grammar

3 Correct the following sentences.

a There are too much traffic in our town.
b I have so a lot of the work to do, I don't know where to start.
c The Netherlands and the Austria are both countries in the European Union.
d Her house, which roof is thatched, is twelfth century.
e John plays piano and he also plays the football, whereas his brother prefers playing the chess.
f Let me give you an advice – don't go on a travel without checking whether you need any visa or not.
g There's a man over there which has been watching us for about half an hour.
h I lived in Las Vegas for ten years and I am still finding it exciting.
i By this time next year I will taught since twenty years.
j He asked me where was the police station.
k I saw a bit of lightning when I was out in the garden.
l Have you got information enough to object about the factory noise?
m He's the one to whom I gave the book to.
n My eldest son who lives in Paris is a physicist.

4 Complete the sentence beginnings a–g with their endings 1–7.

EXAMPLE: **a 5** *He apologised for overcooking the meat.*

a He apologised
b She denied
c The chef claimed
d The customer insisted
e My neighbour warned
f Next time you come, I promise
g The waiter encouraged

1 me that the restaurant was expensive.
2 to make you a cake.
3 overcharging them for the coffee.
4 on seeing the kitchen.
5 for overcooking the meat.
6 them to try the chocolate ice cream.
7 he hadn't forgotten to order the eggs.

Phrasal verbs revision quiz

5 The phrasal verbs here are from Units 1–18. Decide which answer (A, B or C) is correct. Then, if possible, write another correct answer of your own.

1 What could you get over?
   A a bicycle
   B the flu
   C your homework
2 What might take off?
   A a business
   B a walk
   C a coat
3 What kind of thing might you come up with?
   A a talk
   B a suggestion
   C your foot
4 What would you set off on?
   A a weekend
   B a party
   C a journey
5 Where do you check in?
   A at a hotel
   B at a school
   C at a museum
6 What can go by slowly?
   A food
   B time
   C weather
7 If you come across someone or something, is it usually
   A by accident?
   B on purpose?
   C on time?
8 What might you want to cut down?
   A your hair
   B your car
   C your expenses
9 What might you want to get out of?
   A household tasks
   B a bus
   C a DVD
10 What sort of things can go up?
   A prices
   B trees
   C windows

An apple a day ...

1 How often do you get a good eight hours' sleep?

A Every night – and I prefer nine or ten hours.
B Not often – I don't need much sleep.
C I sometimes find it hard to get to sleep.

2 How often do you do any exercise?

A Once a week.
B Every day.
C Hardly ever.

3 What do you usually have for lunch?

A A large meal.
B Salad or sandwiches.
C Nothing.

4 When did you last have a cold?

A I usually have one or two a year.
B I can't remember.
C I get them all the time.

5 How many cups of tea or coffee do you drink a day?

A No more than three.
B I don't drink anything with caffeine in it.
C Between four and fourteen.

6 You have a headache. Do you

A go straight to the doctor?
B take an aspirin?
C hope it will go away?

7 Do you think it's necessary to add salt to your food?

A Sometimes.
B Never.
C Always.

8 Which is true for you?

A I've given up smoking.
B I've never smoked.
C I smoke about five cigarettes or more a day.

9 Which is true for you?

A I think I'm fit and healthy.
B I think illness is all in the mind.
C I sometimes worry about my health.

How did you score?

Mostly As

You are fairly healthy and have a good attitude to life. You <u>should try</u> to watch what you eat a little more, and if I were you, I'd try to do a little more exercise. Too much work and not enough play isn't good for you! I think it's about time you thought about your diet.

Mostly Bs

You are obviously in the peak of condition! I recommend you relax, as you ought to get some rest, even if you don't need much sleep. Overdoing things can lead to illness! Why don't you try doing more reading, or go on holiday – or have you ever thought of playing a musical instrument?

Mostly Cs

Oh dear! It's time you took a good look at your lifestyle. Missing meals and not getting enough sleep and exercise are very bad for you. My advice to you is to start right away – you'd better join a gym. I also suggest cutting down on coffee and drinking more water and fruit juice. Too much caffeine will keep you awake!

Speaking

1 Look at the photos above and say why you think the people have chosen these activities. Then discuss the following questions in pairs.

- Do you prefer to exercise alone or in a class? Why?
- Would you like to spend time in a gym like the one in the photo?
- What do you think of the exercise facilities in your town?
- What do you think is the best type of exercise? Why?

Modals 3: Advice and suggestion

2 How healthy are you? Complete the questionnaire. Do you agree with what is said about your results? Compare with a partner.

3 Underline the verbs and phrases which are used to give advice and make suggestions. One has been done for you in the 'Mostly As'. This is an example of advice. Make a note of what follows the verb or expression.

EXAMPLE: *should* + infinitive without *to*

Look at these problems and, with a partner, give advice and make suggestions. Try to vary the verbs and phrases you use.

EXAMPLE: *I can't stop sneezing.*
ADVICE: *If I were you, I'd take a cold shower.*

a I woke up covered in spots this morning.
b I've burnt my hand.
c I'm hoping to be picked for the local cycling team.
d I think I've broken my wrist.
e I'm going on holiday to a tropical country.
f I'm going to faint.
g I've been stung by a wasp.
h I never seem to have any energy.

4 The expressions *It's time ...*, *It's about time ...* and *It's high time ...* are used to express strong feelings about something that hasn't been done or about something that should happen very soon.

*I think it's about time **you thought** about your diet a bit more.*
*It's time **you took** a good look at your lifestyle.*
*It's high time **you did** some exercise.*

Corpus spot 👁

The *Cambridge Learner Corpus* shows that exam candidates often forget to use the past simple with these expressions.

It's about time I **joined** a serious riding club.
NOT It's about time I ~~join~~ a serious riding club.

When you are talking generally, it is possible to use the infinitive, but only after *It's time*, not after *It's high time* or *It's about time.*

It's time to go home now. (referring to everyone, including the speaker)
It's time I/you/he/she/we/they went home now. (referring to specific people)

What would you say to a friend in these situations?

EXAMPLE: Your friend's hair is too long.
It's time you had a haircut.

a He smokes 40 a day.
b She drives everywhere.
c She watches TV for six hours a day.
d He lost his job six months ago.
e He likes eating chips.
f He's been living with his parents for 30 years.
g Her coat has holes in it.
h She's always borrowing your books.
i He's always late for work.
j Her car is always breaking down.

G → page 174

Vocabulary

Topic set – parts of the body

5 Can you point to these body parts in the photo?

chest
elbow
knee
wrist
ankle
thigh
jaw
waist
eyebrow

6 If A happened to you, what in B would you do?

EXAMPLE: *If I broke my arm, I'd wear a sling.*

A If I ...	B I'd ...
broke my leg	take an aspirin
had a headache	have stitches
cut my knee badly	go to bed
grazed my elbow	take some cough medicine
sprained my ankle	put a bandage on it
had flu	get an elastoplast / a plaster
had a cough	have it put in plaster

Phrases with *on*

7 In the questionnaire on health, the phrase *on holiday* was used. Look at these expressions with *on* and then complete the sentences with a suitable expression.

on offer   on purpose   on duty   on average
on condition that   on behalf of   on balance

a I go to the gym .... two or three times a week.
b I had to accept the prize .... my brother because he was ill at the time.
c I didn't break the vase ....
d I'd hate a job as a nurse or police officer where I had to be .... at weekends.
e I'll do more exercise .... I can watch more TV in the evening.
f .... I prefer running to cycling.
g I always try to buy things which are .... in the shops.

Which of the above statements are true for you?

19.2

Listening

1 Do you know what these forms of alternative medicine are?

homeopathy   osteopathy   reflexology   herbal medicine

2 Acupuncture is a type of alternative medicine. It is used in Chinese medicine. It consists of steel needles being inserted into the skin. Have you ever tried it?

3 How do you think the patients in the photos feel at this moment? What differences do you think there are in the types of treatment being given?

4 **2 15** You are going to hear part of a radio programme about health matters. A doctor is being interviewed about acupuncture. For questions 1–7, choose the best answer (A, B or C).

1 What do we find out about Dr Carpenter's time in Hong Kong?
   A She was there to study acupuncture.
   B She practised acupuncture while she was there.
   C She enjoyed seeing a different approach to medicine.

2 Patients who she recommends for acupuncture
   A should have a blood test done first.
   B are able to choose an acupuncturist themselves.
   C need to go on a waiting list.

3 What does she say happens if you have a problem with backache?
   A You spend some time answering questions.
   B You have a needle inserted into the area which hurts.
   C You are given advice about changing your lifestyle.

4 What does she say happens after the first treatment?
   A You usually feel better.
   B You might feel tired.
   C You have to go to bed.

5 She says people who have acupuncture complain of pain when the needle
   A is put in.
   B is in position.
   C is taken out.

6 What does Dr Carpenter say about acupuncture?
   A It works whether you believe in it or not.
   B It's best to keep an open mind.
   C A negative attitude will stop it working.

7 In 1971 acupuncture received a great deal of publicity because an American reporter
   A went to China to investigate its use there.
   B was given some acupuncture treatment in China.
   C talked to patients who'd had operations without anaesthetic.

Grammar extra

'to have their chests X-rayed'
'to have a blood test done'

Why do you think we say:

I went to the hospital to have my chest X-rayed and have a blood test done.
and not:
I X-rayed my chest and did a blood test.

You can also say *to **get** a blood test done.*

Why do you go to the following?
a a dry cleaner's
b a hairdresser's
c a garage
d a dressmaker
e a tailor
f a manicurist
g a dentist
h a furniture maker

 G → page 174

5 Look at the photo. Have you ever tried yoga? Why? / Why not? For questions 1–12, read the text and decide which answer (A, B, C or D) best fits each gap. There is an example at the beginning (0).

Example:

0 A taken **B** lasted **C** spent **D** passed

0	**A**	B	C	D
	—	▭	▭	▭

Vocabulary

Word formation

6 Look at the sentences, or parts of sentences, below. They are all from the interview on the recording. Change the word in capitals into the right part of speech. Make sure you spell the word correctly.

a You're a great .... (BELIEF) in Chinese medicine, aren't you?

b We referred patients to .... (SPECIALISE) at the local hospital for .... (TREAT).

c When I was a .... (MEDICINE) student, …

d … I saw how .... (EFFECT) acupuncture could be.

e He will insert needles in .... (VARY) parts of your body.

f Some areas are more .... (SENSE) than others.

g Acupuncture has been used .... (SUCCEED) on cats.

h He felt no pain during or after the .... (OPERATE).

Yoga

Yoga is one of the most ancient forms of exercise, originating in India 5000 years ago. Yoga has (**0**) .... many years to become recognised world-wide, (**1**) .... recently much more attention has been (**2**) .... to it because of the ways in which it can benefit health. Yoga can be practised by anyone, at any age, (**3**) .... any physical condition, (**4**) .... on their physical need. For example, athletes and dancers can practise it to restore their energy and to improve stamina; executives to give a much needed (**5**) .... to their overworked minds; children to improve their memory and concentration.

It's a good idea to (**6**) .... with a doctor first if you've suffered from any type of (**7**) .... None of the exercises should cause you any pain, but it's best to start slowly at first. The best (**8**) .... to practise is either in the morning or in the evening. Beginners (**9**) .... it easier in the evening (**10**) .... the body is more supple.

Contrary to what many people believe, you do not need to practise an hour of yoga (**11**) .... day. Just taking ten to fifteen minutes out of your schedule can (**12**) .... to be extremely helpful.

	A	**B**	**C**	**D**
1	although	whereas	if	unless
2	put	paid	allowed	provided
3	at	in	of	on
4	according	matching	fitting	depending
5	pause	break	interval	interruption
6	see	check	control	call
7	hurt	ache	injury	scratch
8	point	instance	time	occasion
9	find	discover	notice	recognise
10	though	when	until	despite
11	each	all	either	several
12	demonstrate	prove	show	turn

Topic set – health

7 Complete the sentences below with one of the nouns in the box connected with health.

bruise bug examination scar
surgery sweat symptom ward

a I found I had .... pouring off me when I got back from my run.

b The doctor told Sally that she would have to have .... on her ankle as it was a bad break.

c 'Go upstairs and along the corridor,' said the nurse. 'Your sister is on .... 11.'

d You can still see the .... where I cut my knee badly three years ago.

e Can you see my .... ? It's beginning to go blue.

f The dentist gave Pete's teeth a thorough ....

g I couldn't go on holiday because I had a .... – it was one that was going round at the time.

h The doctor said he thought the muscle pain was a .... of flu.

Exam folder 10

Paper 1 Part 1 Multiple choice – fiction

In this part of the Reading paper you are tested on a detailed understanding of either a fiction or non-fiction text. (See Exam folder 12 for non-fiction.) There might also be the following types of questions:

- a question which tests global understanding, for example: *What does the text as a whole tell us about the man's character?*
- a question which tests the meaning of a word or phrase from context, for example: *What does the writer mean by x in line 00?*
- a question which tests reference, for example: *What does 'it' refer to in line 00?*

EXAM ADVICE

- Skim the text to get a general idea of what it is about.
- All the questions, except for the global one, are in order, so you can concentrate on each part of the text at a time. The global question will come at the end, but you need to make sure you take **the whole text** into account when you answer it.
- Some of the choices may be true but do not answer the question. Other choices may seem very plausible and even contain elements of the same vocabulary, but do not answer the question correctly.
- The reference question may refer either forwards or backwards, so check carefully on either side of the pronoun to see what it refers to.
- As you read, underline the part of the text which you think contains the answer.

You are going to read an extract from a novel. For questions 1–8, choose the answer (A, B, C or D) which you think fits best according to the text.

1 How did the writer feel when he first woke up?
- **A** certain that it must be a Sunday morning
- **B** sure about what his senses were telling him
- **C** worried that something unusual was happening
- **D** unclear as to what time it was

2 What do we learn about the writer in the second paragraph?
- **A** He was keen to have his bandages changed.
- **B** He was pleased he had not been put on a ward.
- **C** He liked the sense of routine he found in the hospital.
- **D** He felt he no longer needed to be in hospital.

3 What does 'it' refer to in line 16?
- **A** the bathroom
- **B** a guiding hand
- **C** a close forerunner
- **D** the washing process

4 What does the writer say about the location of the hospital?
- **A** It was next to a large office block.
- **B** It was at a busy road junction.
- **C** It was beside a motorway.
- **D** It was at the top of a steep hill.

5 What does the writer mean by 'I restrained it' in line 27?
- **A** He controlled his wish to take a look.
- **B** He held back his need to get out of bed.
- **C** He tried to fight his feeling of fear.
- **D** He checked his desire to cry.

6 How did the writer feel in the fifth paragraph?
- **A** a great deal better after ringing the bell a few times
- **B** ashamed that he was ill in bed
- **C** worried about upsetting someone if he made a noise
- **D** annoyed that he had to rely on other people

7 What does the writer say about Tuesday, May 7?
- **A** The hospital had held a fireworks display.
- **B** A comet made its expected appearance.
- **C** What happened on that day is well documented.
- **D** He had no memory of the unusual happenings on that day.

8 What impression do you get of the writer from the text?
- **A** He is a very shy person who finds it hard to get on with people.
- **B** He worries unnecessarily about things which happen to him.
- **C** He doesn't like being in a situation he can't control.
- **D** He overstates his problems to obtain sympathy.

When a day that you happen to know is Wednesday starts off by sounding more like Sunday, there is something seriously wrong. I felt that from the moment I woke. And yet, when I started functioning a little better, I became doubtful. I went on waiting. But presently I had my first bit of real evidence – a distant clock struck what sounded to me just like eight. Soon another clock began. In a leisurely fashion it gave an unquestionable eight. Then I knew things were wrong.

The way I came to miss the end of the world was sheer accident. I was in hospital. Chance played it not only that I should be there at that particular time, but that my eyes should be enclosed in bandages. This morning I was feeling annoyed because someone should begin to wash and tidy me up at exactly three minutes after 7 a.m. That was one of the best reasons I had for appreciating a private room. In a public ward the proceeding would have taken place a whole unnecessary hour earlier. But here, today, clocks of varying reliability were continuing to strike eight in all directions – and still nobody had shown up. Much as I disliked the washing process, and useless as it had been to suggest that the help of a guiding hand as far as the bathroom could remove it, its failure to occur line 16 was very worrying. Besides, <u>it</u> was normally a close forerunner of breakfast, and I was feeling hungry.

The day outside, I realised now, was sounding even more wrong than I had thought. Why the founders of St Merryn's Hospital chose to build their institution at a main-road crossing upon a valuable office site, I never properly understood. The buses thundered along trying to beat the lights at the corner. Then the released cross traffic would roar as it started up the slight slope. But this morning was different. No wheels rumbled, no buses roared, no sound of a car of any kind, in fact, was to be heard.

I had to fight down the same feeling of fear that I had had when I was a kid crying in the dark and when I had been too scared to put even a foot out of bed. The temptation to lift the bandages – just enough to get some idea of what on earth could be happening line 27 – was immense. But I restrained it. For one thing, it was a far less simple matter than it sounded. It wasn't just a case of lifting a blindfold: there were a lot of pads and bandages.

I yelled and pushed the bell again. It helped to relieve my feelings a little bit. No one, it seemed, was interested. I began to get as much irritated as worried. It's awful to be dependent, anyway, but it's worse to have no one to depend on. Something, I decided, had got to be done. If I were to yell down the passage, somebody ought to show up, if only to tell me what they thought of me. Nothing happened.

Some little while must have passed, but after a bit I found myself looking once more for a possible explanation for the silence. I became absolutely convinced that it was Wednesday. For the previous day had been notable. You'll find it in the records that on Tuesday, May 7, the Earth's orbit passed through a cloud of comet debris. I was in no state to see what happened myself. All that I actually know is that I had to listen to eyewitness accounts of what was considered to be the greatest free fireworks display ever. And yet, until the thing actually began, nobody had ever heard a word about this comet. It was reported in the news bulletins during the day that mysterious bright green flashes had been seen in the Californian skies the previous night. Accounts arrived from all over the Pacific of a night made brilliant by green meteors said to be 'sometimes in such numerous showers that the whole sky appeared to be wheeling about us'.

Extract from *The Day of the Triffids* by John Wyndham.

John Wyndham is the pen name of British writer John Harris (1903–1969). He wrote *The Day of the Triffids* in 1951.

No place to hide

Speaking

1 **Read and complete the Paper 5 Part 3 task below.**

   Look at the five photographs of clues in a police case. Discuss which two clues are the most reliable, giving reasons for your choice. You have about three minutes to do this. It is not necessary to agree with each other, but make sure you have completed the task and not spent too much time on one point.

2 **In Paper 5 Part 4 you are encouraged to broaden and discuss further the topic introduced in Part 3. Discuss the following questions together.**

   a What do you think are the causes of crime? (e.g. unemployment)
   b Do DVDs and TV programmes about violent crime help to cause more crime? Why? / Why not?
   c Should life imprisonment mean 'life'?
   d Is prison really the answer to crime?

Reading

3 **Look at the vocabulary related to crime below. These are all words and phrases that you will see in the article you are going to read. Fill the gaps in the sentences with the word or phrase which fits best. (You may have to change the form of the verb.) Remember to use your English–English dictionary to help you.**

to cover your tracks	a forensic scientist
the suspect	genetic code
the proof	evidence
guilty	to take someone to court

   a My sister studied to be a doctor but then decided she wanted to change careers and become .... , working alongside the police.
   b It's up to the prosecution to find .... that someone committed a crime.
   c Psychologists believe you can tell if someone is .... by their body language.
   d Everyone has a completely different .... unless they are identical twins.
   e When the police have enough .... they will arrest ....
   f It is virtually impossible nowadays .... completely when you've committed a crime – there is always something that will give you away.
   g If you are caught drinking and driving you will be .... and fined.

4 You are going to read an article about detecting crime. Seven sentences have been removed from the article. Choose from the sentences A–H the one which fits each gap (1–7). There is one extra sentence which you do not need to use.

The professionals

When it comes to fighting crime, it is science which is king. Sherlock Holmes was right to spend his time examining every footprint and strand of hair in his search for the criminal. Today, though, things have moved on and scientists have a wider range of techniques they can use.

Modern scientists believe that it is impossible for someone to commit a crime without leaving something behind or taking something away with them. **1** [ ] They may take the form of fingerprints, hairs, fibres from clothing, tiny traces of chemicals, documents, bullets or fragments of glass. This evidence is collected and studied by forensic scientists.

Science is applied to crime-fighting now more than ever before. **2** [ ] In addition, old techniques are constantly being improved so that they can be applied to smaller and smaller traces of materials.

Not all evidence is equal in law. A fingerprint offers definite identification of a person's presence at the scene of a crime. **3** [ ] But even if an item does not offer enough proof to be used in a court of law, it can still assist the police in focusing their enquiries in a certain direction.

Fingerprints have been used to help identify criminals for almost 100 years. **4** [ ] In most cases it works very well, but sometimes different methods are needed.

Forensic scientists can now use a small portable laser, a kind of light beam, to look for fingerprints. The scientist 'paints' the scene of the crime with the laser beam. **5** [ ]

An even more recent technique is called DNA profiling. **6** [ ] Each contains a unique code, the genetic code that determines what we look like and how we develop. The code takes the form of long strings of molecules called DNA, and no two people have identical DNA unless they are identical twins. A technique for reading genetic codes was developed in the 1980s. DNA profiling, or genetic fingerprinting, was seen by the police and forensic scientists as an excellent way of linking suspected criminals with their crimes.

The process of making a DNA profile may begin with a piece of stained clothing found at the scene of the crime. **7** [ ] With a good sample that is rich in DNA, the chance of two people producing the same genetic fingerprint is only one in 2.7 million, which is good enough for a court of law.

line 10
line 17
line 23
line 27

A   In that time, many new scientific research methods have been developed, although the traditional way of dusting surfaces for fingerprints is still used most of the time.
B   The human body is composed of millions of microscopic cells.
C   However, a footprint may only suggest that someone was there.
D   On the other hand, certain scientists specialise in gathering evidence from the scene of the crime.
E   As it sweeps across doors, walls and furniture, any fingerprints present glow because they are fluorescent.
F   As people find new ways to cover their tracks, scientists develop new techniques for linking suspects with their crimes and proving if they are guilty or innocent.
G   A tuft of hair or spots of blood or saliva can be used too.
H   If these traces of evidence can be found, they may provide the proof needed to bring the criminal to justice – that is, to take them to court.

5   What do you think about DNA profiling?

Do you think there should be an international database with everyone's DNA on it? Why? / Why not?

6   The following pronouns are in bold in the article. What do they refer to?
a line 10 – They
b line 17 – they
c line 23 – it
d line 27 – it

20.2

Listening

1 **2 16** Before you listen to the recording, read through the questions and make sure you understand them. You are going to hear a radio news item about the arrest of a robber in the USA. Take notes while you are listening and then in pairs discuss the answers to the questions.

a How long will Curcio have to stay in prison?
b Where was Curcio arrested?
c Why did Curcio steal the money?
d When did Curcio get the idea of the robbery?
e Why did he put an advert on the Internet?
f What did Curcio pretend to do immediately before the robbery?
g How did Curcio escape?
h Why were the police confused?
i What happened three weeks before the robbery?
j What evidence did the police have for arresting Curcio?

What do you think about Curcio and the robbery?

2 Look at these extracts from the story.

a … it stopped outside the bank to unload the money …
b Curcio stopped working and …
c Curcio remembered to remove his wig …
d … a police sergeant remembered getting the report.

What's the difference in meaning between *stop* and *remember* + gerund, and *stop* and *remember* + infinitive?

Corpus spot

The *Cambridge Learner Corpus* shows that exam candidates often make mistakes with the use of *stop* + infinitive and *stop* + gerund.

My advice to you is to stop **working** too hard.
NOT My advice to you is to stop ~~work~~ too hard.

Gerunds and infinitives 2

3 In Unit 7 you looked at which verb or expression took a gerund and which took an infinitive. However, there are some verbs that can take both.

> **No change in meaning**: start, begin, continue
>
> **A very slight change in meaning**: like, prefer, hate, love
>
> With these verbs, the gerund is used to talk about enjoyment – *I like having a mobile phone.*
>
> The infinitive is used to talk about habits and choices – *I like to have the latest mobile phone.*
>
> **A change in meaning**: try, stop, regret, remember, forget, mean, go on

In pairs, talk about the difference in meaning in these pairs of sentences.

1a I tried to stop the thief taking the woman's bag but I failed.
1b The burglar tried climbing through the kitchen window when he couldn't break the door lock.
2a The detective stopped at the top of the hill to look at the footprint.
2b Tom stopped working for the police last year.
3a Pete regrets leaving his car unlocked.
3b We regret to inform you that your stolen bicycle has been found in the river.
4a I remember our house being broken into when I was six.
4b You must remember to get travel insurance tomorrow.
5a Cycling without lights will mean getting a fine.
5b Sally means to write her first detective novel this autumn.
6a The policeman, after discussing personal safety, went on to talk about car crime in the town.
6b Lucy went on talking about having her suitcase stolen all evening.

4 Complete these sentences with the right form of the verb.

a The householder tried .... (fit) a burglar alarm to the house to deter thieves.

b I remember .... (read) about that kidnapping case in the papers some years ago.

c I regret .... (inform) you that your car tax has expired.

d Selling my car will mean .... (walk) home in the dark every night.

e I'm sure Peter didn't mean .... (hurt) the little girl – he only pushed her.

f I wasn't shoplifting – I just forgot .... (pay) for the scarf.

g I regret not .... (tell) the police about my suspicions.

h Although he'd been arrested for drunk driving he continued .... (drink and drive) just the same.

i I like .... (keep) an eye on my neighbours' houses when they are away.

j The policeman talked about robbery in general and then he went on .... (talk) about sentencing.

k I was mugged as I stopped .... (do up) my shoelace.

l Susan tried .... (run) after the pickpocket but although she's a good runner she couldn't catch him.

5 This exercise revises the work done on gerunds and infinitives in this unit and Unit 7. Complete the leaflet with the correct form of the verb in brackets.

Personal Possessions

A thief only needs a moment (**1**) .... (make off) with your valuables. So try (**2**) .... (be) careful at all times. Carry your wallet in an inside pocket, preferably one it is possible (**3**) .... (fasten), not your back pocket. If someone bumps into you in a crowd, it's worth (**4**) .... (check) (**5**) .... (see) that you still have your purse. Try (**6**) .... (avoid) (**7**) .... (carry) large amounts of cash. When on holiday, try (**8**) .... (put) valuables in the hotel safe. If your credit card is stolen, tell the card company immediately. If you delay (**9**) .... (report) the loss, it could (**10**) .... (lead) to a crime being committed in your name. Never let anyone (**11**) .... (know) your PIN number and remember (**12**) .... (sign) any new plastic cards you receive.

G → page 172

Vocabulary
Topic set – crime

6 Look at the vocabulary below about crime. In pairs, decide which is the odd word out in each set and give your reasons.

a get away with	release	hang	let someone off
b illegal	guilty	innocent	suspicious
c robbery	theft	terrorism	arrest
d burglar	criminal	jury	gang
e trial	cell	court	prison
f punishment	offence	penalty	fine
g arrest	accuse	commit	charge

Writing folder 10

Stories 2

In Writing folder 3 you saw how to approach the short story question in Part 2 of Paper 2. Remember to include the sentence you are given, which either begins or ends the story.

1   Look at this question and read the sample answer that follows. Then read endings A, B and C and discuss with a partner which of them would be the best way to end the story.

Your teacher has asked you to write a story for an international magazine.
The story must **begin** with the following sentence:

I couldn't believe my eyes when I opened the front door.

Write your **story**.

I couldn't believe my eyes when I opened the front door. When I had left home that morning, the house had been clean and tidy. Now, everything was lying on the floor in a terrible mess. There were books on the carpet and all the drawers in my desk had been opened and the papers scattered round the room. I realised at once that I had been burgled. I rushed to the telephone to call the police. They told me to keep calm and not to touch anything.

I decided to take a look round to see what had been stolen. The TV was still there and so was the DVD player. I went into my bedroom and that seemed to be completely untouched. The mess was only in the sitting room. I couldn't understand why, especially as nothing was missing.

A
Suddenly, the telephone rang. I picked it up. A voice said, 'Let this be a warning to you!' It was a woman's voice, and it made my blood run cold. I was now really scared. I didn't know what she could be talking about. I tried to dial the police again, but my hand was shaking so much I wasn't able to. Just then there was a ring at the front door.

B
I decided to make a cup of coffee while I was waiting for the police to arrive. Then they rang the doorbell and came in. They spent half an hour looking at the mess and told me that there had been a lot of burglaries in the neighbourhood recently. I felt very unhappy.

C
Suddenly, there was a knock on the door and my sister was standing there with her little boy, Tom. 'Oh dear!' she exclaimed. 'Yes,' I said, 'isn't it terrible? I've called the police and they are on their way.' Tom suddenly threw himself into my arms. 'I'm sorry,' he said. 'It was me, it was me!'

2 It is very important when you are writing a story to keep in the right tense. Make the necessary changes to the verbs in brackets in the following story. What does the writer do at the end that might lose marks in the exam? This story has to end with the sentence: *For Joe, life at the office would never seem stressful again!*

'I can't believe this is happening to me,' Joe thought. He (1) .... (arrive) at the tiny island only hours before and now he (2) .... (find) himself lying on the deck of a small fishing boat. 'What (3) .... (I/go) to do?' he (4) .... (think). He (5) .... (look) forward to coming to the island for months. Anne, his cousin, (6) .... (come) the year before and (7) .... (tell) him how wonderful it (8) .... (be). 'It (9) .... (have) everything you (10) .... (need) for a complete rest, away from the stresses of everyday life,' she (11) .... (say). At this moment Joe (12) .... (want) to strangle her. 'Why (13) .... (I/decide) to follow her advice?' he asked himself. He (14) .... (know) no one on the island and (15) .... (have) no idea why he (16) .... (kidnap). Then he (17) .... (hear) footsteps coming. It (18) .... (be) a man, about fifty years old with short, black hair and a beard. He (19) .... (wear) a sort of uniform – brown shorts, a blue shirt and tie.
  'We (20) .... (decide) to let you go,' the man (21) .... (say). 'A case of mistaken identity,' he (22) .... (continue). 'We (23) .... (be) sorry and (24) .... (hope) you (25) .... (enjoy) the rest of your holiday.' With that, he (26) .... (untie) me and pushed me off the boat. Luckily, I (27) .... (not have) far to swim to the shore. For Joe, life at the office would never seem stressful again!

3 Now discuss with a partner how you could change the parts of the story that are in the different colours.

the place
the person
the ending

Try to think of interesting alternatives and then tell the rest of the class what you have written.

4 Now do this writing task.

You have been asked to write a short story for your college magazine. The story must end with the following sentence:

Sam could hear no one following him, and realised that he was safe at last.

Write your **story** in 120–180 words.

With a partner, think of some ideas for the story.

a The people in the story – how will you describe them?
b The place where the story happens – what is it like?
c The action – how will you describe what happens?

EXAM ADVICE

- Remember to check the spelling, punctuation and grammar.
- Count the number of words you have written.
- Try to keep within 20 words of the upper limit.
- Get used to judging how many lines of your handwriting will make 180 words.

Urban decay, suburban hell

Vocabulary

Collocations

1 Add these nouns to their partner nouns in the categories below. An example is given. Try to use them in the Speaking task in 2.

> art   community
> congestion   construction
> ~~high-rise~~   property
> residents   road
> rubbish   shopping
> street   traffic

Buildings
high-rise blocks
.... value
.... work

Leisure facilities
.... gallery
.... mall
.... centre

Services
.... collection
.... maintenance
.... lighting

Transport
.... jam
.... charge
.... parking

Speaking

2 Follow the instructions below, working in pairs. Time yourselves.

Student A
Compare the photographs, and talk about the advantages and disadvantages of living in each neighbourhood. (1 minute)

Student B
Say which neighbourhood you would prefer to live in. (20 seconds)

Listening

3 **2 17** You will hear an extract from a radio programme called *Challenge the Expert*. Listen to the introduction to decide what profession the expert is in.

4 **2 18** Before you listen to Part 2, read the sentences below to predict what you might hear. Then listen and complete the sentences.

Julia explains that some 1960s architecture came about because of [1   ]

Today, [2   ] regulations are stricter than they were in the past.

Julia used to live in a [3   ] as a child, in a poor part of Bristol.

The [4   ] used for new buildings have improved since the 1960s.

Julia mentions [5   ] as an example of an environmental requirement for new buildings in Britain.

When explaining what she sees as a problem today, Julia refers to the [6   ] as 'urban sprawl'.

Some city centre shops have shut because of [7   ] facilities.

Julia believes that architects should design [8   ] for city centres.

In a multi-use building, there might be [9   ] downstairs.

People are unhappy about damage to their health caused by [10   ] in cities.

Compare your answers with another student. Then listen again to check. Finally, check that your spelling is accurate.

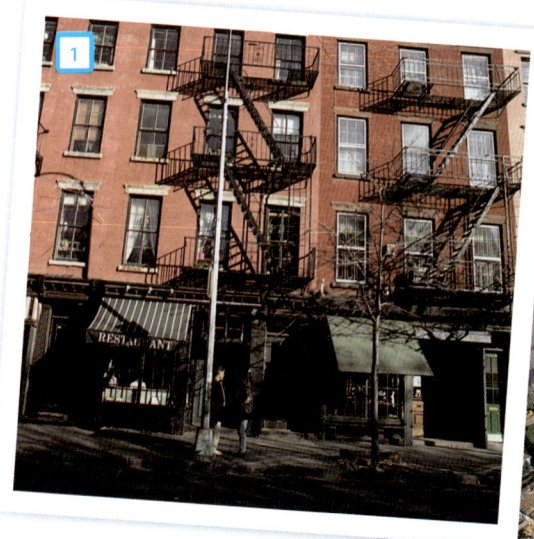

Exam spot

Always check your spelling in Listening Part 2, as answers usually have to be spelled correctly. American spelling is acceptable. Be careful not to make a mistake when transferring your answers. Write clearly on the answer sheet, using capital letters or numbers.

5 **Say whether these sentences about the recording are true or false, explaining why.**

   a Gareth believes that the public are generally given adequate opportunities to comment on planning proposals.

   b Julia's personal experience of below-average living conditions influenced her career choice.

   c Julia argues that urban sprawl has affected both city centres and the countryside.

   d Gareth earns enough to afford a decent property in central London.

   e Gareth admits to Julia that he may change his mind as a result of her responses.

6 **These words with *up* all occurred in the recording. Match them to meanings 1–5. Do you know any other words with *up*-?**

a	uprooted	**1**	maintenance
b	upheld	**2**	expensive
c	upkeep	**3**	made to leave
d	upmarket	**4**	advantage
e	upside	**5**	supported

Speaking

Exam spot

Turn-taking skills are important, especially in Part 4 of the Speaking test, where there is a three-way discussion involving both candidates and the examiner. Part 4 lasts four minutes and each candidate needs to have adequate opportunities to speak, which means being sensitive to the other people in the conversation.

7 **Say whether the purpose of these turn-taking expressions is**

   1 to involve someone in the discussion
   2 to encourage someone to be quiet
   3 to support what someone is saying

   a You clearly know a lot about this, but let's move on.
   b Would you say that this is true in your case?
   c I believe your own view is slightly different?
   d Come on, you're talking rubbish!
   e Well, I have to admit you have a point.
   f I'm going to say something here.
   g What do you think?
   h Absolutely, I couldn't agree more.

Do you consider any of these rude or offensive? In what other ways can a speaker or listener direct a conversation?

8 **Now practise these turn-taking skills. Get into groups of four to discuss the following statements. For each statement, one person in the group should stay silent and time how long each of the others speaks for.**

   a There are both good and bad examples of modern architecture.

   b Living conditions in our cities have got worse.

   c City centres should be traffic-free.

   d Urban sprawl is a serious threat to nature.

Mixed conditionals

1 Look at these two quotes from the recording in 21.1, which are examples of mixed conditionals. Explain what tenses are used and why.

If we were meant to live up in the sky, we would have been born with wings!
If 60s architecture hadn't happened, we would be making similar mistakes today.

In both examples, the second and third conditional forms are mixed.

2 You can use a mixed conditional to talk about a past action affecting a present situation, as in the second example above. Finish these mixed conditional sentences in a suitable way.

EXAMPLE: If we had bought that house, we *would be short of money now.*

a If people hadn't objected to the plans, the building …
b If Tom had remembered to book a table at the restaurant, we …
c If I hadn't seen that programme, I …
d If we had set off earlier, we …
e If she hadn't answered the advert, she …

3 You can also use mixed conditionals to talk about how a different present situation would have affected a past situation, as in this example:

If the city centre was traffic-free, the council wouldn't have needed to build all these car parks.

Finish these sentences in a similar way, using the ideas in brackets.

a If high-rise buildings were of better quality, more people (choose to live in them in the first place)
b If there weren't so many distractions, you (tidy up your bedroom by now)
c If the suburbs were smaller, local taxes (be so high for the last 20 years)
d If the supermarket was open 24 hours, I (go out at 3 am this morning to buy you some paracetamol)

G → page 175

4 Match the sentence beginnings a–f with their endings 1–6. Which sentence contains a mixed conditional? Notice the different ways of expressing a negative condition in a–c.

a **In the absence of** any shops,
b **Without** a police force,
c **Given a lack of** public transport,
d Unless public services were maintained,
e Should all schools be closed,
f If public hospitals hadn't been created,

1 rubbish would pile up on the streets.
2 education could no longer be taken for granted.
3 crime rates would increase dramatically.
4 people would be paying huge sums for healthcare.
5 consumers would have to adopt a different lifestyle.
6 bicycle shops might do substantially more business.

5 Discuss the impact of these problems on a city and its inhabitants. Try to use the sentence openers from 4 and different conditional structures.

a food shortages
b dangerous levels of pollution
c power cuts
d collapse of the banking system due to cybercrime

Vocabulary

Topic set – buildings

6 Read the article about the architect Sir Norman Foster. For questions 1–12, decide which answer, A, B, C or D, best fits each space. There is an example at the beginning (0).

Example:

0 A chose   **B** fixed   **C** dealt   **D** wished

0	A	B	C	D
	<u>—</u>			

The grand designer

When asked to select his favourite building, Sir Norman Foster (**0**) .... a Jumbo jet. His own buildings frequently (**1**) .... materials and technology developed by the aerospace industry. Perhaps his most (**2**) .... building is the Hong Kong and Shanghai Bank, a massive construction of three linked towers 41 (**3**) .... high. His most ambitious European (**4**) .... has been the reconstruction of the Reichstag as the new German parliament building. He has also built a metro (**5**) .... in Bilbao, and two space-age communications towers in Barcelona and Santiago de Compostela.

Foster (**6**) .... in the vertical city, an architect's dream that began a hundred years ago and is still (**7**) .... to be fully realised. He says that the city is in a continuous process of renewal; if buildings cannot (**8**) .... to social or technological change, then unless they are outstanding, they should be replaced. It's all about (**9**) .... the past and the future.

One of Foster's recent (**10**) .... has been to re-design part of a famous London landmark, Trafalgar Square. Aiming to (**11**) .... pollution and improve safety by re-routing traffic away from the north side of the square, he has created an impressive pedestrian (**12**) .... in front of the National Gallery and transformed Trafalgar Square into a truly grand urban space.

1	**A** lend	**B** fetch	**C** borrow	**D** bring
2	**A** famous	**B** known	**C** understood	**D** common
3	**A** flights	**B** levels	**C** storeys	**D** stages
4	**A** activity	**B** project	**C** occupation	**D** post
5	**A** method	**B** plan	**C** routine	**D** system
6	**A** believes	**B** hopes	**C** relies	**D** depends
7	**A** standing	**B** expecting	**C** waiting	**D** resting
8	**A** alter	**B** adapt	**C** fit	**D** match
9	**A** steadying	**B** settling	**C** estimating	**D** balancing
10	**A** trials	**B** challenges	**C** questions	**D** attempts
11	**A** reduce	**B** shorten	**C** dilute	**D** lower
12	**A** site	**B** district	**C** region	**D** area

Word formation

7 There are a number of words containing the prefix *re-* in the article, such as *renewal* and *re-routing*. Make new words from the ones below, using the same prefix. Sometimes words with different parts of speech can be made. Use some of the words to complete sentences a–d.

consider   construct   generate
open   possess   write

a The old industrial city of Duisberg has been .... and now has new, cleaner industries right in its centre, alongside schools and housing.

b Following extensive fire damage, the timber-framed buildings have now been fully .... in their original style.

c The city council's .... of the enquiry into noise pollution has been supported by local residents.

d Anyone who has left the city for the suburbs should .... their move, particularly in the light of how far rents have fallen in the centre.

Paper 1 Part 3 Multiple matching

This part of the Reading paper focuses on your ability to find specific information in a set of texts, or in one text that has been divided into sections. There are 15 questions in all.

For this task, you will often need to locate words and phrases in the text(s) that mean the same as the wording used in the questions. Sometimes more than one text will cover the same subject, so you need to decide which one matches the question wording.

EXAM ADVICE

- Look at the title and any information you are given about the text or texts.
- Skim the texts for their general meaning.
- Read through the questions carefully, underlining any key words and phrases.
- Scan the texts for the specific information you need, rather than reading them in detail.
- Don't be tempted to choose a text simply because it has the same wording as in the question. This may lead you to an incorrect answer.
- When you find an answer in a text, underline that part of the text and write the question number next to it.
- Don't spend too much time looking for an answer. Leave any challenging questions until the end and go on to the next ones.
- When you've finished, go back and look again at any questions you left unanswered. If you still don't know, guess. Never leave an answer blank on your answer sheet.
- Aim to spend up to 20 minutes on this task – even though Part 3 contains half of the total number of questions on Paper 1, they are only 'single weighted', whereas the questions in Parts 1 and 2 count double.

You are going to read a magazine article in which four people talk about driving. For questions 1–15, choose from the people (A–D). The people may be chosen more than once.

Mark your answers on the separate answer sheet.

Which person

chose a car that disappointed a family member?	1
couldn't really afford their chosen car?	2
enjoys driving while listening to music?	3
has never bought their own car?	4
used to imagine driving somewhere fast at night?	5
spends a lot of money on petrol?	6
had to consider the size of the car before buying it?	7
qualified as a car driver in order to compete?	8
complains about their car?	9
had an accident in their car?	10
gives someone close to them a regular lift?	11
remembers one night-time occasion that was special?	12
knows a lot of information about certain cars?	13
gets positive comments from other road users?	14
would like to drive something different?	15

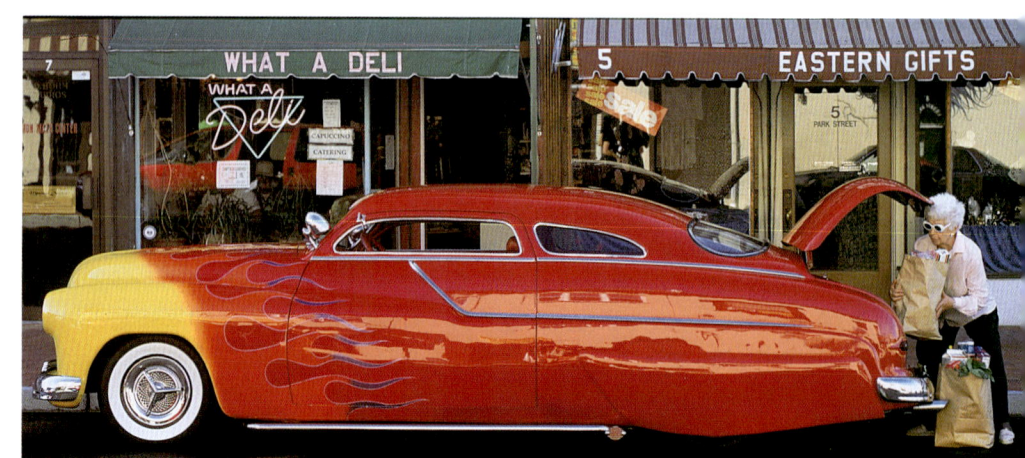

Me and my wheels

Four people talked to us about their favourite vehicles.

A Brett

I dreamt about having the car I drive now when I was at school and almost ruined myself financially to buy it! When I first got it, it had a really loud sound system, and I reversed into a brand-new car because I couldn't hear the horn beeping at me to stop. It has lots of speakers and there's nothing better than driving through the city with all my favourite tunes blasting out. My best moment was when I was at the Glastonbury pop festival and drove it up the hill there after dark. The whole of the site below was blinking with lights and it was a fantastic moment. On the downside, it isn't comfortable on long journeys, and it drinks fuel like a fish. I've got a pair of tiny red, black and green boxing gloves hanging from the mirror. Now that I'm a father, pressure has been put on me to get rid of it. I won't go that far but I do have a Punto now, as the family car.

B Simon

As a child, I used to love memorising facts and few delighted me as much as those about cars. I can still produce all sorts of trivia about 0–60 acceleration times, top speeds, and the engine sizes of all the fastest and most exciting cars. I'm very fond of car magazines because of that, and I go through as many as I can get my hands on! Whenever I visit Britain, I pick some up and enjoy the deliciously technical writing and wonderful shots of car interiors – all those dials! If I couldn't get to sleep as a teenager, I'd pretend to be doing a long journey in the dark in an open-top sports car. But do you know what I currently drive? A VW estate with a small engine. It won't do; I must change my life.

C Marie

I haven't always had four wheels and, in fact, I only learned to drive a car three years ago. I passed my test quite quickly after that and was lucky enough to be given my car – a Mazda sports – as a present. It's very quick off the mark. I really switched to cars instead of bikes in order to join Formula Women, an organisation that's been set up to encourage more women to go into racing. I love the challenge of it all and I know my biking days have helped me to find the best racing line on the track. I've been doing really well recently. Dad comes to all my races and likes to get the crowd behind me! Mum used to worry about the danger involved but she's OK about it now, and she thinks I'm a good road user. Once a week I come and collect her in the Mazda and we go off to do the out-of-town shopping bit together.

D Sonja

My mum was almost in tears when I said I was going to buy the Mini. I'd previously owned an open-top Audi, which she loved being driven around in, but I felt it was time to downsize. I must admit I felt some sadness, knowing I wouldn't be able to drive with the wind whipping through my hair. But I soon got attached to the Mini. When I went for a test drive in one to see if it was really suitable, I realised that they are actually very roomy. Even my husband can fit in it and he's incredibly tall. It's faster than you'd think and I've already received three points on my licence for speeding, unfortunately. Everyone seems to have a great affection for Minis. Drivers always nod and some even start chatting about the car when I'm stopped at traffic lights. My favourite journey is driving home each evening during spring and autumn just as the light starts to fade.

A world of music

Speaking

1 Look at these two photos and discuss their similarities and differences.

2 **2·19** Now listen to the recording, which is an example of Paper 5 Part 2. One student will talk about the pictures for about a minute. Then another student will talk briefly at the end. How do their views differ?

3 What types of music do you enjoy? What do you dislike? Why?

Vocabulary

Topic set – music

4 **2·19** Listen to the recording again and tick any vocabulary you hear in the sets below.

Perform	Performers	Performance
play	musician	concert
take part	orchestra	gig
participate	cellist	festival
join in	conductor	rehearsal
sing a solo	choir	show

Explain the differences in meaning of the words in the 'Performance' column.

5 If a *cellist* plays a cello, who plays these instruments? Be careful with spelling.

a violin
b piano
c drums
d saxophone
e trumpet
f flute

Reading

6 Read the title and the first paragraph of the article. What is a *tribute band*?

7 Skim the main text for general meaning. Then underline content clues, as well as linkers and reference words. Time yourself as you do this.

Glastonbudget – the main event on the musical calendar for tribute bands

The Glastonbury Festival, which takes place in Britain in late June, offers an impressive line-up of famous bands over four days, but tickets aren't cheap at around £200. Glastonbudget, as the name suggests, is a low-priced music festival that specialises in booking tribute bands. A tribute band performs the songs, or 'cover versions', of the particular group they admire, usually copying the group's appearance closely and sometimes playing their music rather well. The tribute band's name is often deliberately similar to the original one, so Dread Zeppelin is a reggae version of Led Zeppelin. There are tribute bands everywhere: Umma Gumma in Brazil, Mun Floyd in Italy, Pink Division in Norway and The Pink Tones in Spain are just four of the many Pink Floyd sound-alikes.

Glastonbudget was dreamed up back in 2003 by Nick Tanner, who runs a village pub in Leicestershire, and his sister. **1** [ ] . Nick loved holding it, as it earned double the money of a normal opening. As the pub wasn't big enough to fit in many more people, Nick suggested looking for another venue.

A year later they found themselves standing in a field, having spent £160,000 in setting up the first Glastonbudget festival. **2** [ ] Due to a combination of hard work, donations and goodwill from the local community, ticket sales have increased steadily. Nowadays, it is a sell-out event, not to mention being the biggest tribute and new music festival in Europe.

Like the budget airlines, there is a system of selling a limited number of low-price tickets: depending on when you book, it's possible to buy a weekend ticket for as little as 99 pence. **3** [ ] Even if they are not big-name acts, this makes it an extremely attractive alternative to Glastonbury.

People who attend Glastonbudget often comment not only on how well it is organised, but on how much of a community atmosphere there is at the event. **4** [ ] Not many festivals can boast a line-up that includes Coldplay, Guns N' Roses, The Foo Fighters and The Killers. Neither can Glastonbudget, although it comes quite close: Coldplace, Guns 2 Roses, The Four Fighters and The Fillers all rocked the main stage this year.

Guns 2 Roses are so close to the original band that when Guns N' Roses lead singer Axl Rose refused to promote the band's latest album, the record company called them in to help. **5** [ ]

Another popular act at Glastonbudget this year was Iziggy, formed by lorry driver Brian Spiers after workmates kept pointing out his amazing likeness to Iggy Pop. Brian – who was mobbed at a recent Iggy And The Stooges show in London – explained that he had had to drop three jeans sizes and get some singing lessons before starting the band. **6** [ ] He's planning to get them removed by laser eventually.

7 [ ] Since the festival's second year, the organisers have featured more and more young, up-and-coming local bands. Closely associated with the Soar Valley Music Centre, the festival also provides training for young people in different aspects of the music industry, from sound engineering to manning the ticket lines.

---

8 Look for the missing information in sentences A–H and decide on your answers. Check that the extra sentence doesn't fit anywhere.

- **A** Singer Gavin Willbourn explained that the band even hosted the album's London launch.

- **B** Despite losing money on that occasion, the festival has gone from strength to strength ever since.

- **C** Having chosen such diverse bands, the organisers were confident of success from the start.

- **D** Near or total strangers become part of a genuinely music-loving festival and enjoy some entertaining bands.

- **E** He also has to spend £50 per gig buying make-up to cover his tattoos because his hero doesn't have any.

- **F** The two were discussing ways to expand the monthly tribute band night.

- **G** This rises to a maximum of just over £50, which includes camping and parking.

- **H** Glastonbudget isn't just about tribute bands though.

9 Discuss these questions in pairs.

- **a** Why are there so many tribute bands performing today?
- **b** Can a cover version ever be better than the original song?
- **c** Would you pay to see a tribute band? Why? / Why not?
- **d** Have music festivals become too commercial?

Concessive clauses

1 Look at these examples from 22.1 and explain the function of the underlined words and the clauses they introduce.

  a <u>Despite</u> losing money on that occasion, the festival has gone from strength to strength ever since.

  b <u>Even though</u> they are not big-name acts, this makes it an extremely attractive alternative to Glastonbury.

  c I love listening to the 12-string guitar, <u>although</u> I can't play one myself.

  d My brother and I listen to each other's albums, <u>even if</u> the bands are sometimes very different.

  e <u>While</u> not at a professional level, I enjoy singing in a local choir.

Match statements 1 to 6 sentences a–e. Some apply to more than one sentence.

1 The same subject is mentioned in both clauses.

2 In this sentence, it is not possible to re-arrange the order of the clauses.

3 The subjects of each clause are different.

4 The first clause has no verb or subject, but the subject is understood.

5 The main clause has a subject and a verb, but the other clause does not.

6 The underlined word is a different part of speech from the other examples.

Corpus spot

Be careful when using the preposition *despite* – the *Cambridge Learner Corpus* shows that exam candidates often make mistakes with this word. Compare *in spite of* in this example.

The singer was excellent **despite** the poor sound system.
OR

The singer was excellent **in spite of** the poor sound system.

NOT The singer was excellent ~~despite of~~ the poor sound system.

2 Join these sentences together using the conjunction or preposition in brackets and making any grammatical or stylistic changes necessary. An example is given.

  EXAMPLE: James has injured his hand. He will play in tonight's concert. (in spite of)
  In spite of injuring his hand, James will play in tonight's concert.

  a The concert was supposed to start at 8.00. The concert actually started at 9.30. (although)

  b The stage was very small. The group did a lot of dancing on the stage. (though)

  c Damon Albarn is in the band Gorillaz. He is still a member of Blur. (despite)

  d I manage to keep up to date by watching YouTube. I can't get to many gigs. (even though)

  e You are allowed to use the school instruments in the music room. No school instruments should be taken away from the music room. (while)

  f We might miss the first band. We'll still get to the festival in time for Arctic Monkeys. (even if)

G→ page 175

Complex sentences

3 Both of these examples from 21.1 begin with a reason, to explain the underlined information. What is the effect of putting the reason first? You may want to look back at the whole text.

  a As the pub wasn't big enough to fit in many more people, <u>Nick suggested looking for another venue</u>.

  b Due to a combination of hard work, donations and goodwill from the local community, <u>ticket sales have increased steadily</u>.

Which sentence starts with a conjunction? What other conjunctions are used in this way?

G→ page 175

4 Example b and examples c and d below illustrate sentence 'fronting', where a phrase containing information relevant to the main clause is put first.

  c Having chosen such diverse bands, the organisers were confident of success from the start.

  d Closely associated with the Soar Valley Music Centre, the festival also provides training for young people in different aspects of the music industry.

Exam spot

Using complex sentences on Papers 2 and 5 may impress the examiners!

5 Read part of an exam answer on the topic of live music. Varying how the sentences begin makes the writing more effective.

> I really enjoy going to places in which you can see a good concert. When I listen to live music, I always have a special feeling of having fun and relaxing at the same time. Sometimes, when I really like the music I am listening to, I forget the real world and start dreaming. Although I like almost everything about music, if I can choose between a classical concert and a blues concert I am going to choose the second one. Seeing blues or soul bands in concert is one of the things that I really enjoy.

Which sentence starts with a concessive clause? Which sentence uses an extended noun phrase as a fronting technique?

The writing could still be improved. Which adverb is used three times? What other adverbs could be used instead?

6 Rewrite the sentences in a–e to produce a single complex sentence. The first word of the new sentence is given in brackets.

EXAMPLE: *The Squier guitar sounds very similar to a proper Stratocaster. It is a low-priced guitar. This is good. (What)*
What is good about the Squier is that although it is a low-priced guitar, it sounds very similar to a proper Stratocaster.

a It was late. We decided not to stay for the final band. (Since)
b The cello, which has been beautifully made by hand and is reddish brown in colour, has an excellent sound. (Beautifully)
c Ellen learnt the recorder for three years. Then she went on to the flute. (Having)
d The trumpeter is technically brilliant. However, his playing has neither energy nor emotion. (Despite)
e The conductor made a mistake. The soloist had to miss out a whole verse. (Due to)

7 For questions 1–12, read the text and decide which answer (A, B, C or D) best fits each gap. There is an example at the beginning (0).

Example:

0 A remains **B** keeps **C** stays **D** continues

0	A	B	C	D
	—			

GEORGE GERSHWIN

George Gershwin, who was born in Brooklyn in 1898, (**o**) ...... one of the world's most popular composers today. He lived and worked in the perfect era for his unique talent to (**1**) .... It was at a time when the Jazz Age coincided with composers like Berg, as well as the first Broadway musicals. Although a gifted pianist, he had only (**2**) ..... reading skills in music, but due to his regular attendance at concerts, he was able to (**3**) ..... up his own repertoire. In 1924, Gershwin worked with his brother Ira on a musical comedy called *Lady Be Good*. This proved to be a successful (**4**) ...... that continued for the rest of his life.

George Gershwin was determined to (**5**) ..... an impression as a serious composer, which he also achieved in 1924. At its New York premiere, one of his most famous (**6**) ....., *Rhapsody in Blue*, received (**7**) ..... applause from an audience that included musical celebrities such as the Russian composers Rachmaninov and Stravinsky. Gershwin (**8**) ..... this success with innovative orchestral works such as *An American in Paris* and, in 1935, the memorable opera *Porgy and Bess*.

No one has been able to match Gershwin's ability to write original works that (**9**) ..... the boundaries of jazz, opera and classical music and his (**10**) ..... on modern music has been enormous. It is appropriate to (**11**) ..... that he made the American composer a respectable (**12**) ..... around the world, at a time when very little American music was being performed. Sadly, Gershwin died at the early age of 38.

1	**A** become	**B** develop	**C** result	**D** invent
2	**A** key	**B** plain	**C** basic	**D** easy
3	**A** grow	**B** pull	**C** move	**D** build
4	**A** company	**B** teamwork	**C** pair	**D** partnership
5	**A** make	**B** get	**C** put	**D** take
6	**A** writings	**B** exercises	**C** designs	**D** compositions
7	**A** hot	**B** wild	**C** deep	**D** full
8	**A** brought	**B** followed	**C** adopted	**D** led
9	**A** enter	**B** split	**C** cross	**D** carry
10	**A** power	**B** direction	**C** control	**D** influence
11	**A** join	**B** mix	**C** add	**D** link
12	**A** figure	**B** body	**C** human	**D** character

DO YOU NEED MORE PRACTICE?
CD-ROM UNITS 21–22

Writing folder 11

Reports

In Part 2 of Paper 2 you may be asked to write a report. This will involve the presentation of mainly factual information, with suggestions or a recommendation. Any report needs to be clearly organised with an introduction and conclusion. Headings usually help to signpost the content and some use of bullet points may also be appropriate. Reports are often written in an impersonal style, using the passive.

1   Read the following exam question and its answer. Then rewrite the answer, making the improvements suggested in a–d.

   a   What would you add at the beginning and end of the report?

   b   How could the highlighted headings be improved?

   c   Why are the underlined parts of the answer inappropriate to a report? How could the passive be used to address this?

   d   Where you see the symbol §, use a conjunction to join the two sentences together, making any other changes necessary.

Every year, you help at a local music festival, which takes place outdoors over one weekend. The organisers want to improve the festival and have asked you to write a short report. You should comment on the facilities that were available at this year's festival and make recommendations for next year.

Write your **report**.

Dear Organisers

Here is my report

_____

The place in town where you hold the festival

The site this year was disappointing, mainly because it wasn't large enough. There was some car parking. § Many people had to park over two kilometres away.

Eating

There was some choice of catering at the site. § Very little vegetarian food was offered. Also, my friends and I had to go to one end of the field for food and then we ran over to the opposite end for a drink. This drove us nuts!

The programme

People seemed to enjoy the performances. § Each band should be allowed more time on stage.

The cost

Several members of the audience thought the tickets were unusually cheap. § The price could be raised next year. This would help us, wouldn't it?

Recommendations

You need a bigger site and better-organised catering – some changes to the timing of the event too.

_____

151 words

2 You could be asked to write a report about shopping facilities in your town or city. If so, you should think carefully about the group of 'shoppers' you are writing the report for. This is different from the target reader of the report, who will be specified – for example, the festival organisers in the last question, or your boss at the tourist office.

For each target group below, decide which types of shopping it would be suitable to focus on, choosing from a–j. Some will be used more than once. Remember to consider the advantages or disadvantages given in brackets and to recommend things that are realistic in the time allowed.

Target group

1 American exchange students on a limited budget
2 Elderly tourists visiting as a group one weekend
3 Business people spending a free hour after their appointments
4 Families camping outside the town for a week

Types of shopping

a an exclusive gift shop (in the main square)
b a large toyshop (limited parking)
c a central stationery shop (open late)
d the Saturday crafts market (very colourful)
e a discount computer warehouse (plenty of parking)
f a sports equipment store (good value)
g a supermarket on the edge of town (massive)
h a music store (very noisy)
i the university bookshop (discounts available)
j an art gallery (includes a coffee shop)

3 Now read this exam question.

Some British students are on an exchange programme at your college for a month. The college has asked you to write a report on local shopping facilities for the teacher who is in charge of the group. You should give advice on best value for money, including areas such as food, study materials and souvenirs.

Write your **report**.

4 Match definitions a–j to these words about money and shopping. Which two are adjectives?

bargain   brand   budget   competitive   economical   expense   fortune   purchase   savings   stock

a as good as or better than other prices, services, etc.
b something that is on sale for less than its real value
c a lot of money
d something that you buy or the act of buying something
e not using a lot of money
f the money that you keep in an account
g not expensive
h the money that you spend on something
i a type of product made by a particular company
j all the goods that are available in a shop

5 Now add some of the words from 4 in phrases a–f, making the nouns plural where necessary. You can use these phrases in your report in 6.

Food
a luxury/ low-cost .... of
b .... prices

Study materials
c in / out of ....
d on a tight ....

Souvenirs
e (not) cost a ....
f hunt for ....

6 Plan what you are going to write, starting with the ideas in 2. Remember that you are writing to the teacher, not the students, so your report should be fairly formal.

7 Write your report, using suitable headings and including an introduction and conclusion.

Speaking

1   In pairs, look at the photographs. What is each photo of?
    Decide which set of words goes with each photograph.

    a   a storm, thunder, a flash, lightning
    b   to be stranded, torrential rain
    c   a peak, ash, an eruption, gases
    d   cracks, to tremble, to shake

2   Ask and answer the following questions.

    a   Have you ever experienced a natural disaster? If so, what was it like?
    b   Have you ever seen a natural disaster reported on the television?
        If so, which?
    c   Do you think there is anything you can do to avoid a natural disaster?

Listening

3   **2 20** You are going to hear an interview with a woman, Liz, who
    together with her friend, Dave, had a frightening experience when
    they were camping. For questions 1–10, complete the sentences.

Dave thought at first that the cloud was the result of a [   ] 1
Liz says that what she saw was different from a [   ] 2
Liz thought it was odd because it was completely [   ] 3
The heat melted the [   ] 4 of the coffee pot.
Dave and Liz tried at first to reach [   ] 5
Dave and Liz had been protected in the hole by [   ] 6
Dave and Liz put their [   ] 7 round their heads to help them to breathe.
It was hard to walk because of the depth of the [   ] 8
There was an awful smell similar to [   ] 9
Liz now regrets not having a [   ] 10 with them.

Vocabulary

Phrasal verbs with *off*

4 Match these phrasal verbs you heard in the interview with their meaning.

removed   began the journey exploding

1 It was like a bomb *going off*.
2 We *took off* our shirts.
3 When we *set off* it was difficult to breathe.

Now complete the following sentences, choosing a phrasal verb that means the same as the word or words in brackets. Make sure you use the correct tense.

tell off	call off
let off	cut off
show off	wear off
send off	log off
break off	

a Tom (spoke angrily to) the boys for throwing stones at the windows.
b The Prime Minister's visit to Australia has been (cancelled) because of the floods at home.
c Anne (put in the post) fifty job applications before she got an interview.
d The excitement of living in New York soon (disappeared) and then I felt homesick.
e The village was (isolated) because of the flooding.
f My sister (ended) her engagement to Pete yesterday.
g The thief was (not punished) by the magistrate as it was his first offence.
h I (broke the connection with) my laptop and went to bed at about midnight.

Words often confused

5 In the following sentences there are two words or phrases which are often confused by students. Decide which one is correct, then write another sentence to show how the other word or phrase is used.

a We waited for the emergency services but *at the end / in the end* our neighbour rescued us from the floods.
b Our two-way radio was *invaluable / priceless* during the storm.
c You don't see many people taking risks outdoors *nowadays / actually*.
d Questions about another eruption were *raised / risen* at the meeting.
e *Lie / Lay* down and try to rest until the weather improves.
f *Tell / Say* me the story about how you coped after the earthquake.
g I'm an excellent outdoor *cook / cooker*.
h My camping gear was *stolen / robbed* yesterday.
i I *damaged / injured* my leg when I was running for shelter.
j My friend was very *sympathetic / friendly* when I broke my arm.
k Jean is so *sensible / sensitive* that she cries whenever she watches a disaster movie.

6 For questions 1–12, read the text below and think of the word which best fits each gap. Use only one word in each gap. There is an example at the beginning (o).

An Unchanging Planet?

If you think of Earth (0) _AS_ a stable and unchanging planet, think again. Nearly five billion years after it was first formed, the Earth is still developing – (1) .... alarming ways. Unlike earthquakes, which strike (2) .... warning, volcanoes build up (3) .... months and are usually easier to predict. But their spectacular climax is no (4) .... devastating. A volcano can erupt in many different ways and it can spill out a variety of materials. Mild eruptions spurt gas, steam and hot water and are (5) .... geysers. Larger volcanoes shoot out ash and large chunks of hot rock into (6) .... atmosphere, and enormous fountains of glowing red hot lava that flow (7) .... the sides of the volcano. This liquid lava quickly thickens into a steaming sticky carpet (8) .... can travel 150 km before it stops and turns solid. Lava floods (9) .... fire to and destroy (10) .... that stands in their way. Famously, in AD 79, the Roman city of Pompeii (11) .... covered in lava and ash, preserving buildings and some of their contents to (12) .... day.

I wish / If only

1 In the recording, Liz says that she wished she'd taken a radio with her.

You can use *wish* / *if only* + past perfect tense to talk about a wish or regret in the past.

What other things do you think Liz wished after the eruption? Suggest five other things she might have said.

EXAMPLE: *I wish we had chosen a*
different place to camp.

Now talk together about things that you personally regret doing or not doing in the past.

I wish I hadn't gone to that boring party.
If only I had worked harder for the test.

2 When Liz says, 'if only we could get in the tent, we'd be safe' she is saying what she felt at that particular moment.

You can use *wish* / *if only* + past simple or *would*/*could* to talk about a wish or a regret in the present.

Now write down ten things that you wish for right at this moment. Compare your sentences with a partner.

EXAMPLES: *I wish I was/were on a*
beach instead of in class.
I wish I could have
something to eat.

Note: You can't say: *I wish I would /*
He wishes he would / They wish they
would, etc.

3 After *wish* and *if only*, *would* can be used to complain about or criticise a person or situation.

EXAMPLES: *I wish it would stop raining.* – It's raining at the moment and I want it to stop.
If only my neighbour would be quiet. – She's making a lot of noise at the moment.
I wish he would stop smoking. – I want him to stop smoking now (for example because the smoke is getting in my eyes).

Is there anything bothering you at the moment? Write down a few examples using *would*.

4 *Wish* is often confused with *hope*.

I hope I see you soon.
I wish I could see you soon.

Hope usually takes a present tense with a future meaning. When we use *hope* we usually don't know or can't tell the outcome, whereas with *wish* we do know the facts and they are the opposite of what we want.

Decide on the correct alternative in the following sentences.

a I *hope* / *wish* the rain stops soon.
b I *hope* / *wish* you can come to my party.
c I *hope* / *wish* I could speak Arabic.
d I *hope* / *wish* Peter would finish writing his book.
e I *hope* / *wish* I had remembered to bring the sleeping bags.

> ### Corpus spot
>
> Correct the errors that exam candidates have made with *wish* and *hope* in these sentences from the *Cambridge Learner Corpus*.
> **a** I wish I had know it two days ago.
> **b** I wish you were there with us.
> **c** I hope you would be able to give me some more information.
> **d** I wish you can come to Japan.
> **e** I wish that you have a good time.
> **f** So, I hope I could help you out a little bit.
> **g** I wish I haven't said that.

5 Here are some other expressions followed by the past tense.

a *as if* / *as though*
It wasn't like a smoke cloud, it was as if it were alive. – It wasn't alive.

b *would rather*
This takes an infinitive without *to* or a past tense.
I'd rather not tell you what really happened.
I'd rather you didn't ask me about the experience.
(Don't confuse *I'd rather* and *I'd better* (= I had better) – they mean different things.)

Say what you *would rather do* in each situation.

EXAMPLE: *Would you like to go camping?*
– *I'd rather stay in a hotel.*
– *I'd rather we stayed in a hotel.*

a Would you like to come with us for a pizza?
b Would you like to study engineering?
c Would you like to travel to the Moon?
d Would you like me to teach you Latin?
e Would you like me to buy you an iPod?

6 For the following questions, complete the second sentence so that it has a similar meaning to the first sentence, using the word given. Do not change the word given. You must use between two and five words, including the word given.

1 I regret not taking the park ranger's advice.
TAKEN
I .... the park ranger's advice.

2 I think it's better for the children to stay inside in bad weather.
RATHER
I .... inside in bad weather.

3 What a pity we didn't see any wildlife on our trip.
ONLY
If .... wildlife on our trip.

4 I don't like living in an earthquake zone.
WISH
I .... somewhere else.

5 Don't walk so fast, I can't keep up with you!
WISH
I .... walk so fast, I can't keep up with you!

6 I'd prefer you not to repeat what I've just told you.
RATHER
I .... repeat what I've just told you.

Ⓖ→ page 175

Vocabulary

Word formation

7 Liz and Dave had to 'unroll' their trousers to empty out the ash that had collected in them.

What sort of things do you:

a untie?   **f** unearth?
b unbutton? **g** unfasten?
c undo?   **h** unlock?
d unwrap?   **i** unwind?
e uncover?

Topic set – weather

8 Fill in the missing letters for these weather words.

a The Mid-West states of the USA suffer from TO_ _ _D_ _S.
b A typhoon is a type of T_ _P_ _ _ _ storm.
c It gets B_ _L_ _G hot inside the club when it's full of dancers.
d The weather F_ _ _C_ _ _ for tomorrow is quite good.
e My fingers were F_ _ _ _I_ _ cold after building the snowman.
f It P_ _ _ _D with rain all day, so we couldn't play tennis.
g H_ _ _ _C_ _ _S usually occur in the Caribbean.
h DR_ _ _ _T occurs when there isn't enough rain.
i Britain has a D_ _P climate, whereas parts of India are often H_ M_ D.

Exam folder 12

Paper 1 Part 1
Multiple choice – non-fiction

In this part of the Reading paper you are tested on a detailed understanding of the text. For more information and advice on multiple-choice tasks, consult Exam folder 10 (multiple choice – fiction).

1   You are going to read an extract from a newspaper article.

    Skim through the text – what is it about?

2   Now look at questions 1–8. Choose the answer (A, B, C or D) which you think fits best according to the text.

    Underline the part of the text where you think the answer is.

1   What is the problem the writer has at the beginning of her holiday?
    A   The weather is not good enough for painting.
    B   She's brought the wrong materials with her.
    C   There are no animals to paint.
    D   She can't reproduce the exact colours.

2   The writer hid her work because
    A   she believed Royale paints better.
    B   it wasn't good enough to sell.
    C   she thought it would disappoint Royale.
    D   it was only a quick sketch.

3   What does the writer mean by the phrase 'what I am up to' in lines 38–39?
    A   What I am painting.
    B   What I will give him.
    C   What I can teach him.
    D   What I might do.

4   What does the writer say about her previous painting holiday?
    A   She preferred the teacher she had had then.
    B   The landscape was more familiar to her.
    C   Her technique had improved much faster.
    D   She had been able to complete a number of paintings.

5   The writer says that Susan Scott-Thomas
    A   looks at things in a different way from her.
    B   is a very capable person.
    C   is not as good at cooking as her.
    D   was a solicitor before going to Africa.

6   What does 'it' refer to in line 85?
    A   the holiday
    B   the country
    C   the colour and shape
    D   the finished painting

7   What is a suitable title for the article?
    A   An unsuccessful holiday
    B   Painting the natural world
    C   Learning to work with others
    D   Travelling in a different country

8   What is the writer's purpose in writing this text?
    A   To encourage people to take up painting as a hobby.
    B   To persuade people to visit Zimbabwe.
    C   To describe how she combines her hobby with a holiday.
    D   To criticise the organisers of her African holiday.

By the middle of the second day I know I'm in trouble. In front of me the land stretches up and away towards a distant hill, and into the space, between that summit and me, is crowded one of the most vivid concentrations of colour I have ever seen. It starts with the trees. The wet season is only a few weeks off and, almost as if they can smell the coming rains, they have put out their leaves. They are no ordinary green and the dry grasses beneath them are ablaze with golds, browns and reds. I want to recreate this scene with watercolours. Although I can make a try at it with words, trying to paint it in my sketch book is another matter altogether. I've already made one attempt: a series of zigzags in orange and red, with bluish trees placed across them, which now lies face down in the grass beside me.

I've put it there because the last thing I want right now is for someone else to come along and look at it. A young man called Royale walks up the hill. Royale is a sculptor, and, with several other local men, produces pieces of work in the local stone. Recently, and quite suddenly, this work, and that of several other local co-operatives, has acquired an international reputation. I certainly don't want a man capable of such things looking at my own awful brush-strokes. So I put my foot, as casually as I can, on the finished painting beside me and we resume the conversation started earlier in the day.

line 38 I want to talk to Royale about his life here. He, however, is only interested in <u>what I am up to</u>. To begin with, it seems that he considers me a fellow artist, and for a moment I find myself staring into the depths of embarrassment. But when he asks me, 'What is painting like?' I realise that this professional artist has never painted anything in his life before. He just wants a go with my colours.

When I signed up for this holiday, I was hoping for an experience like the one I had had four years earlier in Wales. That was my first painting holiday, and I loved it. Two things made it great. First was the teacher, a man called Robin, who showed me that what is important about drawing and painting is not the finished article but the process of completing it. The second element of that week was the place. I grew up in places like that, and I connected with it immediately. But it was stupid of me to think that I could reproduce the experience down here, deep in the Southern Hemisphere. Zimbabwe is not a part of me, nor I of it. Trying to draw it for the first time, from a standing start, is like trying to start a conversation in Swahili.

There were compensations. The holiday was wonderfully organised by a friend of mine – Susan Scott-Thomas. Admittedly, there are some rather large differences between us – she's extremely wealthy and she inherited a farm in Africa when she was in her mid-twenties, and instead of taking the easy option of becoming a solicitor and staying in London, she came out to reclaim the land and rebuild the decaying farmhouse. In the process, she learnt how to lay foundations and make clay bricks. All of which she did while I was just about mastering making sauce for pasta.

Even my disastrous painting didn't detract from enjoying the holiday. Painting really forces you to look at things, to consider their shape and colour. And even if <u>it</u> is line 85 a disaster, that process of looking and thinking and transferring those thoughts into movements of your hand leaves an imprint of what you have seen. By the end of the week I have still not produced anything to hang on my walls, although there is a drawing of a local schoolboy of which I am rather fond, not because it is much good, but because it was so challenging to do.

24.1 Anything for a laugh

Speaking

1 Work in pairs. Stop your partner after one minute and answer the short question.

First long turn (photos 1 and 2):

Student A
Compare the photographs and say what makes something funny on film.

Student B
Which type of film do you prefer to watch at the cinema?

Second long turn (photos 3 and 4):

Student B
Compare the photographs and say what is important when watching live performances.

Student A
What kind of live show would you like to attend?

Reading

2 You are going to read four 'urban myths' – modern-day stories, usually humorous, which people enjoy telling each other at parties or at the pub. First, read questions 1–15.

In which urban myth does someone

need to withdraw money?	1
have an injured pet?	2
appear unconcerned?	3
mistake a person for a criminal?	4
have urgent treatment?	5
have a conversation in an elevator?	6
go to a restaurant?	7
intend to use public transport?	8
disobey a request?	9
have to make a hard decision?	10
break the rules?	11
try to hide something?	12
order someone to leave their job?	13
receive an apology?	14
have something taken from them?	15

3 Now scan the four texts for the answers, ignoring the highlighted words. Compare your answers with another student.

A

A woman was looking forward to an important dinner party, where her guests would include her husband's new boss. She wanted to serve a really special meal, so she bought a whole salmon, which she cooked and prepared beautifully. The dinner party started well, and the woman received many compliments about the starters she served. At a suitable moment, she went out to get the fish from the kitchen, where she found a rather horrifying sight: her cat was sitting on the work surface, tucking into the fish. She shooed the cat away and, in a state of total panic, hastily disguised the damage with some carefully placed slices of lemon and cucumber. Then she took the salmon through, to gasps of admiration. However, when the woman went to the kitchen to make the coffee, she found her cat writhing around on the floor in obvious pain. Convinced that the salmon was to blame, the poor woman went back in to tell her guests the truth. They all rushed off to hospital to have their stomachs pumped. The woman had only just returned home when the doorbell rang. It was the milkman, who explained that he was just calling to see if the cat was all right. It turned out that he'd dropped a metal milk crate on its head that morning.

B A young man had been out for the evening in central London and was making for Charing Cross station to catch his train home, but then decided he would rather have something to eat first. Checking his pocket, he found he only had about £5. It was a difficult choice: go home or get a quarterpounder with all the trimmings. Then he remembered he had his cash card, so all was well. He bought himself the burger, which he had already started to eat when he reached the cashpoint machine. He put in his card, put the snack down next to the keypad, punched in his numbers and waited for the cash to come out. Instead, the screen flashed up: 'Sorry, you have used the wrong number. Do you wish to try again?' A bit nervous, he keyed in another number. Again the message appeared. He was convinced that the first number was right, so he keyed it in carefully. No sooner had he finished than a message came up, saying his card had been retained. This was not the only thing he lost either, for then the glass shield came down, locking away his delicious burger.

3

4

4 Which do you think is the funniest of the four urban myths? Are any of them not funny at all, in your view? Explain your reasons to another student.

5 Work out the meaning of the **highlighted** words in the text from the surrounding context. Then use some of them in a–j.

   a The walkers sensed movement and suddenly a huge bear .... out of the trees just ahead of them.

   b The hotel .... their passports for the duration of their stay.

   c Take that .... look off your face – it's me in disguise!

   d Murray .... the ball in the air badly and decided not to play the serve.

   e The baby's birth had been difficult and Jane looked exhausted, so her father .... everyone .... to allow her to get some rest.

   f Rob cooked an amazing Sunday lunch of roast beef and ....

   g We .... the bill between the three of us, as it was Gregor's birthday.

   h You can't go to a job interview dressed like that – you look so ....!

   i Thousands of villagers are thought to be .... their homes, fearing the worst after the second earthquake.

   j When we moved out of the apartment, we packed everything into large wooden .... , which we stored at my parents' place.

C

An English couple who were driving around the USA were spending a few days in New York. They'd had some great evenings out on the town, including a show on Broadway and an Italian meal on the Lower East Side. They'd been a bit anxious at first, having seen all those violent shoot-'em-up cop shows on TV, but by the final evening, they were really enjoying themselves. They drove back to the hotel, parked in the basement car park, and waited for the lift up to reception. It was quite dark and rather scary. Suddenly, a huge man with a Rottweiler **loomed** out of the shadows. The lift came and the couple hurried in, followed by the man and his dog. As the doors closed, the man shouted, 'Get down, lady! Rather than put up a fight, the petrified couple **tossed** all their money at him and threw themselves on the floor. When the lift arrived, they scrambled to their feet and ran out in a panic. To their surprise, when they checked out the next day, the receptionist explained that a man had already **settled** their account, and she handed them an envelope. Inside was all the money they'd given the 'mugger' and a note saying: 'I'm real sorry about scaring you yesterday, and I hope paying your bill has made up for your **ordeal**. By the way, Lady is the name of my dog.'

D

Back in the 1980s, when businessman Robert Maxwell owned the *Daily Mirror* newspaper, he lived above their offices in London. One day, Maxwell, who was in the luxurious **penthouse** flat at the top, was coming down in the lift. At the next floor he was joined by a young lad in a rather **scruffy** suit, who happened to be smoking. Maxwell was furious to find one of his employees ignoring the company's no-smoking policy. The lad was promptly told to extinguish his cigarette, but rather than doing so he started blowing smoke in Maxwell's face. Maxwell angrily insisted that he put it out immediately. 'No way,' said the lad, and carried on puffing. At this, Maxwell demanded to know how much the lad earned a week. On being told £200, he took £400 in cash from his pocket and handed it to the lad, who looked totally **bewildered**. Maxwell said 'I'm giving you two weeks' notice. You're fired! Get out of my offices now.' 'Don't worry, mate,' said the lad, **fleeing** through the lift doors with his **wad** of cash, 'I'm going – I work for Telecom anyway!'

Grammar extra

rather

Look at these examples from the four urban myths and then answer questions a–c below.

1 But rather than doing so, he started blowing smoke in Maxwell's face.

2 At the next floor he was joined by a young man in a rather scruffy suit.

3 ... but then decided he would rather have something to eat first.

4 It was quite dark and rather scary.

a In which example could you use *instead of*? Which word apart from *rather* would you also have to omit?

b In which example is *rather* used to mean *prefer*? Which word has to be used as well? What word could be added to these words to give the opposite meaning?

c In which two examples is *rather* used in the same way? What similar word is also used in one of these examples?

G → page 176

The grammar of phrasal verbs

> A phrasal verb consists of a main verb and a *particle* – an adverb or a preposition. You have met many phrasal verbs throughout this course (pages 164–165 have a list of these). Now it is time to understand their grammar, which affects word order.

1 **Look at these examples from 24.1. Which two contain intransitive phrasal verbs (verbs which have no object)?**

   a A woman was looking forward to an important dinner party.
   b Her cat was tucking into the fish.
   c She shooed the cat away.
   d It turned out that he'd dropped a metal milk crate on its head.
   e He put the snack down next to the keypad.
   f He keyed it in carefully.
   g No sooner had he finished than a message came up.
   h Rather than put up a fight, the petrified couple …
   i I hope paying your bill has made up for your ordeal.
   j Maxwell insisted that he put it out immediately.

2 **Examine the word order for the transitive phrasal verbs in 1. Can the position of the object be changed in any of the examples? If so, give the alternative word order.**

EXAMPLES: **a** A woman was looking forward to an important dinner party.
   no change possible
   c She shooed the cat away. ✓
   She shooed away the cat.

3 **Check your ideas by matching examples a–j to these statements.**

   1 When a two-part phrasal verb is intransitive (has no object), the verb and the particle cannot be separated by other words.
   2 When a pronoun is used as the object of a two-part phrasal verb, it always comes before the particle.
   3 When a noun is used as the object of a two-part phrasal verb containing a preposition, the object has to come after the preposition.
   4 When a noun is used as the object of a two-part phrasal verb containing an adverb, it can generally come before or after the adverb. There are one or two exceptions, one of which is example … .
   5 In a three-part phrasal verb, the object cannot come between the two particles.

4 **Complete the sentences using the phrasal verb in brackets and a suitable noun or pronoun.**

   EXAMPLE: *My friend* has talked me into doing a 15-km run *at the weekend.* (talk into)
   a Please .... – you've watched far too much already. (turn off)
   b Sooner or later you'll have to tell me the truth, so let's .... , shall we? (get over with)
   c It was getting foggy, but they .... in the distance, which had its lights on. (make out)
   d That story .... driving in an open car for life! (put off)
   e While we were living in Sweden, we .... quite well. (pick up)
   f If there are any words you don't understand, ... in a dictionary. (look up)
   g I've just .... to that question! (work out)
   h You know you really should have .... before now – it's not good owing so much money. (face up to)

G → page 176

Corpus spot

These three-part phrasal verbs with *up* are frequently used by exam candidates. Match them with the noun phrases to check your understanding of them.

catch up on	his expectations
come up with	your bad moods
keep up with	some sleep
live up to	the international news
put up with	some good ideas

PV → page 164

5 Match the first lines (a–o) and second lines (1–15) of these jokes. Then take a vote to decide on the three funniest ones, giving reasons for your choices.

a What do you call someone who hangs around with musicians?

b Every time I drink coffee I get a stabbing pain in my left eye.

c When a man has a birthday, he takes the day off.

d What's the definition of a modern artist?

e I ended up as the teacher's pet.

f What's the best way to make the landlord paint your apartment?

g Did you start out as an actor?

h What's the best way to stay out of the army?

i Why did you wake me up? It's still dark.

j My brother and I are inseparable.

k What are you doing in my tree, young lad?

l A Hollywood couple have finally worked out their divorce settlement.

m Would you please open up the piano?

n Old pickpockets never die.

o What would you do if you were in my shoes?

1 One of your apples fell down and I'm putting it back.

2 No, as a little boy.

3 Clean them up.

4 She couldn't afford a dog.

5 In fact, it takes six people to pull us apart.

6 I can't – the keys are inside.

7 Well, take the spoon out of the cup.

8 Join the navy.

9 Someone who tosses paint on a canvas, wipes it off with a cloth and sells the cloth.

10 A drummer.

11 Well, open your eyes!

12 Now they can get married.

13 Move out.

14 They just steal away.

15 When a woman has one, she takes a year off.

6 Read this biography of Jim Carrey. For questions 1–12, think of the word which best fits each gap. Use only one word in each gap. There is an example at the beginning (0).

Example: 0 MUCH

A funny man with a funny face

Jim Carrey's humour is very (**0**) .... his own brand. It is often slapstick, sometimes a (**1**) .... tasteless, but always extremely funny. Carrey, who was born in Canada in 1962, believes that his sense of humour developed (**2**) .... his teenage years. This was his way of dealing (**3**) .... a difficult period in his life. His father had lost his job and Carrey junior had to earn money and study (**4**) .... the same time.

Carrey first performed live when he was 15, at Yuk Yuks, a famous club in Toronto. Even (**5**) .... he failed to make his audience laugh on this occasion, he kept working on his material and within four years became the club's top comedy act. He later moved to Los Angeles to tour the clubs there. From 1990, he starred regularly in an American TV show, (**6**) .... one of the many characters he played was Fire Marshall Bill, who always went (**7**) .... in smoke! Sadly, this character finally had to (**8**) .... dropped because of complaints that his fire act might have a bad influence on children.

Carrey's first feature film was *Ace Ventura: Pet Detective*, one of his (**9**) .... popular films. Another early film, *The Mask*, was the perfect vehicle (**10**) .... his weird humour. Other films (**11**) .... then have included *Batman Forever*, *The Truman Show* and *Yes Man*. His earnings (**12**) .... estimated at around $20 million per film.

Writing folder 12

Transactional letters and emails 3

1   You may have to correct facts in a Part 1 task. Read this article and the notes made on it. Decide on the four main points that need to be covered in a letter to the editor.

NO GREAT LAUGHS AT FESTIVAL OF FUN!

Say who I enjoyed

The comedy on offer at this year's Festival of Fun has been very disappointing indeed. I cannot think of a single performance that has been memorable, in contrast to last year's wonderful line-up of stars from stage and screen. It seems that the organisers have cut down on spending this year, selecting unknown and second-rate acts on the cheap!

There have been just too many dull and predictable performances: the pathetic slapstick routines of Forbes and Company, the unfunny stand-up comedian Linda Ritson, whose jokes were extremely poor, and the dreadful comedy duo Holmes and Watson, who were clearly under-rehearsed.

Disagree with this

Give my opinion

Saturday's audience was shocked to the core by Ted Grainger's rude and offensive jokes. To make him top of the bill was a big mistake and it was interesting to see how many people walked out soon after he came on stage.

This year's event was a total disaster. It's probably not worth holding another one next year!

Explain why this festival is important

2   Now read this sample answer. Apart from the opening paragraph, it is a well-written letter. However, one content point is missing. Which one?

Dear Editor

I want to point the finger at whoever wrote the article about the Festival of Fun, published in yesterday's Daily News. In fact, I couldn't get my head round the article. Your journalist has produced an inaccurate report and I don't see eye to eye with him.

For a start, the journalist says there were no memorable performances. Perhaps he was absent on Friday evening, when some excellent acts were on offer. For example, I found Larry Hatfeld (who is in fact a very well-known comedian) extremely funny.

Ted Grainger's political humour is described as 'offensive', but the majority of the audience found him very entertaining. I didn't notice many people leaving, either, in contrast to what your article claims!

This annual event is important because it gives local comedians opportunities to try out their work. The organisers have done a good job this year and will, I'm sure, do the same again next year.

Yours faithfully

Izzy Edwards

3   What do the first three idioms in the box have in common? Why is their use inappropriate in this letter? Rewrite the first paragraph of the letter, including the fourth idiom instead of the other three.

> **English idioms**
>
> Point the finger at someone – accuse someone of something
> Get your head round something – understand something
> See eye to eye with someone – agree with someone
> Be economical with the truth – deliberately not tell the whole truth

Use idioms sparingly – less is more! Also, try to follow this advice.

- Be careful to use the correct pronoun.
- Make sure the tense fits the sentence.
- Check that any preposition you have used is correct.

4   Now do this similar Part 1 task.

You see this newspaper article about a concert which you enjoyed recently.
You decide to write to the editor, correcting the facts and giving your own point of view.

GOOD SOUND SYSTEM – SHAME ABOUT THE BANDS!

Last night's annual *Talentspot* concert at the Juniper Theatre was a huge disappointment. None of the bands who performed there were worth watching. An excellent sound system was provided by the theatre, too, so the performers had no excuse. If this is the best that local bands can do, I would rather stay at home and listen to CDs!

Support local music?

First on stage was the group Acid Rain, whose twenty-minute performance was appalling. The microphone used by the singer was of poor quality – I couldn't make out any of the words she sang. Next came Dingbats, who couldn't even agree on what to play – the bass player was arguing with the lead guitarist for much of the time!

Not their fault – say why

Disagree because ...

Down and Out, the final act, is exactly how I felt by the end of the evening. This second-rate group performed an unambitious collection of songs, supported by a useless drummer and a guitarist who knew a total of three chords! I hope the organisers wash their hands of this embarrassing event next year!

Explain why event is important

Write a **letter** of between 120 and 150 words in an appropriate style. Do not include any postal addresses.

Units 19–24 Revision

Topic review

1 Answer these questions, giving your own opinions. If you are working in pairs or groups, remember to use turn-taking skills.

  a What should someone do to lose weight?
  b When should you tell someone it's time for them to leave a party?
  c Even if someone has committed a crime, is prison the best form of punishment?
  d What are the advantages and disadvantages of living in a city?
  e If you were woken up by an earthquake, what would you try to do?
  f Do you think the Internet has increased or decreased crime? Why?
  g Which would you rather watch, a comedy programme or the news?
  h What do you hope to do after you have passed Cambridge First?

Vocabulary

2 Read the statements or questions and choose the best option, A, B or C.

  1 Someone has given you a present. Should you
    A uncover it?   B unfasten it?   C unwrap it?
  2 If you caught flu, would you have
    A a bug?   B a bruise?   C a sweat?
  3 Which performer would you not see at a classical recital?
    A a violinist   B a cellist   C a bass guitarist
  4 You are driving in torrential rain and a tree falls across the road 200 metres in front of you. Are you in danger of being
    A cut down?   B cut off?   C cut out?
  5 You see someone take another person's bicycle. Do you
    A arrest them?   B charge them?   C accuse them?
  6 If you don't see eye to eye with someone, do you
    A hate them?   B disagree with them?
    C find out about them?
  7 What would you do if your little brother breaks your mobile?
    A tell him off?   B send him off?   C show him off?
  8 You need a plaster. Do you have
    A flu?   B a cut?   C a cough?

3 The twenty words below have all appeared in Units 19–24. Decide what they are with the help of the information given and then use one from each set to complete the sentences a–e.

  • two verbs to do with illness or injury:
    1 S P _ A _ _
    2 C _ _ _ H
  • three words to do with volcanoes:
    3 E _ U _ _ _ _ _
    4 _ _ H
    5 L _ _ _
  • four musical instruments:
    6 O _ _ _
    7 _ I _ _ O
    8 _ U I _ _ _
    9 _ L _ _ E
  • five nouns to do with crime and punishment:
    10 R _ _ _ _ _ Y
    11 _ O U _ _
    12 _ _ R G _ _ R
    13 T _ _ _ L
    14 F _ _ _
  • six words for parts of the body:
    15 E _ _ B _ _ W
    16 _ A _ S _
    17 _ _ W
    18 _ N _ E
    19 _ L B _ _
    20 T _ _ _ H

  a She picked up the shiny silver .... and began to play her favourite piece.
  b This belt is a bit tight around my .... – I must have put on weight!
  c The city of Pompeii was destroyed by the .... of Vesuvius in 79 AD.
  d It is very easy to .... your ankle when running to the back of the court for a difficult ball.
  e You will get a .... if you cycle without lights in our town.

4 Complete the story with a phrasal verb from the box in the correct form.

bring in	call up	end up	miss out on
put off	take aback	take on	work out

If the Royal Marines had drummed one thing into Sergeant Ken Murgatroyd during his twenty-two years of service, it was the importance of seizing opportunities. After he left the Royal Marines, his new job in telesales involved **(1)** .... computer companies. However, one morning he rang the direct line of Neil Corbould, a senior assistant to the film director Steven Spielberg, by mistake. Within minutes Mr Murgatroyd had been **(2)** .... for a leading role in the war film *Saving Private Ryan*.

No one was more **(3)** .... than Mr Murgatroyd. Mr Spielberg needed to **(4)** .... someone who could **(5)** .... how to make the scenes as realistic as possible. Mr Murgatroyd, who was one of the navy's foremost authorities on landing manoeuvres, was perfect.

'I hadn't even heard of the film when they gave me the job. I was trying to sell an Internet database, when I pressed a wrong button and **(6)** .... talking to Spielberg's assistant. I told him I had made a mistake, but out of curiosity asked him what kind of work he did. When he told me, I thought, I can help with that.'

Working with celebrities didn't **(7)** .... Mr Murgatroyd at all. 'In fact, I found all the Hollywood types very pleasant. I don't think they had ever worked with someone like me before. I wouldn't have wanted to **(8)** .... an opportunity like that.'

Grammar

5 Read the text below and think of the word which best fits each gap. Use only one word in each gap. There is an example at the beginning **(0)**.

How to make a small fortune

Have you ever wished you had some savings to fall back **(0)** ..ON.. ? Perhaps you already have something put aside for a rainy day, but if **(1)** .... , here are some unusual ways to make a pile **(2)** .... cash. Look critically at your old toys. Very **(3)** .... remain in a condition that is good **(4)** .... for them to be sold, **(5)** .... that a pre-1950, well-looked-after teddy bear can be worth **(6)** .... to £2,000. Musical instruments can also raise **(7)** .... large sum, sometimes unexpectedly. Hazel Morgan hadn't played her violin for more **(8)** .... forty years, so she decided to sell **(9)** ....
To her surprise, the violin itself was valued **(10)** .... £2,500 and the bow, despite **(11)** .... in bad condition, was expected to fetch even more. Fine wines can also be highly profitable, and even **(12)** .... your investment doesn't prove as big an earner as you hoped, you can still enjoy drinking the wine!

Speaking folder

Paper 5 Speaking

The Speaking test is an opportunity to demonstrate your level of English. Don't be too worried about making mistakes – you are not only assessed on your accuracy, but also on your range of grammar and vocabulary, your pronunciation, and your ability to communicate with other people in discussion.

EXAM ADVICE

- Try to be relaxed and cheerful – it will take less than 15 minutes!
- Ask the examiner if you are unclear about an instruction.
- Don't be afraid to spend a few seconds thinking, in order to plan what you are going to say.
- Give detailed answers in Part 1, rather than answering the examiner's questions in a single word.
- Listen carefully to the other candidate's long turn in Part 2 so that you can make a comment when asked.
- Keep going during your own long turn, remembering to compare and contrast, rather than describe an individual picture.
- Be sensitive to the other candidate in Part 3 and use turn-taking skills to ensure you both work towards completion of the task.
- Interact both with the other candidate and the examiner in Part 4. Here, you have the chance to broaden the discussion, so take the initiative and show them what you know.

Now put all the advice into practice in this complete Speaking Test.

Part 1: Answer these questions.
How do you like to spend your free time?
Do you go shopping because you have to, or because you enjoy it?
What kind of music do you prefer to listen to?
Can you describe a work of art that is special for you?

Part 2: Look at these pictures, which show two celebrities.

Student A: Compare the photographs and say what would be the advantages and disadvantages of being famous.
Student B: Talk briefly about how your life differs from that of a celebrity.

Now look at these pictures, which show two different parts of the world.

> **Student A:** Compare these photographs and say which place you think would be the more difficult to live in, and why.
> **Student B:** Talk briefly about which place you would prefer to live in.

Part 3: Look at the picture together. It shows a living room which doesn't have enough furniture in it. Talk about the problems with the room and decide together on which *three* things you would buy to improve it.

Part 4: Now discuss these questions.

How important is it for a room to be comfortable?

Which of your possessions are particularly special to you?

Is it useful to have a computer at home? Why? / Why not?

Will more people work from home in the future? Why? / Why not?

What are the advantages and disadvantages of having an office at home?

Phrasal verb list

This list covers the phrasal verbs practised in *Objective First Student's Book*, with definitions taken from the *English Vocabulary Profile*. (The Unit and page numbers are given in brackets.) Where the position of the object can be moved, you will see both options given, for example **call off sth** or **call sth off**. Note that some phrasal verbs occur both with and without an object, for example **break (sth) off**. Remember that phrasal verbs without an object cannot be separated, for example **fall apart**. Several phrasal verbs have more than one meaning and the words in capital letters show you which meanings are covered in the course, for example **take off** AIRCRAFT, SUCCESSFUL.

add to sth PUT WITH to put something with something else (U1, 11)

book (sb) into to arrange for someone to stay at a hotel (U3, 23)

break down If a machine or vehicle breaks down, it stops working. (U19, 125)

break off (sth) or **break (sth) off** to end (something) suddenly (U23, 149)

call off sth or **call sth off** to decide that a planned event, especially a sports event, will not happen, or to end an activity because it is no longer useful or possible (U23, 149)

call sb up to telephone someone (U18–24, 161)

calm down to stop feeling upset, angry, or excited, or to make someone stop feeling this way (U5, 36)

catch up on sth to do something that you did not have time to do earlier (U24, 156)

check in HOTEL to go to the desk at a hotel in order to say that you have arrived, and to get the key to your room (U3, 23)

check out to leave a hotel after paying your bill (U3, 23)

come across sth SEEM to find something by chance (U18, 117)

come down FALL to fall and land on the ground (U5, 36)

come out BECOME AVAILABLE If a book, record, film, etc comes out, it becomes available for people to buy or see. (U18, 117)

come up MOVE TOWARDS to move towards someone (U24, 156)

come up with sth to suggest or think of an idea or plan (U18, 117)

consist of sth to be formed or made from two or more things (U15, 101)

cut down sth or **cut sth down** REDUCE to eat or drink less of something, or to reduce the amount or number of something (U1, 11)

cut down sth or **cut sth down** REMOVE to make a tree or other plant fall to the ground by cutting it near the bottom (U4, 28)

cut off sb/sth or **cut sb/sth off** to cause a person or place to become separate, or cause someone to be or feel alone (U23, 149)

do without (sb/sth) to manage without having someone or something (U7, 50)

dress up FORMAL to put on formal clothes for a special occasion (U1, 11)

end up to finally be in a particular place or situation (U5, 35)

face up to sth to accept that a difficult situation exists (U24, 156)

fall out (with sb) to argue with someone and stop being friendly with them (EF 4, 52)

fill in sth to write the necessary information on an official document (U3, 24)

find out (sth) or **find (sth) out** to get information about something, or to learn a fact for the first time (U2, 18)

fit in with sth If one thing fits in with another thing, they look pleasant together or are suitable for each other. (U1, 11)

get away HOLIDAY to go somewhere to have a holiday, especially because you need to rest (U3, 23)

get away with sth to succeed in not being criticized or punished for something (U8, 56)

get down to sth to start doing something seriously and with a lot of attention and effort (U8, 56)

get in VEHICLE ARRIVING If a train or other vehicle gets in at a particular time, that is when it arrives. (U3, 23)

get into sth BE CHOSEN to succeed in being chosen or elected (U8, 56)

get on (with sb) (UK) If two or more people get on, they like each other and are friendly to each other. (U8, 57)

get out of sth/doing sth to avoid doing something that you do not want to do, especially by giving an excuse (U8, 56)

get over sth/sb GET BETTER to get better after an illness, or feel better after something or someone has made you unhappy (U8, 56)

get sth over with to do or finish an unpleasant but necessary piece of work or duty so that you do not have to worry about it in the future (U24, 156)

get through sth FINISH to use up or finish something (U2, 17)

go ahead ALLOW something that you say to someone to allow them to do something (U1, 11)

go ahead START to start to do something (U18, 117)

go back to return to a place where you were or where you have been before (U1, 11)

go by TIME If time goes by, it passes. (U18, 117)

go for sth CHOOSE to choose something (U1, 11)

go off EXPLODE If a bomb or a gun goes off, it explodes or fires.(U23, 149)

go off sth/sb to stop liking or being interested in someone or something (U18, 117)

go on HAPPEN to happen (U1, 11)

go out LEAVE to leave a room or building, especially in order to do something for entertainment (U1, 11)

go over sth to talk or think about something in order to explain it or make certain that it is correct (U1, 11)

go through sth to experience a difficult or unpleasant situation (U18, 117)

go up INCREASE to become higher in level (U1, 11)

hang around (with sb) to spend time with someone (U24, 157)

keep (sb/sth) away to not go somewhere or near something, or to prevent someone from going somewhere or near something (U6, 41)

keep on doing sth to continue to do something, or to do something again and again (U6, 41)

keep sb in to make a child stay inside as a punishment, or to make someone stay in hospital (U6, 41)

keep sth down NO INCREASE to stop the number, level, or size of something from increasing (U6, 41)

keep to sth NOT CHANGE PLANS to do what you have promised or planned to do (U6, 41)

keep up (with sb/sth) UNDERSTAND to be able to understand or deal with something that is happening or changing very fast (U1, 11)

keep up (with sb/sth) SAME SPEED to move at the same speed as someone or something that is moving forward so that you stay level with them (U6, 41)

key sth in to put information into a computer or a machine using a keyboard (U24, 154)

let off sb or **let sb off** to not punish someone who has committed a crime or done something wrong, or to not punish them severely (U23, 149)

live up to sth to be as good as someone hopes (U4, 29)

log off to stop a computer being connected to a computer system, usually when you want to stop working (U23, 149)

look after sb/sth to take care of or be in charge of someone or something (U17, 111)

look at sth EXAMINE If someone, usually an expert, looks at something, they examine it (U17, 111)

look for sth/sb to try to find someone or something (U17, 111)

look forward to sth/doing sth to feel happy and excited about something that is going to happen (WF2, U17, 109)

look into sth to examine the facts about a problem or situation (U17, 111)

look up sth or **look sth up** to try to find a piece of information by looking in a book or on a computer (U24, 156)

look up to sb to respect and admire someone (U17, 111)

make for swh to move towards a place (U24, 154)

make up for sth to reduce the bad effect of something, or make something bad become something good (U24, 156)

make out sth/sb or **make sth/sb out** to see, hear or understand something or someone with difficulty (U24, 156)

miss out on sth to fail to use an opportunity to enjoy or get an advantage from something (U19–24, 161)

pick up sth or **pick sth up** to learn a new skill or language by practising it rather than being taught it (U24, 156)

pull away START MOVING If a vehicle pulls away, it starts moving. (U5, 36)

pull on sth CLOTHES to put on clothes quickly (U1, 11)

pull up If a vehicle pulls up, it stops, often for a short time. (U5, 36)

put down sth or **put sth down** to put someone or something that you are holding onto the floor or onto another surface (U24, 154)

put off sb or **put sb off** to make someone dislike something or someone, or to discourage someone from doing something (U24, 156)

put out sth or **put sth out** STOP BURNING to make something that is burning, such as a fire or cigarette, stop burning (U24, 155)

put sth together or **put together sth** JOIN PARTS to create something by joining or combining different things (U1, 11)

put up sth to show or express a particular type of opposition to something (U24, 156)

put up with sb/sth to accept unpleasant behaviour or an unpleasant situation, although you do not like it (U24, 156)

save up (sth) or **save (sth) up** MONEY to keep money so that you can buy something with it in the future (U1, 11)

send off sth or **send sth off** to send a letter, document or parcel by post (U23, 149)

set off to start a journey (U3, 23)

slip on sth or **slip sth on** to quickly put on a piece of clothing (U1, 11)

slip out If a remark slips out, you say it without intending to. (U24, 154)

stand out NOTICE to be very easy to see or notice (U1, 11)

start out to begin your life or the part of your life when you work, in a particular way (U24, 157)

stop over to stay at a place for one night or a few nights on the way to somewhere else or before returning home (U3, 23)

take after sb to be similar to an older member of your family (U11, 74)

take back sth or **take sth back** [THING] to return something to the place you borrowed or bought it from (U1, 11)

take off AIRCRAFT If an aircraft takes off, it begins to fly. (U3, 23)

take off SUCCESSFUL to suddenly become successful (U11, 74)

take off sth or **take sth off** to spend time away from your work (U24, 157)

take out sth or **take sth out** to remove something from somewhere (U11, 74)

take sth off or **take off sth** REMOVE to remove something (U1, 11)

take sth on to accept a particular job or responsibility (U19–24, 161)

talk sb into (doing) sth to persuade someone to do something (U12, 80)

tell off sb or **tell sb off** to speak angrily to someone because they have done something wrong (U23, 149)

tell sb/sth apart to be able to see the difference between two very similar things or people (U12, 81)

turn on sth or **turn sth on** to move the switch on a machine, light, etc so that it starts working, or to start the supply of water, electricity, etc (U2, 16)

turn out BE DISCOVERED to be known or discovered finally and surprisingly (U24, 154)

turn up sth or **turn sth up** to increase the level of sound or heat that a machine produces (U2, 16)

wear off If a feeling or the effect of something wears off, it gradually disappears. (U23, 149)

work on sth to spend time repairing or improving something (U24, 157)

work out sth or **work sth out** CALCULATE to do a calculation to get an answer to a mathematical question (U24, 157)

work out sth or **work sth out** PROBLEM to understand something or to find the answer to something by thinking about it (U24, 156)

Grammar folder

Unit 1
Comparison
There are various ways of making comparisons in English.

1 Comparative and superlative adjectives
Regular adjectives of one syllable have forms like these:

Adjective	Comparative	Superlative
young	young**er**	(the) young**est**
large	larg**er**	(the) larg**est**
slim	slim**mer**	(the) slim**mest**

Note that if an adjective ends in a single vowel and consonant (not *w*), the final letter is doubled, as in *slim* above. Some common examples are:
sad, big, thin, fat, hot, wet.

Two-syllable adjectives ending in a consonant followed by the letter *y* are formed like this:

Adjective	Comparative	Superlative
dirty	dirt**ier**	(the) dirt**iest**

Some common examples are:
angry, busy, easy, funny, happy, heavy, silly, tiny.

Most other two-syllable adjectives and all longer adjectives form their comparative and superlative forms like this:

Adjective	Comparative	Superlative
careful	**more** careful	(the) **most** careful
casual	**more** casual	(the) **most** casual
outrageous	**more** outrageous	(the) **most** outrageous

Some common two-syllable adjectives have both forms:

Adjective	Comparative	Superlative
simple	simpl**er** OR **more** simple	(the) simpl**est** OR (the) **most** simple

Other examples are:
clever, common, cruel, gentle, likely, narrow, pleasant, polite.

Irregular adjectives have the following forms:

Adjective	Comparative	Superlative
good	better	(the) best
bad	worse	(the) worst
far	farther/ further	(the) farthest/ furthest
old	older/ elder	(the) oldest/ eldest

2 Adverbs of degree
These adverbs of degree can be used in front of comparative adjectives:
a bit, a good deal, a great deal, a little, a lot, much, rather, slightly.
This T-shirt is a bit cheaper than the others because it's last year's design.
Helen is much more intelligent than the rest of the group.

These adverbs of degree can be used in front of superlative adjectives:
by far, easily, much, quite.
You're easily the cleverest person I know!

3 not as ... as
This structure is used to compare two things or people. A less common form is *not so ... as*.
Sally is not as tall as her brother.

4 Comparative and superlative adverbs
Comparative adverbs are usually formed by adding *more* to the existing adverb:

commonly	→	more commonly
readily	→	more readily

Superlative adverbs are usually formed by adding *(the) most* to the existing adverb:

commonly	→	(the) most commonly
readily	→	(the) most readily

A few adverbs are not formed with *more / most* and consist of a single word for both the comparative and superlative forms. Here are some common examples:

badly	→	worse	→	worst
close	→	closer	→	closest
early	→	earlier	→	earliest
far	→	farther/further	→	farthest/furthest
fast	→	faster	→	fastest
hard	→	harder	→	hardest
near	→	nearer	→	nearest
well	→	better	→	best

Unit 2
Adverbs
Most regular adverbs are formed by adding *-ly* to a related adjective:
quick → quickly, endless → endlessly
Adjectives ending in double *ll* just add *y*:
full → fully
However, there are sometimes spelling changes when an adverb is formed in this way:
-le becomes *-ly*: gentle → gently, remarkable → remarkably
-y becomes *-ily*: easy → easily, cosy → cosily
-ic becomes *-ically*: tragic → tragically, automatic → automatically
-ue becomes *-uly*: true → truly

Some irregular adverbs do not end in *-ly*:
fast, hard, late, well.

The adverbs *hardly* and *lately* have different meanings from *hard* and *late*:
I worked hard on the project all day.
I hardly had time to stop for a coffee all day.

I finished the work late in the evening.
I've put in some long hours at work lately.

Review of present tenses

Uses of the present simple tense

- Permanent situations
  Most people access the Internet for information.
- Habitual situations
  I check my emails twice a day.
- In time clauses
  Once you finish your work, give me a ring.
  We usually play tennis until it gets dark.
- In zero conditionals
  If you use all seven letters in the board game Scrabble, you get fifty extra points.
  Steam forms when water boils.

Uses of the present continuous tense

- Temporary situations
  I'm living at home until I find my own flat.
- Developing situations
  Traffic is becoming heavier and heavier.
- Events happening now
  Sit still while I'm talking to you!
- Events in the near future
  Tim's leaving for Hanover next week.

See Unit 10, Review of future tenses (page 170), for further information about the present simple and present continuous tenses.

Stative verbs are not normally used in continuous tenses. The commonest of these are:
admire   be   believe   belong   consist   dislike   doubt
fit   forget   guess   hate   hear   imagine   include
keep   know   like   love   mean   prefer   realise
recognise   remember   seem   smell   sound
suppose   taste   understand   want   wish
*She **keeps** talking when I'm trying to watch TV.*
*We **wish** we could be with you right now.*

Unit 3
Modals 1: Obligation, necessity and permission

Strong obligation: *must* and *have to*, *have got to* (Informal)

Present and future	must	have to	have got to
Past	had to		

1 **must**
   Must is used to talk about strong obligations in the present and future that are imposed by the speaker.
   You must brush your teeth before you go to bed.
   I must arrange to have my windows cleaned.
   (It is also used to talk about laws: *Drivers must obey traffic signals.*)

2 **have to/have got to**
   Have to/have got to are used to talk about strong obligations in the present and future that are not imposed by the speaker.
   I've got to do some homework tonight. (My teacher says so.)
   If in doubt whether to use *must* or *have to*, use *have to*. Do not use *I've to*, which is incorrect.

3 **had to**
   Had to is used to talk about past and reported obligations:
   I had to help on the farm when I was young.
   We were told we had to get a visa before we left on holiday.
   There are also other ways to express obligation:
   to make someone do something
   to be compulsory

Weak obligation: *should ought to*

Present and future	should do ought to do
Past	should have done
	ought to have done

There is no difference in meaning between *should* and *ought to*.
You ought to/should write home more frequently.
In the past *should have done* and *ought to have done* are often used for criticism or regret, because an action didn't happen:
We should have bought/ought to have bought your sister a card for her birthday.

Asking for and giving permission: *can could may*

Can is the more usual way of asking for and giving permission.
Could is a bit more polite and *may* is quite formal:
Can/may/could I borrow your bike?
Yes, you can/may.

Other ways of asking for and giving permission are:
to allow someone to do
to permit someone to do
to let someone do

Prohibition: *mustn't can't*

Present and future	mustn't can't
Past	was not to couldn't

Mustn't and *can't* are used when something is forbidden:
You mustn't cross the road without looking.
Elizabeth can't go out this evening – her father says so.

Other verbs which can be used are:
to forbid someone to do something
to ban someone from doing something
to not allow someone to do something
to not permit someone to do something
to not let someone do something.

It is also possible to use an imperative:
Don't cycle on the pavement!

Unit 4
as and *like*

(See also grammar summary in Unit 4)

Like can be used as a preposition and is followed by a noun (*like a house*), a pronoun (*like it*), or a gerund (*like swimming*). It is used to give a comparison:
Your house is like our house/ours. (is similar to ours)
My bed is so hard it's like sleeping on the ground.

As can be used as a preposition to tell you what job or function a person or thing has:
As a chef, I have to cook one hundred meals a day.
I used the tin as a cup to drink out of.

Please note these other uses of *as* and *like*.
It's like living in a palace, living in your house. (It's not a palace.)
As a palace, Windsor is very impressive. (It is a palace.)

As is used in prepositional phrases:
At my school, as at most schools, pupils were expected to respect their teachers.

Some verbs can be followed by an object and *as*:
He is known as a generous person.
I don't regard learning a language as optional.

Like and *such as* can be used to mean 'for example':
I enjoy films like/such as thrillers.
I dislike sports such as/like skiing.

As can be a conjunction and is followed by a subject and verb:
She cut up the vegetables as I had taught her. (in the way I had taught her)

In British English it is becoming more common to hear *like* followed by a subject and verb. *Like* followed by a subject and verb is acceptable in American English:
I don't speak like he does.

Unit 5
Table of common irregular verbs

INFINITIVE	PAST TENSE	PAST PARTICIPLE
become	became	(has/had) become
bet	bet	bet
burst	burst	burst
buy	bought	bought
cut	cut	cut
draw	drew	drawn
drive	drove	driven
eat	ate	eaten
feel	felt	felt
find	found	found
get	got	got
hear	heard	heard
hit	hit	hit
hold	held	held
keep	kept	kept
know	knew	known
leave	left	left
lose	lost	lost
put	put	put
run	ran	run
say	said	said
see	saw	seen
send	sent	sent
set	set	set
shake	shook	shaken
shut	shut	shut
sink	sank	sunk
speak	spoke	spoken
spend	spent	spent
swim	swam	swum
take	took	taken
tell	told	told
think	thought	thought

Review of past tenses
Past simple

This is used to talk about events in the past which:
- occurred at a particular time
  The Titanic sank in 1912.
  I drove back from London last night.
  This indicates a completed action in the past with a fixed time phrase.
- happened regularly
  Matthew spent most weekends at tennis tournaments.
  She burst into tears every time she heard his name.
  Note that *would* and *used to* are also used to talk about the past in this way – this is dealt with in Unit 8 (page 169).

Past continuous

This is used to talk about events in the past which:
- had a longer duration than another action
  I was cutting up vegetables in the kitchen when I heard it on the six o'clock news.
- were temporary
  Norwich were losing two-nil, with only five minutes to go.

  It is also used to set the scene in a story: *The sun was shining when the old man set off from the cottage.*

Present perfect

This is used to talk about events or a period of time which:
- started in the past but are still true or are still continuing
  We've lived here for eight years.
  Ellen has eaten no meat since she was six.
- happened in the past but have an effect in the present
  They've cancelled tonight's concert so we'll have to do something else.
  I've heard from Iain again.

Past perfect

This is used to talk about events which:
- happened earlier than something else
  Ken sat in the dark miserably and thought about what he had said to his girlfriend.
  Once I had finished my exams, I started clubbing again.

  Note that the past perfect needs to be used when it is important to show a time difference.

  Unit 14 deals with the perfect tenses in more detail (page 172).

Unit 6
Conditionals with *if* and *unless*

These are normally used to talk about possible events and the effects of them. There are four main types:
- Zero conditional
  Not a true conditional, as the events described both happen.
  If I stay up late, I feel awful the next day.
  When the moon passes between the earth and the sun, there is an eclipse.
  If/When + present tense | present tense
- First conditional
  Used to talk about likely events in the future if something happens.
  If I pass Cambridge First, I'll have a big party!
  If you don't stop talking, I'll send you to the head teacher.
  If + present tense | future tense *will*

- Second conditional
  Used to talk about unlikely or impossible situations.
  If I won the lottery, I'd give all the money to Oxfam.
  People might behave differently if they had the chance to repeat their lives.
  If + past tense | would, could, might
- Third conditional
  Used to speculate about the past.
  If we'd had more money, we'd have gone to the States last year.
  If you'd told me the truth in the first place, I wouldn't have asked the teacher.
  If Tom had taken his guitar, he could have played with the band that night.
  If + past perfect | would have, could have, might have + past participle
  (Unit 21 deals with mixed conditionals.)

Unless is a conjunction meaning 'if not', so the clause following *unless* never contains a negative verb form:
I'll see you at the station at 7.00 unless I hear from you.
Unless we book train tickets in advance, we won't get a discount.

Unit 7
Gerunds and infinitives 1

The gerund

The gerund is a verb which is used as a noun. It can be the subject of a clause or sentence: *Climbing the hill took them all day*, or the object: *I consider learning to save to be an essential part of growing up.*

You use the gerund:

- after certain verbs and expressions, especially those expressing liking/disliking:
  I don't mind getting up early in the morning.

  Common examples:
  like   love   enjoy   adore   fancy   feel   don't mind
  detest   hate   loathe   can't stand   dislike
  finish   avoid   give up   keep   miss
  suggest   consider   imagine
  it's not worth   it's/there's no use   there's no point (in)

- after all prepositions except *to*
  (Some exceptions to this rule are: *to look forward to doing, to object to doing, to get used to doing.*)
  On hearing the news, she burst into tears.

- after adjective and preposition combinations
  Steven is fantastic at cooking Thai food.

  Common examples:
  good/wonderful/fantastic/bad/awful/ terrible at
  happy/pleased/glad/anxious/sad/worried about
  afraid/frightened/scared/terrified of
  interested in
  keen on
  capable of
  proud of

  Another common use is with the noun *difficulty* (*to have difficulty in*).

- after verb and preposition combinations
  I don't approve of people drinking and driving.

  Common examples:
  insist on   approve of   apologise for
  consist of   believe in   succeed in
  accuse someone of   congratulate someone on

- after phrasal verbs
  I gave up playing tennis when I hurt my knee.

The infinitive

The infinitive is used:

- after certain verbs
  I learnt to speak Spanish in Valencia.

  Common examples:
  afford   agree   ask   choose   help   hope   want
  intend   pretend   promise   expect   prefer   used

- after certain adjectives
  I was surprised to see him at the party.

  Common examples:
  difficult   possible   happy   certain   simple

- after verbs which follow the pattern verb + someone + *to do* + something
  I asked her to open the window.

  Common examples:
  encourage   permit   allow   persuade   teach   force

- to express purpose
  I went to the shops to get some bread.

The infinitive without *to*
This is also used after modal auxiliaries (*can, must*), after *let, had better* and *would rather.*
Make has no *to* in the active, but adds *to* in the passive:
I made him go to school /He was made to go to school.

Unit 8
used to and *would*

Used to and *would* express habitual actions in the past.
- *Used to* is followed by the infinitive and is used for actions which no longer happen. It is used for permanent situations as well as habitual actions.
  I used to have a tricycle when I was five years old.
  John used to have long hair before he joined the army.

  The negative is *didn't used to*, though sometimes *didn't use to* is used.
  I didn't used to go abroad for my holidays before I won the lottery.

- *Would* is used for past habitual actions which were repeated. *Would* takes an infinitive without *to.*
  I would get up for work at seven, then get the bus at seven-thirty.

- *Get/Be used to doing* means to get or to be accustomed to. It can be used with all tenses and is always followed by a gerund (an *-ing* word).

Unit 9
Modals 2: Speculation and deduction

- *could, might, may* are used to speculate about something the speaker or writer is unsure about:
  It could be a sea eagle, though the feathers look too dark.
  That star you're looking at might in fact be Jupiter.
  The answer may be to readvertise the job.

- *must* is used to indicate certainty:
  That car must be doing over 50 mph at least!
  It must be possible to make a booking on the Internet.

- *can't/cannot* and *couldn't/could not* are also used to indicate certainty, in relation to impossible ideas and situations:
  It can't be her birthday – she had a party in August.
  You cannot be serious!
  They couldn't possibly be here before lunchtime.

- *couldn't/could not* can also be used in questions, sometimes with *possibly*, to speculate about something:
  It couldn't possibly be a case of mistaken identity, could it?
  Couldn't it be a computer error?

- *could have, might have, may have* are used to express uncertainty about something in the past:
  It could have been Greg you saw on the bus – he often catches the 206.
  The dinosaurs might have survived without the meteor impact.
  I think I may have met you before.

- *couldn't have / can't have* are used to express certainty that something in the past was impossible or didn't happen:
  He couldn't have damaged your bike – he was with me all evening.
  It can't have been raining, as the path is completely dry.

- *must have* is used to express near-certainty about something in the past:
  It must have been cold that winter.
  Jan must have arrived home by now.

Order of adjectives

Opinion adjectives always come before descriptive adjectives:
the brilliant French film 'Le Bossu'
an appalling old brown tracksuit
Descriptive adjectives generally follow this order:
size shape age colour nationality material
a small oval brooch
the young American film star
It is unusual to have four or more adjectives together –
a separate phrase is more commonly used:
a slim-cut black leather jacket with a classic Italian look

Unit 10
Review of future tenses

There are many ways of talking about the future in English. Sometimes, more than one tense is possible, with no change of meaning.

The future simple tense *shall/will* can be used for:

- future plans
  I'll give you a ring sometime.
- definite future events
  Our representative will meet you at the airport.
- predictions based on general beliefs
  Mass space travel will soon become possible.

- offers or promises relating to the future
  I'll prepare some salads for the party.
  I'll do my homework after this episode of 'The Simpsons'.

  Remember that the future simple is also used in the first conditional.

The 'going to' future can be used for:

- future plans, particularly if they are likely to happen soon
  I'm going to clear out the kitchen cupboards at the weekend.
- intentions
  James says he's going to work harder.
- predictions based on facts or events in the present
  It's going to snow tonight.

The present continuous tense can be used for:

- imminent future events
  I'm having a meeting with Charlotte at two o'clock.
- definite future arrangements
  Johnny's starting school next September.

The present simple can be used for:

- events based on a timetable or known date
  The plane leaves at 09.45.
  'Twelfth Night' opens on Saturday at the Arts Theatre.
- future intentions
  NASA plans to send further rockets to Mars.
- definite planned events
  The new pool is due to open in April.

The future continuous tense is used:

- to indicate certainty, when we are thinking ahead to a certain point in the future.
  Tom will be sharing an office with Fran.

The future perfect simple is used:

- to refer to events that have not yet happened but will definitely do so at a given time. This tense also conveys the idea of completion at some point in the future.
  This time next year I'll have finished my course.
  Space tourism will have become a reality by 2010.

The future perfect continuous tense is used:

- to indicate duration.
  At the end of June, Henry will have been working here for sixteen years.

Unit 11
Past and present participles

The past participles *bored, interested, thrilled*, etc. are used when we want to talk about how people feel:
I was thrilled when I received her birthday invitation.

The present participles *boring, interesting, thrilling*, etc. are used to describe what causes the feeling:
The film was so boring that I fell asleep.

Unit 12
The passive

The passive is used:

- when the action is more important than the person doing it:
  The film is loaded into the camera automatically.
- when we don't know who did something:
  The camera was put together in a factory.
- frequently, in news reporting, scientific writing and other kinds of writing where we are more interested in events and processes than in the person doing the action:
  A factory was set alight during the weekend and two million pounds' worth of damage was caused.

Formation of the passive

The passive is formed with the verb *to be* and the past participle of a transitive verb. For modals it is formed with the modal + *be* + past participle.
Get can sometimes be used informally instead of *be*.
It is used with all tenses except for the present perfect continuous and the future continuous.
Compare these sentences:
A *George Eastman invented the Kodak camera.*
B *The Kodak camera was invented by George Eastman.*

Sentence A is active and follows the pattern of Subject (George Eastman), Verb (invented) and Object (the Kodak camera).
Sentence B is passive and the pattern is Subject (the Kodak Camera), Verb (was invented) and Agent (by George Eastman).
Sometimes there are two objects:
My uncle gave me some money for my birthday.
It is more common to say:
I was given some money by my uncle.
than:
Some money was given to me by my uncle.

The agent *by*

It is sometimes unnecessary to include the agent – if for example we don't know who did something or it is obvious from the context of the sentence who did it:
She was arrested for speeding. (It's obviously going to be by a policeman so it's not necessary to include it.)

The infinitive

When the situation is in the present and the sentence needs to be impersonal, you can use the passive form of the verb plus the infinitive:
The President is believed to be in contact with the astronauts.
In the past we use the passive plus the past infinitive:
He is said to have poisoned his opponents in order to gain power.

Unit 13
Reporting

When direct speech is reported, it becomes indirect speech. There is usually a change of tense in the indirect speech, which is called 'backshift':
'I want to go home straightaway,' said Jennifer.
Jennifer said that she wanted to go home straightaway.

'Can I show you my stamp collection?' asked Billy.
Billy asked if he could show me his stamp collection.

'After Robert left primary school, he grew up very quickly,' said his mother.

Robert's mother said that after he had left primary school, he had grown up very quickly.

When something is reported that is a general truth, there is often no tense change:
'Girls' exam results are generally better than boys',' the head teacher admitted.
The head teacher admitted that girls' exam results are generally better than boys'.

There are a number of different reporting verbs in English. Here is a list of common ones, showing the structures they can take:

accuse + of + -ing
Mary accused Nick of deliberately forgetting to tell her.

admit + to (optional) + -ing; admit + that (optional)
The company admitted to selling banned products.
I admit that I was to blame.

apologise + for + -ing
James apologised for being late.

argue + for + -ing; argue that (optional)
The department argued convincingly for having extra staff.
Sally argued that it was unnecessary to delay the expedition.

claim + that (optional)
Newspapers are claiming that Mr Blair was told in advance.

deny + that (optional); deny + -ing
He denied his part in the crime.
Kirsty denied hiding the files.

explain + that (optional)
Geoff explained that there was no more money available.

insist + on + -ing; insit + that (optional)
The children insisted on staying up late.
Keith insisted that the project was too difficult.

promise + that (optional); promise + to + infinitive
Mum promised she would pick me up at 4 pm.
Jackie has promised to look after the cats while we're away.

refuse + to + infinitive
The MP has refused to comment on these rumours.

say + that (optional); in passive, 'is said' + to + infinitive
People said that the flames were visible ten miles away.
The CD is said to include many new songs.

suggest + that (optional); suggest + -ing
Vera suggested that they should seek sponsorship for the exhibition.
Hugh suggested contacting everyone by phone.

urge + to + infinitive
Owen urged them to keep calm.

warn + that (optional); warn + to + infinitive
His sister warned us that he might not come.
The police warned people not to use that part of the motorway.

Unit 14
all and the whole

All is used with plural nouns and cannot be used on its own with a singular noun. You cannot say *All company is moving.* Instead you say *The whole company is moving.*

The whole is not used with plurals. You cannot say *The whole businesses are affected by computerisation.* Instead you say *All businesses are affected by computerisation.*

Note that it is possible to say *Whole businesses are affected …* without the definite article, but this gives a change of meaning: you are now referring to each individual business.

Possessive pronouns are also used with *whole*:
Your whole career has been ruined.

You can use *of the* with both *all* and *the whole*:
All of us were sad to leave.
The whole of the world is watching the event.

Perfect tenses

See other units for information about:
- the present perfect tense, the past perfect simple tense (Unit 5)
- the future perfect simple and continuous tenses (Unit 10)

Present perfect continuous tense

This is used to emphasise the duration of a recent or ongoing event:
Lars has been talking about his own experience – does anyone share his views?
I've been learning Italian for six years.

Past perfect continuous tense

This is used to emphasise the duration of a past event:
I'd been working for the same company for twelve years and it was time to move on.

Unit 15
Countable and uncountable nouns

1 A noun can be either countable or uncountable. Uncountable nouns cannot be made plural, and they only have one form. They take a singular verb. Uncountable nouns are often the names of things or substances or abstract ideas which cannot be counted.
Examples of common uncountable nouns:
accommodation, traffic, news, bread, milk, wine, information, advice, electricity

2 Some nouns can be countable and uncountable and have a difference in meaning:
a *Her hair is very long.* Uncountable noun meaning the hair on her head.
b *There's a hair in this sandwich!* Countable noun.

a *Coffee grows in Brazil.* Uncountable noun for the product.
b *Would you like to come round for a coffee?* Countable noun meaning 'a cup of coffee'.

a *I haven't got enough paper left to finish this composition.* Uncountable noun.
b *Run out and buy me a paper will you?* Countable noun meaning a newspaper.

3 Uncountable nouns can be limited by using a countable expression. *A bit* or *a piece* are often used with uncountable

nouns, although it is usually better to use a more specific expression.
a piece/slice of cake
a clap of thunder
an item of news
a loaf of bread

4 Determiners can be used with countable and uncountable nouns.
Singular countable nouns can use *a/an* and *the*.
A new table was delivered this morning.
The man next door is a chef.

with uncountable nouns	with countable plurals
how much	how many
a lot of	a lot of
lots of	lots of
little	few
a little	a few
some/any/no	several
the	some/any/no
plenty of	the
a large amount of	plenty of
a great deal of	a large number of

5 There is an important difference in meaning between *a few/few* and *a little/little*:
a *I've seen little improvement in your work recently.*
b *I've seen a little improvement in your work recently.*
Sentence **a** is considerably more negative than *b* in tone. Compare:
a *There were few people at the meeting.* (It was disappointing because not many people were there.)
b *There were a few people at the meeting.* (There weren't many people there, but there is no suggestion that more were expected.)

some, any and no

In general we use *some* in positive sentences and *any* in negative sentences and questions:
I bought some new CDs this morning.
Did you get any bread at the supermarket?
I haven't had any breakfast this morning.

However, *some* is also used in questions when we offer something to someone:
Would you like some cake?

We also use *some* when we expect the answer to be 'yes':
(In a tourist office) *Do you have some information about the museum?*

Any is often used to show we don't have a preference:
You can take me to see any film at the cinema – I don't mind which.

With *no, nothing* or *nobody/no one* we use a positive verb:
I saw nobody when I went swimming this morning.

Unit 16
The article

1 We use the indefinite article *a/an* before a singular, countable noun. It is used when we are talking about something in general or when it is mentioned for the first time:
I saw a man outside the bank selling watches.
A pet can be a good companion for the elderly.

The indefinite article is also used for jobs:
My aunt is a doctor.

2 The definite article *the* is used in the following ways:
- when something has been referred to before or is common knowledge:
  I wouldn't buy a watch from the man standing outside the bank.
- when there is only one of something:
  the Earth, the Sydney Opera House.
- with rivers, seas, oceans, mountains, regions, national groups and countries which are groups of states:
  the United States, the Netherlands, the Atlantic, the Himalayas, the Irish
- with buildings:
  I'm going to the prison to visit a prisoner.
  He's in the office at the moment.
- with species:
  the cat, the polar bear
- with superlatives:
  the biggest tower in the world, the greatest sportsperson, the most important question
- with musical instruments:
  I play the piano.
- when talking specifically about something:
  The life of an airline pilot is hard.

3 There is no article:
- With most streets (except for *the High Street*), countries, single mountains, towns, cities (except for *The Hague*), lakes:
  Austria, Mont Blanc, Tokyo
- When talking about sports:
  I play football well.
- When a noun is used generally:
  Life is hard.
- With illnesses:
  She's off school with chickenpox.

4 Expressions
You go *to prison* if you have been found guilty of a crime. You go *to hospital* if you are ill.
You go *to the prison* or *to the hospital* to visit someone there or to work.
Other expressions which don't take an article include:
to go to bed, to have lunch/dinner/breakfast, to go on holiday, to go to work, in October, to hold office, etc.

Unit 17
Relative clauses

There are two types of relative clause: **defining** and **non-defining**. A defining relative clause gives essential information about the subject of the sentence. A non-defining relative clause gives additional but non-essential information. In other words, this information could be omitted without affecting the sense of the sentence:
The girl who is studying to become a vet is called Sarah.
Sarah, who is 20, is studying to become a vet.
As these examples show, punctuation is used in non-defining clauses but is absent from defining clauses. It is very important to use commas accurately in relative clauses, as inaccurate use may change the meaning of the sentence:
The sports facilities which are not in regular use will be sold.
The sports facilities, which are not in regular use, will be sold.
In the first example, only the sports facilities which are not being used will be sold, whereas in the second example, all the facilities will be sold, as none are being used.

Relative pronouns

In defining relative clauses, you can use:
- *who* or *that* when talking about people
  The boy who is playing is county champion.
  The teacher that I met is Head of Maths.
- *which* or *that* when talking about things
  Colours which can be worn are black, navy and grey.
  The book that I recommend costs £8.50.

The relative pronoun can be left out when it is the object of the verb in the relative clause, as in the second example of each pair above. It must be included when it is the subject of the relative clause.

In non-defining clauses, you use:
- *who* when talking about people
  Ned, who plays the violin, is living above a music shop.
- *which* when talking about things
  The new brand of shampoo, which is selling well, contains only natural ingredients.

That cannot be used, because there is no linking of the clauses, unlike in sentences containing a defining relative clause.

Instead of using a relative pronoun, *where, when* or *why* can be used after a noun. It is possible to omit *when* and *why* in defining relative clauses:
The hotel where we stayed had a beautiful garden.
Christmas is the time (when) many people start thinking about their next holiday.
That's the reason (why) she's so upset.
In non-defining relative clauses, *when* and *why* cannot be omitted:
I moved to London in 1975, when I started teaching.

Relative pronouns

who or *whom*?

Both pronouns are used in relative clauses. *Whom* is a formal word, which can only be used as the object of a verb or with a preposition:
Ruth Gresham, who cannot sell her house as a result of this new rail route, says she will seek compensation.
The people for whom this new housing development is planned are unhappy about the lack of public transport.

whose

This pronoun is used to refer to both people and things:
Professor Newton, whose latest book on urban sprawl has had excellent reviews, will open the conference.
This revolutionary new car, whose energy comes from solar panels, is expected to go into production shortly.

Unit 18
enough, too, very, so, such

enough can be used:
- after an adjective or adverb
  The room wasn't large enough to hold everyone.
  You haven't worked hard enough this term.
- before an uncountable or plural countable noun
  The car has enough space for five people and their luggage.
  There are not enough girls doing science subjects.
- as a pronoun
  Enough has been made of this in all the papers.

- with a modifying adverb
  There is hardly enough memory in the computer.
- with certain adverbs for emphasis
  Funnily enough, we heard from him only last week.

too and very

These words are often confused. Here are the main uses.

- each can be used in front of an adjective or adverb, but *too* indicates an excessive amount of something, whereas *very* is just an intensifier:
  It is too cold in winter for many plants to survive.
  It is very cold in winter but a few plants do manage to survive.
- *too* can be used to show that two things or people have something in common:
  Dictionaries are useful at school and in the home too.
  You're Swedish too, aren't you?
  Note that here *too* always comes at the end of a clause.
- *too* can be used for emphasis:
  Computers are much more powerful than they were, and less expensive too.
- *too* can be used with a quantifier:
  There are too many loose ends to this story.
  A lot of people earn too little money to pay tax.

so and such

These words are also confused sometimes.
- Both can be used for emphasis and to express the same idea, but in different grammatical structures:
  It rained so much that most of the area was flooded.
  There was such a lot of rain that most of the area was flooded.
- *such* is used with *as* in giving an example of something:
  Dairy ingredients such as cheese and milk are best avoided.

Unit 19
Modals 3: Advice and suggestion

Giving advice

You should	try to watch what you eat.
You ought	to get some rest.
You'd better	book a place in the gym.
If I were you,	I'd try to do more exercise.
My advice to you is	to go to the doctor's.

Making a suggestion

I suggest	(that) you (should) cut down on coffee.
	cutting down on coffee.
I recommend	(that) you (should) relax a little more.
	relaxing.
What about / How about	doing some reading?
Why don't you try	doing some reading?
Have you thought of	playing a musical instrument?

It's time …, It's about time …, It's high time …

After these phrases we use the past simple tense, even when we are talking about the present or the future:
It's time you went to bed. – You need to go to bed now.

It is also possible to use an infinitive with *to* after *It's time* if we are speaking in general terms rather than to particular people:
It's time to go. – Everybody needs to go now.

to have/get something done

Compare: *I cut my hair.* – I did it myself.
I had my hair cut. – Someone else did it for me.

A *have* + object + past participle
B *get* + object + past participle

Both of these forms are used, but B is more informal than A.

Unit 20
Gerunds and infinitives 2

Some verbs can be followed by both a gerund and an infinitive. Depending on the verb, this can result in a change in meaning.

No change in meaning

Verbs such as *start, begin, continue, attempt, intend, be accustomed to, be committed to, can't bear.*
These can be used with either a gerund or an infinitive with no real change in meaning:
The audience started to clap when the performance finished.
The audience started clapping when the performance finished.

Slight change in meaning

Verbs such as *like, prefer, hate, love*
Compare:
I like swimming. – In general.
I like to swim in the morning. – Talking about a habit.

Note that in American English, the infinitive is used more often than the gerund for both meanings.

After *would like, would prefer, would hate* and *would love*, an infinitive is used for a particular occasion or event:
Would you like to dance?

A change in meaning

Verbs such as *try, stop, regret, remember, forget, mean, go on.*

try
I tried to open the window, but it was stuck. I couldn't do it as it was too difficult.
It was hot, so I tried opening the window. I did it as an experiment to see if some fresh air would help.

stop
I stopped the car to get some petrol. Purpose.
I stopped going to that garage when they put their prices up. I didn't go there any more.

regret
I regret to tell you that we have no more rooms available. Giving bad news.
I regret not making more friends when I was at school. For past events.

remember and **forget**
I remember/never forget going to New York on Concorde when I was quite small. This happened in the past.
I must remember / mustn't forget to buy a newspaper while I'm out shopping. This still hasn't happened.

mean
I mean to work hard at university. Intention.
It will mean going to the library more often. This is what it involves. This is the result.

go on
When I've finished shopping, I think I'll go on to see a film.
A change of activity.
Please don't stop, go on showing us your photos. Continue.

Unit 21
Mixed conditionals

- *If* + past tense (second form) with *would(n't)/might(n't)/ could(n't)/should(n't)* (third form):
  If I weren't so busy all the time, I could have come along.
  This is used when a change in a present situation would have affected a past situation.

- *If* + past perfect tense (third form) with *would(n't)/might(n't)/ could(n't)/should(n't)* + infinitive (second form):
  If you had told me about the skiing trip, I would be there with you now!
  This is used when a change in a past situation would have caused a different present situation.

Unit 22
Concessive clauses

These are used in English to give contrasting information to the information in the main part of the sentence.
James insisted on playing in the match, despite feeling ill.
A number of different conjunctions can be used in front of the concessive clause:

although	even if	even though
much as	though	whereas	while

Much as and *whereas* are less commonly used and occur mainly in formal written English.
I prefer to buy free-range eggs, even though they are more expensive.
Although we were very tired, we watched the whole of the play.

The prepositions *despite* and *in spite of* are also used to introduce contrasting information:
Robyn went ahead with the concert despite having a sore throat.
In spite of arriving at the festival early, we couldn't get near the stage.

Sometimes it is possible to reduce the concessive clause by leaving out the main verb.
Although very tired, we watched the whole of the play.
You should only do this when the concessive clause refers to the subject of the main clause. So, for example, you would not say:
Although very boring, we watched the whole of the play.

Remember that *despite* and *in spite of* cannot be followed by a main verb. You cannot say:
Despite he was late, John had another cup of coffee.
Both can be followed by a gerund or a noun:
In spite of being late, John had another cup of coffee.
Despite the time, John had another cup of coffee.
You can add *the fact that* and follow this by a verb clause:
Despite the fact that he was late, John had another cup of coffee.

Complex sentences

It is possible to draw attention to information by 'fronting' it in a sentence. Fronting often improves the cohesion and naturalness of a piece of writing. So, for example, a reason clause, which explains information in the main clause, can present information in a logical way by coming first:
As the organisers had paid attention to detail, the festival was a great success.
Since I had bought an extra ticket for the concert, I invited Mike to go with me.

Conjunctions commonly used in reason clauses are:
as, because, since

Unit 23
I wish / If only

Talking about the past – things you regret doing/not doing:
wish / if only + past perfect
I wish I hadn't been so rude to my mother last night.

Talking about the present – things that haven't come true now and things that might come true in the future:
wish / if only + past simple
I wish I were/was lying on a beach somewhere instead of being here.
I wish I could speak Japanese.
Both *were* and *was* are acceptable but *were* is more formal.

Talking about irritating habits – things which are annoying you:
wish / if only + would
He wishes his daughter would wear smarter clothes.

as if / as though

Both *as if* and *as though* mean the same.
To talk about 'unreal' situations you use the past tense after both *as if* and *as though*:
He looks as if he's tired. He is tired.
He looks as if he was/were exhausted. He isn't tired.

would rather

Would rather + past simple is used to talk about the present or future:
I'd rather you didn't go to the disco tonight.

Would rather + past perfect is used to talk about the past:
She'd rather they had gone to an Italian restaurant.

Would rather + infinitive without *to* is used to talk generally about the present and future:
The government would rather not give out too many benefits to young people.
Do not confuse this phrase with *had better*, which means 'should'.

Unit 24

Uses of *rather*

- Used as an adverb, in the same way as *quite*:
  Eddie Izzard's humour is rather surreal at times – elephants on skis, that sort of thing.
  Some comedians are quite direct and indeed rather rude to their audiences.

- Used with *would* to mean 'prefer':
  I'd rather go to a live show than watch a video.
  John says he'd rather not come with us, as he's very tired.

- Used as a prepositional phrase to contrast two things or situations:
  The jokes were about society in general rather than being purely political.
  Rather than stay at home watching TV, he got changed and went off to the party.

- *Rather* can also be used as an adverb immediately before a verb of thought or feeling, to express an opinion politely:
  I rather think his recent success has gone to his head.
  I rather like your hair cut short.

The grammar of phrasal verbs

Phrasal verbs consist of a main verb and a particle (which is an adverb or a preposition).

- When used intransitively (that is, without an object), the verb and particle of a phrasal verb cannot be separated:
  The engine cut out and they drifted on the waves.

- When the particle is an adverb, transitive phrasal verbs can usually either be separated or followed by a noun as object; they are always separated by a pronoun as object.
  He keyed the number in carefully.
  He keyed in the number carefully.
  He keyed it in carefully.

  Could you put the drinks down on that table?
  Could you put down the drinks on that table?
  Could you put them down on that table?

- When the particle is a preposition, no separation is possible:
  The lorry ploughed into a barrier.
  My older sister keeps getting at me!

- For three-part phrasal verbs, no separation is possible:
  The sparkling blue sea more than made up for their difficult journey.
  I was really looking forward to that concert – what a shame it's been cancelled.